Introduction

The origin of this diary is simple. In Summer 1979 my friend Basil Rooke-Ley persuaded me to try the experiment of keeping a diary for three months. He kept insisting, 'You meet such interesting people.' I think that he was right but I had not thought of them in that light until then. I duly complied and at the end of three months produced a record which seemed to give pleasure to those who read it.

My particular egotism does not take the form of supposing that what amuses my family and friends will necessarily appeal to a wider public. It needed the familiar charm of George Weidenfeld to persuade me to try my hand at a Diary for the year 1981 with a view to publication.

In the event I wrote, deliberately, three times as much as was likely to be needed. Sally Mapstone, my editor at Weidenfeld, performed what seems to me to be a first class feat of selection and compromise.

I may be asked how candid is the resulting self portrait. I have read many diaries, modern and not so modern. Among those I have enjoyed most were the Diaries of Harold Nicolson. But we now learn from James Lees-Milne's revealing biography that a large and vital section of his life was omitted from the published and, I believe, the unpublished Diaries. I do not think that even the most inquisitive scrutineer of my private life would be able to dig up anything half as exciting.

I have observed what seemed to be the modern conventions about what use can be made of private conversations. If in doubt I have placed charity and a desire not to cause pain beyond any desperate desire to tell the whole story. As regards my own feelings I have assumed that there is a limit to what can properly be laid bare – whether of joy or sadness, tenderness or antagonism.

I will offer one word to anyone who is not an habitual diarist; it requires a great deal of persistence. One hopes that the pleasure given to others will make it seem worthwhile afterwards. But, in the meantime, I can honestly say that keeping it has added a new dimension of interest, an extra spice of enjoyment to the events recorded here.

My first acknowledgement must obviously go to the discerning and accomplished Sally Mapstone and to her colleague Elizabeth Burke. After that to my wife who kept me inexorably to my task. Then, in connection with the manuscript, to my inestimable colleague Gwen Keeble and, as so many times before, to the invaluable Barbara Winch; to a new ally in Kitty Chapman and to an old one in Matthew Oliver and to all the victims mentioned below. I add my gratitude to Gwen Brown, assisted by Ellen Grinter, who have preserved us for so many years at Bernhurst and to those who have looked after us so capably at Chesil Court in Chelsea.

Much has happened since I finished this diary; much more will happen before the book reaches the public. At the moment the Falklands crisis fills every heart and mind; one can only pray that peace and justice prevail.

Diary of a Year

DIARY
OF A
YEAR

Lord Longford

Weidenfeld and Nicolson
London

To Elizabeth
and my Labour colleagues
in the House of Lords

First published in Great Britain by
George Weidenfeld and Nicolson Ltd
91 Clapham High Street
London SW4

ISBN 0 297 78049 2

Printed in Great Britain by
Butler & Tanner Ltd
Frome and London

Thursday, 1 January 1981

I have resolved to keep a diary for one year. So here it begins. What is my prime objective for 1981? To finish a better man than I am at the moment, though I shall never in this life know whether I have attained that end. In other words, I aim to grow in love of God and man. But at once the old unanswerable question raises its head. Isn't this concentration on one's own spiritual progress too self-centred to be the highest of purposes?

We all know that it is self-centred and dangerous to concentrate too much on becoming prime minister or on making a fortune, but are there no analogous dangers in concentrating on one's own spiritual progress? Is not a life spent in fighting self-centredness itself self-centred? The problem will always haunt me. Mercifully I am aware that there are plenty of people (in my own church Cardinal Hume and our parish priest, Father Docherty, are the first to spring to mind) who strike a balance in practice between too much and too little concentration on their own spiritual welfare. They would, I am sure, be the last to claim such an achievement, but whatever balance they strike if I could discover and live it, it would be more than enough for me.

In my own case there is the whole area of family life, duty and love where my performance, though it might pass muster externally, could be vastly improved. This is the fiftieth year of my totally fulfilling marriage to a woman of transcendent gifts of mind and heart and character. How can I ever respond adequately to my good fortune in sharing life with Elizabeth?

On the worldly plane what can be expected of an old fellow (Evelyn Waugh's phrase applied to himself when not much over fifty) of seventy-five? We are aware that Gladstone at seventy-five had not completed his second administration. He would not begin his third until he was eighty-three. Churchill was seventy-five in 1949, eagerly awaiting the recall to Downing Street, which did not come till two years later. All that sounds very encouraging. But I am also aware that of my dozen best friends at Oxford or just afterwards nine are now dead. Roger Chetwode, Ronnie Shaw-Kennedy, Peter Fleming, Freddy Birkenhead, Basil Dufferin, Hugh Gaitskell, Evan Durbin, Evelyn Waugh, and Patrick Gordon-Walker. (I will add Dick Crossman, wonderfully gifted and life-enhancing, though our relationship was more ambiguous.) Only three survive: Esmond Warner, Aidan Crawley and Roger Nickells. Of course my close friends David Astor and Nicko Henderson are much younger. Quintin Hailsham, his mind more incisive than ever, is on sticks. So is David Exeter, the only Olympic gold medallist with whom I can claim cousinship. When I go for my four-mile walks with a little jogging down the hills I realize that I am one of the lucky ones. But I remember also what my old housemaster, C.M. Wells, said to me as we parted for the last time after lunch at the Turf Club. He was ninety-two, I was in my late fifties. I said to him a shade patronizingly, 'I hope you will be all right, sir', to which he replied as incisively as ever, 'I might die at any moment, but so, my good fellow, might you.'

For thirty-five years in the House of Lords I have watched middle-aged men growing old, in some cases very old. Every now and then they disappear from our midst without much warning. Manny Shinwell and Fenner Brockway in their nineties are phenomenally vigorous. Tony Benn's father in his eighties was the sprightliest and most mischievous member of the House. On one occasion he provoked Quintin Hailsham, then Leader of the House, into carrying a resolution that he 'be no longer heard' to his (Wedgie Stansgate's) infinite pleasure. But veterans such as these are exceptions. I conclude myself that after seventy, for example, one's brain can work as clearly and one may speak at least as well. One's experience can add to one's wisdom. But in only one case in a thousand, if that (Charles Forte occurs to me), is the kind of stamina required for sustained administrative work or endless public appearances what it used to be. Now we have Ronald Reagan and Michael Foot reaching the top in their late sixties. I shall be fascinated and delighted if they prove me wrong.

Such grave possibilities no longer concern me directly. My chairmanship of Sidgwick and Jackson ends today after a ten-year run. (I remain a director and shall still be found on the premises.) I lack, alas, the temperament of the Queen Mother who seems able to think of all periods of her life as 'very happy years'. Certainly she makes them happy for all who meet her. But whatever my worries during the last ten years (I am a fairly consistent worrier) the hours spent in Sidgwick and Jackson and with colleagues and staff there have been unfeignedly happy. I should doubt whether there has been quite so happy a team in publishing, and publishing is on the whole a happy profession. Gwen Keeble, my private secretary, and William Armstrong, the managing director, have been the special sources of my own happiness, and William has never allowed the anxieties inseparable from publishing at the moment to obscure his sunny nature. Bill Procter, Margaret Willes, Nikki Stace, Nigel Newton, Bill Williams, Jane Heller and the others make up a fine team. On the whole I have had more kudos as chairman of Sidgwick and Jackson than I deserve. I was chosen in 1978 as one of six great English publishers for a *Sunday Times* photograph. But really that was absurd. In retrospect, I should have tried to persuade them to put William Armstrong in my place. One famous publisher refused to participate because another famous publisher would be taking part; that sounds a bit petty, but in publishing feelings of that kind are regarded as part of the fun.

I have not left my personal stamp on Sidgwick and Jackson even to the very limited extent that I left it on the National Bank when I was chairman from 1956 to 1963. In the National Bank I was roughly in the position of a minister in a government office, but I was never as much as that in Sidgwick and Jackson. I was officially part-time and no self-respecting minister would accept or be allowed such a label. I was engaged in many other public activities, such as the major inquiry into pornography. Except in terms of public relations I saw my achievement as carried out through William, though no doubt in various imponderable ways I strengthened and encouraged the others. Charles Forte, who has been such a wonderful supporter of S & J, now takes over (I presume) as chairman. He will always be of the utmost value to Sidgwick and Jackson.

Friday, 2 January 1981

Religious reading for today St Luke Chapter 10. I extract the sentence, 'Wherever you go into a house first say Peace be with this house.' I interpret this as meaning whenever you meet someone show yourself friendly and genial. No one who travels as much in trains and buses as I do is unaware that British people refrain from speaking to each other unless introduced. Shall I set out to break this tradition? In the Lords there is a good deal of mateyness, almost of back-slapping. But it was not until I cut my head recently and wore a large piece of plaster for some while that all sorts of peers, some of them unknown to me, came to me and spoke to me in the friendliest fashion. So perhaps the British are glad of an excuse to be more friendly than the convention authorizes.

People ask what I am going to do now that I have retired. I put them off by saying that I have retired now quite often. From Christ Church in 1945, from government (compulsorily) in 1951, from the National Bank in 1963, from the Wilson Cabinet in 1968.

The *Daily Mirror* quote me correctly though inadequately as saying that my New Year's resolution is to drink less, though I admit getting pleasure from drinking with friends. Opinions canvassed included those of Brezhnev, Lord Denning, Richard Ingrams and a showbiz medley. The *Mirror* had no space to report my rather vague answers to the questions they put me about my plans for 1981. They obviously had in mind my retirement from the chairmanship of S & J. I hadn't got time, in any case, to go through my regular activities outside the office. The daily visit to the New Horizon Centre (of which I was one of the founders in 1968 and am still chairman) for instance, the endless correspondence with prisoners and others in trouble, the fairly frequent visits to prisons and suchlike places. And then, as usual, I am engaged on a book. My joint work on Ulster with Anne McHardy, four years the *Guardian* correspondent in Northern Ireland, is almost ready for the publishers. Anne has been a delightful colleague with much first-hand material at her fingertips. The difference of background, standpoint, etc., not to mention age bracket – her age is roughly half mine – have not produced as many complications as might have been expected. But I foresee the need for some very intelligent editing before the book sees the light.

Of course I shall go on working for penal reform and individual prisoners. I much admire the work of the All-Party Penal Affairs Group led by Robert Kilroy-Silk. I hope to be rather more helpful to them in the future. Nineteen-eighty has at least seen the beginnings of pressure by the Home Secretary on the judges. He is beginning to urge them to send fewer people to prison and send them for shorter sentences, ours being absurdly long by international standards. But the mental torture undergone by the long-term prisoners including life prisoners has not yet begun to percolate widely. The recent news about Myra [Hindley] has been discouraging. She was convicted for her share in the appalling Moors murders in 1965, though I have

4

always been convinced that her participation was far less than the public were allowed to suppose. She has proved herself in prison a woman of strong character and deep religious feeling. She wrote to me at the end of 1968 and I have been visiting her at three-month intervals ever since, first in Holloway and for the last years in the ineffable women's wing at Durham. It was constructed originally for the most dangerous men but rejected as too inhumane.

She has still not been allowed by the Home Office to be considered for parole. The European Commission has now turned down her appeal. James Fawcett, the President and our dear friend, has told me that our highly technical submission might not have been the cleverest approach in a strictly legal sense. There is what he calls a 'gap' which makes it difficult for them to say that any particular length of sentence is inhumane. He seemed to think that we would have had and might still have a better chance by a straightforward emphasis on the accepted fact that she is not dangerous and is at present harshly confined. When I saw Myra just before Christmas she was more depressed than I has seen her for a long time. The news of the rejection of her submission was an additional blow. She feels an overwhelming urge to make a protest which in her case would mean going into solitary confinement. I begged her not to take this step at any rate until she had seen her admirable young solicitor (Mike Fisher). She said that if he were to come to see her in January she would hold her hand; and he has since agreed to see her this month.

Back to my 1981 agenda. I say to myself I really must make an altogether new effort for the cause of mental health, not that I have never done anything at all. Years ago I was chairman of the National Society for Mental Health and for a short while treasurer of the Richmond Fellowship which under the phenomenal inspiration of Elly Jansen has by now built up a whole network of half-way houses helping mental patients back into the community. I have written the introduction to two of Peter Thompson's books arising out of his four years in Broadmoor. I know where I want to concentrate: on mental after-care. I had dinner last Tuesday with Peter Thompson, and we began to lay plans for a new inquiry. Peter launched the Pakenham–Thompson Inquiry into prison after-care twenty years ago and performed indispensable services to the Inquiry on victims in 1977–8. But I must not, in any case, fail to make early contact with Elly Jansen and the Mental After-Care Association of which I have been a patron for many years. It may be that there is some small way in which I can help them.

At the beginning of a new year I cannot help recalling a prediction I made within a fortnight of Mrs Thatcher's victory: 'She won't last two years.' I did not mean that she would be ousted by the Labour Party but by her own colleagues. I was calculating when I forecast her downfall that she could never dominate her Cabinet as she clearly wished to dominate them unless her policies were rapidly and patently successful. And few could claim today that that has happened. Which is not to deny that it may yet come about. If she is ejected, it will be through a combination of disgruntled businessmen and Conservative MPs or candidates in marginal constituencies. If I have, therefore, to make an Old Moore's prediction I guess that she will still be there at the end of 1981. She won't be unless she modifies her present monetarism quite considerably, yet she is not without greatness.

Saturday, 3 January 1981

Rather a day for recognition – four individuals or couples at Charing Cross Station. One man accompanied by his mother joined me in my railway carriage and asked me for the secret of my 'peace of mind'. I do not in fact rate myself highly for that quality, but my new friend had spent a good deal of time in mental homes during the last two years so perhaps I had something to teach him. I suggested a regular course of religious reading to move his mind away from current anxieties. I honestly believe that he will follow this advice. At any rate for a time, perhaps for ever.

Religious reading for today Luke Chapter 11 and most of Beauty for Ashes. Luke 11 includes a rather abbreviated version of the Lord's Prayer omitting the appeal to be delivered from evil. I offer up the whole prayer with that last appeal particularly on entering a New Year. There are some sins of commission to be resisted. Drinking too much, for example, but far more sins of omission. That leaves me with the thought that I must decide at my present advanced age which are real sins of omission and which are sins in my imagination.

Sunday, 4 January 1981

Dinner with Malcolm and Kitty Muggeridge last night. Four old friends really enjoying themselves though Kitty and Malcolm, who rise at 5 a.m. or earlier, nodded off more than once. They seldom do this when they come to us; the sleepy head here is more likely to be me. Something no doubt to do with the rival stimuli.

Malcolm is having a splendid Indian summer just now. The book about him by Ian Hunter, though the author is judged unexciting, is selling 'amazingly well' I was told in Hatchards. I repeated this to Malcolm, slightly adapting the language. He and I profess to be bored by books about ourselves, no doubt with equal honesty. The BBC are doing an eight-part series based on his endless television programmes over the years. Collins are bringing out the diaries that he has kept for half a century, off and on. He was recently on the *Start the Week* programme with Michael Foot and Alan Taylor and on *Any Questions* with Enoch Powell. He is still very much a star though he talks of himself as having retired from the world. I am sure that he has done nothing to promote the recent publicity.

How to explain the continued interest in him at seventy-eight? He is a splendid performer on radio and television, just as he is a scintill-ating journalist. What is remarkable is that his Christian conversion, in itself anathema to most of the communicators, has not diminished the interest in his message. He himself will never accept the crude fact of the conversion. In a deep sense since Cambridge there has always been Christianity within him, but no one who got to know him for the first time as I did twenty years ago would have called him a Christian champion at that time, or indeed a Christian at all. Since then he has proclaimed Christianity all over Britain, the USA, Canada and Aus-tralia to much effect. Again twenty years ago no one would have called him an ascetic, in fact the opposite, but drink, meat and fish and smoking have long since been abandoned. He gives us to under-stand in his writings that he has had many intimate friendships with women. But his long and loving marriage to Kitty is at its zenith.

I asked him yesterday about the basis of his Christian convictions. Malcolm says that for him religious truth must be reached through the imagination. The revelations offered in the Bible, though he is not a fundamentalist, help him towards it. But in the end the deepest truths about God and Christ can only be understood and expressed in imaginative and artistic terms. Even our most successful attempts to provide explanations will seem quite puerile in the world to come. This last contention fits in well with Malcolm's ever stronger convic-tion about the infinite unimportance of this world compared with the next one. I don't know anyone, any layman at any rate, who is more sure of his ground here. The fact that he has proved and is still proving an immense success here below is often treated as a matter for cynicism. I see it as a credit to him and an indication that current taste is not so bad after all. Elizabeth adds the thought that Malcolm's good-natured, witty pessimism (in a worldly sense) is just what the public enjoys these days, though that is certainly not the reason why Malcolm has adopted this posture.

He is indeed, in the worldly sense, a super pessimist, arguing more or less seriously that the whole place is going to the dogs and incidentally that any particular leader, and Margaret Thatcher at the moment, is clearly doomed. The best that he can say of any prominent person (including Michael Foot, for example, of whom he is very fond) is 'Poor old Michael, I have a feeling that he has shot his bolt.' Or, in one case, 'There's nothing really wrong with him except that he is mad.' But none of this discourages him in the least. He really does believe so strongly in the mercy of God that he can say with Mother Julian 'All will be well' (he has in mind of course the next life). For him religion is an unqualified consolation. Kitty is just as religious as he is (I tell her that in addition she is a nature mystic) and just as happy.

Monday, 5 January 1981

Left Bernhurst, which has been our country home since 1950 (I inherited it in 1938). Came up to London in Elizabeth's car – no trains for 'industrial reasons'. William, assisted by myself in my new role of rank-and-file director, gave lunch to Ned Sherrin at the Garrick. Ned, a brilliant figure in his own fashion, a kind of show business Isaiah Berlin, equally at home in theatre, films and TV and as producer or writer. Tall, balding and very, very quick in his responses. The idea of a book did not advance very far; his memoirs seem to be more or less committed to George [Weidenfeld]. He is going to let us see a book already written about great song writers and we shall go on from there. I very much hope that he will finish by doing something for us. When I tentatively mentioned a book on TV, he and William agreed that the public are much interested in TV stars and watching TV, but not in books about it. His group had been defeated by that of Peter Jay for breakfast television. He reckoned that Peter Jay lent a responsibility that no one else could provide. I have known of Peter Jay's brilliance since he was a small boy at the Dragon School. Though larger than any of his contemporaries, I have never particularly associated him with responsibility, but I suppose everything is relative.

Ned Sherrin is writing or, as he said, putting together a musical 8 about the Mitfords. He said that the Mitford I know least, the Duchess of Devonshire (she is fifteen years younger than I am), is wheeling the others into line and ironing out any little family difficulties. What an astonishing interest has suddenly broken out in the Mitfords! When it comes to doing books, films, musicals, etc., it appears that Nancy's writing is a tremendous bonus. Curiously I have never enjoyed her books particularly, but every kind of person from my Uncle Eddie downwards (who placed her on a level with Evelyn Waugh) has proved me wrong. Nancy and Elizabeth developed a beautiful pen friendship at the end of Nancy's life. There was a genuine mutual admiration between them as writers. It has been a real delight working with Diana, and before he died getting to know Tom [Sir Oswald] Mosley, in connection with Diana's book about the Duchess of Windsor. I remember Decca best from the days when she was married to Esmond Romilly, and full of mischief along with him and Philip Toynbee. But later, much later, I gave her lunch at the Gay Hussar to talk about penal reform, now that she is a professor in the social sciences.

When I got round to sport, Ned Sherrin told us that he had played in a cricket match in Connecticut last summer and made fifty not out, in his fiftieth year. We both dwelt happily on Harold Pinter's passion for cricket which we found very appealing.

Tuesday, 6 January 1981

The dismissal of Norman (St John-Stevas) from the Cabinet is bad news for anyone who cares for the arts, or, if such people exist, parliamentary procedure. The simplest explanation is that he was an expendable 'wet', but the story of his personal relationship with Margaret Thatcher, whom he popularized under the title of 'the Blessed Margaret' or 'the Leaderene', must be revealed later. When tackled recently about her in the Garrick, he replied in a manner that was, on the face of it, fulsome, but could easily be understood to be ironic. One hazards the guess that in Cabinet he was a disconcerting opponent to the true believers. Curiously enough it was only yesterday that Ned Sherrin remarked how successful he felt his recent interview with Norman had been. 'I always enjoy teasing Norman', he commented, and Norman always enjoys being teased. At times I have compared Norman to Disraeli, but there was something much harder and less spiritual about the latter gentleman.

To the Arts Club for an exhilarating lunch with the President of the

Portrait Sculptures and others, including my old (young) friend, Judith Bluck, of Hurst Green origination. She did busts of me and Elizabeth in 1967. I am no judge of sculpture, but Judith has done wonderfully well professionally and deserves the success she is obtaining. A certain John Nevill, nephew of Rupert Nevill, who runs galleries in Canterbury and Bath, did some sprightly talking. His wife, also present, had known Margaret Thatcher at Oxford. There was a general pro-Margaret feeling, if only because she was ready to 'do something', unlike most recent leaders. Someone observed that she had no sense of humour. Nevill replied that we in Britain had been suffering from an excess of humour. I found myself secretly agreeing with him.

In the context of the artistic occasion, I was about to open the Annual Exhibition of the Portrait Sculptures. Nevill recalled a speech made by Winston Churchill at the annual Academy banquet round about 1950. 'If I met Picasso,' he proclaimed, 'I'd kick him down Piccadilly!' The President, Munnings, when his turn came was not to be outdone. 'I'd do the same,' he said, 'with Matisse.' The point of the story, I assume, was that we have advanced beyond that state of barbarism. I worked frantically during lunch to dredge up something to say. I persuade myself that my remarks went down well. My line was that everyone ought to have their children sculptured. I was able to exploit the presence of some charming small children in the foreground. The boards of business houses, I went on, would do better to have their retiring chairmen sculptured rather than painted. They could not look more unglamorous and it was just possible that their solidity might give them a new attraction. I bemoaned the departure of Norman recorded above, as I found afterwards did all those I spoke to. He is clearly regarded as an aesthete among philistines; but in an average parliament an aesthete's prospects are never promising.

Wednesday, 7 January 1981

Lunch at White Hart, a nearby pub, as guest of an ex-prisoner who had come from Cleveland in North Yorkshire to talk to me, though not to ask for my assistance. Aged thirty-three, married with three children, deeply and actively religious, he had suffered from nervous trouble at various times. A climax was reached when he began sending out bogus calls to the ambulance and fire service. Today he explains these aberrations no doubt rightly as cries for help.

Not surprisingly, he was placed in a mental hospital, but astonishingly when he was fit to appear in court he was sentenced to nine months' imprisonment, of which he served six. He was mocked by the other prisoners for his peculiar form of criminality. They thought it very funny to point out to him that the charge for telephoning had now gone up. Physically, he was bullied to the point where he sought protection under Rule 43. He pays unstinted tribute to the support given him through all this by the local Catholic community and in particular by the Bishop of Middlesbrough, Bishop Harris. Bishop Harris is the penal affairs bishop to whom I am in danger of being less than generous. I cannot get out of my mind his long connection with the Home Office. But whenever I meet him I am aware that I am in the presence of a man of immense compassion. At a recent conference, Bishop Harris reminded us that Christ had a special tenderness for 'baddies'. So far I have failed dismally to get any branch of the Catholic hierarchy interested in Myra Hindley. At least half a dozen prison chaplains have become very fond of her. One who visited Durham has said that when he acquires a parish and she is free, he would be glad to have her to live in his house.

Thursday, 8 January 1981

After lunch at the Garrick, fell in with some of the blither spirits: Kingsley Amis, Dominic Harrod and Ronnie Harwood among them. General agreement that Norman, our fellow member, had scored sharply off Mrs Thatcher in the exchanges which followed his dismissal from the Cabinet. Dominic Harrod claimed to admire Mrs Thatcher but did not consider her really clever, and Norman had been too smart for her. I did not mention that I had rung Norman the day before and asked him to do a book for Sidgwick and Jackson. He had seemed ready to discuss it over lunch but somewhat preoccupied. It was not till next day that I realized that he had not only been involved in acrimonious correspondence with the Prime Minister, but in television and radio appearances. I remarked rather ineptly that he might feel like Wolsey who wished that he had served his God as well as he had served his King. Norman took it quite well, but I can't think why I said it.

Kingsley was being congratulated on his CBE. He attributed it to a conversation following his first meeting with the Prime Minister. An unknown youngster asked him what he thought of her. He made some enthusiastic noises. He turned out to be speaking to one of her intimate acolytes (this way of explaining any honours that one acquires is *comme il faut*). Some discussion as to why so few writers were knighted. Everyone was aware that Evelyn Waugh had refused the CBE. Priestley had told Kingsley some while ago that he had refused everything except the OM, 'but the b——s won't give me that'. Later they must have relented. Ronnie Harwood, certainly the best conversational catalyst in my experience nowadays (alas, I see David Cecil so seldom), complained not quite seriously that his lack of a university education stood in the way of his achieving honours. He consoled himself with the thought that Harold Pinter, a great friend and RADA-trained, had achieved a CBE.

Friday, 9 January 1981

Six o'clock yesterday evening to the Ritz Casino for William Hickey party. Astounded to find a middle-aged taxi driver who didn't know where the Ritz was – he had an idea that it was in the Strand. Shades of Evelyn Waugh in the early thirties! I couldn't resist telling the doorkeeper at the Ritz about the ignorance of the taxi driver. He was suitably unmoved. 'You never know what you will find behind the wheel these days, milord.' Could only spend thirty minutes at the party in view of commitment to address Young Humanists. Spent most of it with someone I really like, Diana Dors, who disproves the theory that plump women can't be glamorous. Her husband Alan provides a striking contrast, slim and dark and naughty-looking. I congratulated him on his coat, silk and braided, with appropriate stock. I gather that the coat has cost £250, but in this ruined country that figure doesn't seem to bother anyone any more.

I had made friends with Diana in a Southern Television programme on pornography. Diana was nominally chairman but played a vibrant part in discussion, almost too much on my side. In an earlier programme of hers Willy Hamilton had attacked the monarchy. Alan, an ex-professional boxer, was said to have threatened him afterwards. He told me that I had got it all wrong. He had only used violence once recently and then under extreme provocation. He had taken his young son into the bar of a hotel in Blackpool with a view to introducing him to the trade union leaders during the TUC conference. Unfortunately by that time the latter gentlemen had had their fill of port and brandy. Alan took it on himself to tell them that this was no way to serve the interests of the toiling masses. They retaliated by summoning three bouncers, but Alan soon laid them low. He was eventually removed by the police.

On to the Young Humanists. Not more than a dozen present, and young middle-aged rather than young. But nice serious men (no women). I enjoyed myself thoroughly in their company. My topic was Christian and Humanist approaches to penal reform. Both groups believe in what Christians call the duty to one's neighbour, Humanists without the support of a belief in a deity. On the ethical side Christians have sin, forgiveness and the infinite worth of an immortal soul. What about the Humanists? Answer, nothing very coherent. But at the end of the evening the right words came to me for my adieu: 'If you can't believe in God, humanism is the next best thing.' Everyone went away happy, assuring me that they and I were equally attached to the individual human person.

This morning New Horizon as usual. We are exceptionally lucky in our present team of workers. Asked Vaughan Jones (co-ordinator) to draft some ideas for the All-Party Penal Affairs Group, who are now concentrating on young offenders. Last year we saw something like three thousand young people with problems, mostly homeless. Vaughan reckons that the great majority have been in trouble with the law, though only a small number are yet involved in serious crime. Most of our 'visitors' are between eighteen and twenty-five but Vaughan has had experience of younger age groups with analogous problems. I know he'll turn out something really valuable.

Lunch at Beoty's. Anne and I were guests of John Curtis, George's very receptive and capable lieutenant, who introduced us to our young editor-to-be, Sally Mapstone. Smallish, eyes bright behind gold-rimmed glasses, most acceptable. We had let them have the first and the last chapters of our book which it was agreed provisionally to call *Ulster*. The problem of keeping up to date with events moving so fast is insoluble in theory. John had the clever idea of leaving a page or two at the end for last-minute insertions. We must all do the best we can.

Saturday, 10 January 1981

Back to the office yesterday afternoon; shown by Margaret Willes, our chief editor, with an air of great secrecy a MS. regarded not unreasonably as highly secret. William had asked me to look at it so I was annoyed when Margaret, to whom I am much attached, made a great song and dance about my not reading it until she had obtained permission from William. I said that she made me feel like King Lear and told her that I should be heading my diary 'The Decline and Fall of the Chairman'. I made far too much fuss about a tiny irritation but it is not easy to adjust instantaneously to reduced status.

Sunday, 11 January 1981

Read a good deal of George Herbert, including Helen Gardner's introduction to my edition. Helen used to be thought delightful, but rather dowdy, in the old days at Oxford, but now with her smart white hair and stylish glasses she represents a form of elderly chic which attracts strongly. Her introduction contains one particularly striking sentence: 'The deepest pain is the pain of feeling useless, of having nothing to give where so much has been given; and this Herbert knows to be the real nerve pain of egoism.' What is she driving at here? Does she mean that it is a symptom of egotism? If so, is she right? I remember Harold Laski, then a highly popular demagogue, saying to me after I had thanked him for a speech on my behalf at Oxford, 'It makes me feel a little less useless than usual.' I always felt very fond of him afterwards.

Read Herbert's long poem 'The Sacrifice'. No one can ever have expressed more poetically what it means to share the suffering of Christ on the Cross. Afterwards went over as usual at twelve o'clock to our little Catholic church which is locked up between services. As often before, I prayed before the figure of Jesus Christ set on the wall of the tower. If only I could feel a hundredth part of what Herbert felt. Though I accept the death of Christ on our behalf without intellectual difficulty, it is only on rare occasions, most obviously on Good Friday, that I share a little of Herbert's feeling.

Telephone call from Bishop Harris whom I had rung up with a view to a meeting. His domicile in Middlesbrough makes it difficult. He was sweetness itself, making me more guilty than ever about my criticism of his 'Home Office standpoint'. I pleaded with him to do something significant about Myra. I said, I hope not too bitingly, that if she were an Anglican I would be taking up her case with the Archbishop of Canterbury. As it is she is very much one of ours, receiving Communion twice weekly.

Bishop Harris asked me whether the attitude of Mrs West, the stricken mother, was known to me. I said that she had often expressed her intention of harming Myra if she had the chance, but surely that should not affect the question of Myra's parole. Bishop Harris agreed. But Dennis Trevelyan, head of the Prison Department, had mentioned the same point without pressing it. I suppose that it is fed into the Home Office computer as a factor working against parole. I have in fact had several poignant meetings with Mrs West, including one after a television programme and one in my office. If I am asked how I can reconcile my sympathy for victims with that for criminals, I answer (I hope not too pretentiously) that I would see my attitude as that of the average clergyman.

Monday, 12 January 1981

To the office. Michael Whitaker at twelve; his daughter was brutally murdered some years ago. He was the life and soul of our committee on victims which reported in 1978 and the inspiration behind my Private Member's Bill which got a Second Reading and a Committee Stage in 1979. Michael is now pushing ahead under his own steam in Yorkshire, the best outlet for his articulate passion. I and others have agreed to act as sponsors. Not for the first time we asked ourselves why victims and their friends are such a weak lobby. We agree that it is the reluctance of victims and their relatives to appear in public as such. Michael is an exception and I should think that his friends and relatives have not been over-enthusiastic. But nothing will stop him and in my small way I shall never desert him.

Tuesday, 13 January 1981

Margaret and I gave dinner at Victor's to two of our potential best-sellers, Jon Snow and Diana Mosley. Elizabeth was also present to the general satisfaction. Margaret even suggested their doing a book together.

Jon, the son of an Anglican bishop, was sent down from Liverpool University for student rebelliousness. I gave him his first job as co-ordinator of the New Horizon Youth Centre, where his success was memorable. He really set the place on the map. Later Jack Profumo, a member of the council of New Horizon, offered him the key position of Warden of Toynbee Hall, a striking honour for a young man of twenty-eight. But Jon chose broadcasting and has become a real television star, reporting dramatic and dangerous events in all parts of

Asia and Africa, including Afghanistan and Iran. He has covered many of the Pope's activities, including his visit to Ireland where I met him at Phoenix Park and Knock.

Elizabeth and I were much excited when he became engaged to Anna Ford. We gave them lunch at the House of Lords. I was all set to go to the wedding in London and the reception in Gloucestershire. Then the engagement collapsed. Perhaps Jon has not quite finished his years of adventure. Today he was just off to El Salvador for three weeks. We agreed that when he got there it would be strange to think of this little lunch in the cosy security of the House of Lords. Jon is now thirty-four. I am flattered that he still keeps in close touch with me. We have a left-wing community of aspiration which bridges the gulf of years. I tell him that he is too soft to what he calls the Russian presence in Afghanistan. But he speaks with confidence about that country, not only from recent but earlier knowledge.

Jon and Diana arrived before the rest of us. He had no idea who she was. When he discovered later in the evening, he was surprisingly thrilled to think that she had known Lytton Strachey, Evelyn Waugh, Churchill and Hitler, not to mention her going to prison during the war without committing an offence. Yet I can't think of anyone who is basically so anti-Fascist and so firmly left of centre as Jon. He is in no way pro-Soviet but argues that their performance in Afghanistan is at least intelligible.

Diana told Margaret afterwards that she had been very depressed, but the dinner had cheered her up. It is only a few weeks since her husband died. At dinner she drew on her large reserves of courage without apparent effort, as she has done many times in her life. At Sidgwick and Jackson we want her to do a book of essays about the exciting people she has known. I argued strongly that she ought to begin with Tom if only because he is bound to be so much in her mind at the present time. She writes very well, as do all the Mitfords. She has become very fond of Margaret, who will persuade her to do the book if anyone can.

There was a time when many people spat at the mention of Tom Mosley, but today he is respected increasingly. Diana has never lost the affection and admiration of her many friends. I recalled that the first time I had seen Tom was at the home of the Astors, Cliveden, in summer 1930 when he had just left the Labour Government and delivered one of the greatest resignation speeches of the century. He was still only thirty-four. At Cliveden everyone treated him as a man of destiny, but he committed the fatal error of starting his new party. After that there was no room for him in British party politics and his movement into Fascism had a grim inevitability.

My next encounter was at the Fascist punch-up in the Carfax Assembly Rooms in 1936, which Diana and I agree must never be referred to, but somehow gets frequently mentioned. Then dinner in 1963 with the Mosleys in London after Victor Gollancz and I had written to *The Times* to protest against the beating up of Tom at one of his East End meetings. Then another long gap in our relationship till Margaret and I went over to see them at their house near Paris to discuss a book by Diana about the Duchess of Windsor, which in the event proved most successful. Lunches etc. in London followed. I was going to lunch with them just about the time that Tom died. Diana insisted that he had deep compassion for the underdog and brought up a telling example of his resignation from the Conservative Party because of the Black and Tans in 1921. Not doubting that, I still have to think of him as possessed of a violent temperament when he was young. In old age he was mellow and almost gentle and especially good with the young. It was not difficult to remember that he had been one of the great lady-killers of his time. His gifts as a parliamentarian and demagogue had been exceptional in the old days and he adjusted to television effectively. Diana, though she no longer possesses her youthfulness, has acquired a distinction which one feels is not unconnected with suffering.

Wednesday, 14 January 1981

Elizabeth and I dined last night with the Crawleys, Aidan and Virginia. Also present were their children, Randal and Harriet, and among others an ex-Fellow of All Souls, close associate at one time of Jacob Rothschild, and it may be about the most academically distinguished young man in international finance. The idea seemed to be that I should be collectively grilled about my continued adherence to the Labour Party. This duly occurred, but Aidan was kind enough to say afterwards that the young people did not realize that I was much tougher than I look. To be honest I get almost too much of a kick out of that kind of situation.

I was pressed repeatedly to say that I was worried about the threat to democracy in the present left-wing drift of the Labour Party. That I declined to do, but readily conceded that I was much disturbed by what seemed on paper like a tendency to abandon Western defence altogether. At my age the question of leaving the Labour Party did not arise. In any case, one had complete freedom of action in the House of Lords. If I were in my early forties like David Owen, I might or might not decide to make my life's contribution outside the official party. Whatever my age, I could not visualize joining a Jenkinsite centre party.

Eleven a.m. today, meeting of the Young Delinquents Group of the All-Party Penal Affairs Committee. Eight or nine impressive and certainly dedicated people, John Hunt, Jack Donaldson, and Robert Kilroy-Silk, chairman of the main committee, among them. On the last few occasions, I arrived last and felt badly 'out of it'. This time, arrived first and felt myself right in the centre. Do these feelings of mine, no doubt shared by others, affect one's behaviour at committee meetings? Suspect they do. But great committee men, like John Maud [Lord Redcliffe-Maud], I am sure rise above them.

Gave lunch to Mary Warnock, of the Warnock Report, before the debate on the handicapped. I was later to describe her as the 'dynamic philosopher and headmistress'. Just before lunch Pat Llewelyn-Davies, our glamorous Chief Whip, had asked me to wind up the debate for the Opposition. For twenty-two years I spoke from our Front Bench on one side or the other of the floor, frequently winding up, but for thirteen years this kind of honour had not come my way. Felt an unexpected sense of exhilaration and at the same time relaxation on being asked back to my old perch, although like Cinderella I would disappear from it as the day ended.

The debate was notable for the presence of over thirty speakers, five of them in wheelchairs. Sue Masham, opening, left an indelible impression, not only from what she said but for what she is, and for the life of dedication modestly hinted at. The Duke of Buccleuch was impressive, rather differently. Lord Winstanley, winding up for the Liberals, said of him, 'I knew him in the House of Commons before his accident and I have known him since. He seems to me exactly the same very popular chap.' I suppose that he was a good deal older than the others before he was struck down. When I came to speak I repeated one thing I had said when I carried Alf Morris's Bill through the Lords in 1970: 'Suffering, while it often degrades, can often ennoble.' I wound up by insisting, as indeed the Archbishop of Canterbury had done, that if there had to be cuts, the disabled being most vulnerable should not bear their share.

Plenty of kind things were said to me about my speech; that is the way of the House of Lords, but taking all the circumstances into account I felt that I had come through well. Lord Snowdon, who had spoken himself, said to me afterwards, 'You were so cool and urbane.' He had done and is doing an immense amount for the disabled. It was not difficult for me, therefore, to pay a counter-compliment. I should hope that the debate in which so many speakers had demanded better treatment for the disabled would be not without influence.

Thursday, 15 January 1981

Management committee meeting (S & J). Found myself unpleasantly testy when Margaret pressed me as to why I had not approached Frankie Donaldson about the book we hoped for from her. My irritation to be accounted for, I suppose, by my present lack of facilities in the absence of Gwen, except on Tuesdays. Rather ashamed of myself, though a certain amount of innocent amusement was caused. Margaret said that she would try to forgive me. She is very good-tempered but rather sensitive. I suppose that I am also rather sensitive and not so good-tempered.

Frankie is looked on by all of us as a potential best-seller since her *Edward VIII* and the resulting television programme. She really does seem keen on doing a book for us. I went down to Churchill College with her to look at the Esher papers, but in the end she felt that wasn't for her. Frankie herself has said that there must be an exciting book in Ann Fleming, in view of her husbands and countless important friends from Anthony Eden to Evelyn Waugh. This is what I must follow up if I am not to incur the further wrath of Margaret.

Working lunch while Sebastian Coe and David Miller, his collaborator, presented their book to us and our sales representatives. Sebastian Coe, though only twenty-four, reminds me strongly of Prince Charles. I can well believe that he is everyone's darling. He is, of course, the good guy of athletics, whereas Steve Ovett has been cast, or has cast himself, for the bad one. The book is very readable and sensible and informative. I honestly don't think it could be much improved on. I found myself, however, vaguely worrying about the life of anyone who has trained for several hours every day to do such a monotonous thing as putting one foot in front of the other somewhat faster than anyone else over certain distances. His father's obsessional drive to make him a world champion is edifying in its way, but I could not help being reminded a little bit of Joe Kennedy and his passion that one of his sons should be President.

Myra's solicitor, Michael Fisher, to tea. He goes to see her on Monday. He handed me the text of the reply of the European Commission turning down her submission. Naturally, I shall study it urgently. Mike and I agree that we must now concentrate on the next application to the Home Office for Myra to be considered for parole; a further application to the European Commission might be counter-productive at this stage. Mike wants a really good submission drawn up by a QC. He thinks that Myra's previous advisers have left her to do the job too much herself. He agrees with me, however, that her own gifted writing ought to come into it somehow. Otherwise she is just a digit and a digit with a terrible crime on her record.

I agreed with him that there were some unfortunate phrases in her personal testament, 'society owes me a living', etc. But he agreed with me that her so-called 'arrogance' had kept her going and enabled her to obtain an Open University degree. Mike said that he had never known a prisoner who had shown remorse. I told him that he had not known Shane O'Doherty, who has publicly repudiated the IRA and apologized to his victims. It would indeed be helpful if Myra could send a similar apology to Mrs West. But Myra clings to her own sincerity which makes it harder.

Mike has been acting for Tuite, the IRA prisoner who burrowed his way out of Brixton, a staggering feat. He told me that he had never liked a prisoner more. He felt that he would one day be a member of an Irish cabinet (cf. De Valera, Kenyatta, Nehru, etc.). He had taken great pains to plant his bomb at night and give warnings that would prevent loss of life. The police, apparently, had much respect for him. It was quite true that he was a master of disguise. By now he was almost certainly in Ireland. The last thing he said to Fisher, who of course had no idea that he would escape, was significant: 'I can't think why I ever came to this country.'

Friday, 16 January 1981

'Reps' meeting (S & J) 10–1, plus working lunch. Became bored and depressed during first two hours. Mind went back to Cabinet days when thoughts of lunch alone sustained me. Felt that I ought to get my word in (as in those days) in order to show that I was not sulkily aloof. Made one or two interventions, not very happily. Began to wonder whether I ought to stay on as director of S & J if this is all the contribution I can offer.

Then matters improved for me. William mentioned an issue, the inevitability of leaks, where he said that he and I differed. I spoke up strongly. I can still remember the occasion when *Private Eye* carried the perfectly true story of my saying my prayers in the Sidgwick and Jackson lavatory. William bet me a bottle of sherry that a leak would not occur in this particular matter. I accepted the offer. General jollity. I was back in the family at once. Not an exciting meeting from any standpoint but a necessary procedure.

Monday, 19 January 1981

Lunch today for Michael Luvaglio at the Gay Hussar. Michael did twelve years in prison for a murder which I and everyone who has looked into it agree he did not commit. Took an Open University degree while a prisoner. His 'colleague' in the alleged murder called Stafford, an older man with a criminal record, was released on parole with Michael. Recently he announced that he was guilty after all and that Michael, though he did not participate, was present. A little later Stafford announced in another newspaper that this was just a cock-and-bull story, dredged up because he was short of money. Meanwhile Michael fights on to clear his name, strongly supported by various eminent persons, including his solicitor, Sir David Napley.

Michael is now working for the handicapped, kindly attributing to me and The New Bridge, of which I am President, the opportunity. The New Bridge, an association to help ex-prisoners, was founded by myself and others, including Bill Hewitt, C.H. Rolph of the *New Statesman*, and Edward (Lord) Montagu, in 1955. Before Christmas he went into hospital with a lump on one side of his neck, the size of an egg, no one knowing whether it was or was not malignant. It turned out mercifully not to be. But now a lump has appeared on the other side. He will require an operation in September. His religious faith is striking. He is ready to face whatever may be the outcome.

At the next table were Bernard Levin and William Rees-Mogg. A coincidence here. On the way to the Gay Hussar had contemplated ringing William this afternoon and asking permission to write an article or, failing that, a letter to *The Times* on 'Why I remain Labour'. The opportunity was now almost literally on my plate. William's first reaction was to do an article of 900 words on the lines suggested. Later he slightly amended the invitation – 800 words from me as one of four or five writers on 'The Crisis in the Labour Party', the article to appear on Saturday morning, the day of the Wembley Conference. Have done a first draft. One problem is to indicate firmly that I am not leaving the party in the foreseeable future without malevolence to the efforts of the Social Democrats.

I only just caught the number 11 bus from Chelsea Town Hall to Sloane Square this morning, throwing my bag on to the platform and jumping on afterwards. The young Scottish conductor observed, 'I don't take very kindly to people who throw their bags at me.' I had the sense to apologize at once. Later, as we went on our way, I remarked to him, 'I wasn't throwing my bag at you. I hope you realize.' 'I know that,' he replied, 'but you might have hit someone.' I said, 'But there wasn't anyone but you on the platform'. He said, 'But there might have been.' I desisted.

Wednesday, 21 January 1981

Dinner at Grillions, famous dining club, where Gladstone once dined alone with a bottle of champagne. It meets every fortnight during the parliamentary session. A small attendance but, being asked to take the Chair, I enjoyed myself even more than usual. Situated Willie Whitelaw on my right hand and was impressed with a fresh sense of his positive niceness. When I have visited him (twice) on deputations have felt the warmth of his welcome almost too much. But close up the real man comes through. Willie assured us that his top priority was the reduction of the prison population. Someone suggested that the Crown Court judges with their reactionary sentencing policy were the 'niggers in the woodpile'. I told Willie that it would be a tragedy if his biographer had to describe him as a great potential Home Secretary sabotaged by the Crown Court judges. He smiled discreetly.

I had no idea that he was such a brilliant raconteur. One story he told us about Lord Brookeborough's memorial service had me laughing aloud, which I don't do easily. The gist was that hardly anyone would shake hands with or speak to anyone else because of the way Stormont had been suspended. The Lord Mayor of Belfast refused to shake hands with Whitelaw, the Home Secretary, or Heath, the PM, who in any event was not speaking to anyone much. 'I will speak only to the Queen's representative', said the Lord Mayor pompously and hid behind the pillar. The Queen's representative was Field Marshal Sir Gerald Templar who was furious at having to come to Belfast for the occasion. The Lord Mayor, emerging from behind the pillar, held out his hand to Templar who snapped out, 'And who the bloody hell are you?' Later Whitelaw was visited by Lady Brookeborough, who had already demonstrated her displeasure on the occasion mentioned. She refused to shake hands with Willie. By the end of their conversation he had won her over to the point where she held out her hand. 'Oh no,' he said. 'You must apologize to Her Majesty's Secretary of State [himself] before I shake hands with you.' Which she duly did, and in the end a handshake was effected.

Saturday, 24 January 1981

Elizabeth motored me to the Wembley Conference Centre for the Labour Party special conference. Pleased to see my article in *The Times* along with five other contributions: I had plenty of criticisms to offer, particularly of the unilateral possibility and of course the block vote, but I concluded, 'So long as I can work for the causes I believe in *within* the Party, I cannot see myself leaving it' (an ending, incidentally, supplied by Elizabeth). Shirley Williams moving, but rather too much in detail, which is her strength and weakness; Scargill predictably hard-left. Can't pretend that many people at the conference spoke to me about my piece (not much time to have read it). Roy Hattersley, however, went to sit by Elizabeth in the guest seats. When I joined them he remarked gracefully, 'I have come to sit by the wife of the author of *The Times* article.' Later he referred to one of the speakers as taking the Hattersley–Longford line (or was it Longford–Hattersley?). Elizabeth summed the whole thing up as we drove home. 'They', meaning the Left, 'have over-reached themselves.' Her political instinct has always been very acute. May it be so this time.

The drama of the day centred round the proportion of the electoral college that would be allocated to the MPs. They dislike the college as much as I do but are resigned to it. One of my neighbours, John Morris MP, recently Secretary of State for Wales, opined that if the Foot compromise (50 per cent for PLP) were adopted, he doubted whether defections would take place, unless and until MPs were undermined in their constituencies. He added, however, that if the Executive's proposal were adopted (33 per cent for MPs) he thought that the conclusion would be drawn that the Left were in no mood for reasonable compromise. A number of parliamentary defections was then probably inevitable, though he would not be among them. In the event the result was worse for the PLP than their worst fears: only 30 per cent for themselves against 40 per cent for the unions and 30 per cent for the constituency parties. We must expect defections.

Told Elizabeth that I felt I was looking at it all from afar off. The MPs and peers, though ex-officio delegates, were, like the visitors, in the gallery. What I meant was that the debate seemed to have even less relevance than usual to the crucial decisions, that these were being cobbled up somewhere else by half a dozen trade union bosses. But the speeches were good-tempered and vigorous. David Owen, whose wife sat next to Elizabeth (he joined them after his speech), was brave and shrewd without touching the emotions of the conference. He possesses genuine fire – synthetic fire is all too common. He is a potential leader, though not ripe for it yet. Frank Chapple made a more effective speech (on the right side) because more frankly prole-tarian. The flavour of the conference was more assertively proletarian even than usual. Many, perhaps half, of the delegates could not have passed as working-class at any time in their adult lives. Yet whenever the proletarian note was struck, it was the winner.

Michael Foot, who wound up the proceedings, is an entrancing orator full of spontaneous humour appearing to flow out of his thoughts as he proceeds. I have recently read his book of essays. Far the best is his portrait of his father, a west-country solicitor, active radical and inspired preacher. Yesterday, Michael was a preacher far more than a leader, though he was accepted with rapture in the latter capacity. He had just got badly beaten – his compromise of 50 per cent for the MPs being spurned. He accepted the result gracefully but shrewdly stressed the non-infallibility of conferences and the possibility of their decisions being reversed.

He has certainly had a unique career. No office of any kind until he was sixty-two, having at some earlier point been deprived of the Labour whip for a while. Now he is loved by everyone in Labour circles and liked by everyone who knows him at all. Today he seemed to be suffering from every conceivable physical disability. His eyes were obviously troubling him; Elizabeth and I, sitting in the circle and not priding ourselves on our hearing, agreed that he seemed to gasp for breath. He walks with a stick since his near-fatal car accident and broke his ankle recently. He looks about a hundred in spite of his white locks being shorn. Yet his speech yesterday was a masterpiece.

Tolerance is no doubt one of his best qualities. Here he must be thought to be superior to Hugh Gaitskell, though Hugh was a more real statesman. Hugh cared passionately for certain great causes. He would have given his life for Anglo-American co-operation in defence of the free world and for resistance to Soviet imperialism. Michael has championed unilateralism for many years but he is a more flexible type altogether. He told us that a new approach must be discovered to reconcile multilateralists and unilateralists. Nonsense, of course, but in yesterday's context it was possibly the right sort of nonsense.

Supposing that a real initiative is to be taken within the party to reverse today's lamentable decisions, who will emerge as the 'rescuing genius'? Certainly not Roy Jenkins who burnt his Labour boats long ago. The Gang of Three just possibly, but they seem much more likely to 'quit'. Denis Healey is on paper the obvious candidate. A man of immense ability, deputy leader of the party and a member in that capacity of the National Executive. There is a general feeling that he failed to take his chance at the time of the last conference. It would be a surprise if he takes it now. I hope everyone is wrong about him. Roy Hattersley is the dark horse. I am sure that he is alive to every nuance of the situation and does not lack guts; he probably reckons that it is unwise to present them in public.

Monday, 26 January 1981

Religious reading Mark 8: 'The Son of Man must suffer much and be rejected by the elders, the chief priests and the teachers of the law. He will be put to death, but three days later he will rise to life.' And then a verse or two afterwards: 'If anyone wants to come with me, he must forget himself, carry his cross and follow me.' The Cross and suffering are deep in Christian spirituality and ethics. Clem Attlee, my hero, once said to Kenneth Harris, when asked about religion, 'Accept the Christian ethic, no use for the mumbo-jumbo.' But Christian ethics do not confine themselves to the golden rule, love your neighbour as yourself, which could be regarded as glorified common sense. Leaving our humility and forgiveness for the moment, they introduce the strange ideas of the Cross and suffering which, as my revered head-master, Dr Alington, used to say from the pulpit at Eton, are 'uncommon nonsense'.

Wednesday, 28 January 1981

Meeting of the Youth Committee of the Penal Affairs Group. Promised them a powerful document from Vaughan Jones, coordinator of the New Horizon, next week. Hoped they didn't mind social workers' jargon. All cried out that they detested it. Generally agreed that I had given Vaughan's paper quite a build-up.

Lunch at the Garrick. Sat opposite John Vaizey who, along with Ronnie Harwood sitting on his right, provides the best fun available. John has had a heart operation lately but, astonishingly, he is running three miles a day, covering twelve miles if you count walking and swimming – all part of the cure. I am bound to say he looked very pale, though as lively as ever. Teased John, not for thr first time, on having accepted a Labour peerage and now taking the Tory whip. He cheerfully retorted that he had had letters in hospital from *both* Maggie Thatcher and Harold Wilson. Much hilarious chatter about the Gang of Three, etc. I forecast that their position would be weaker a year from now than it seems to be at the moment. No one seemed to dissent. All of us drank Ronnie Harwood's health, he having won the *New Standard*'s prize for the best play of the year.

An excellent talk at the Lords, after a private meeting, with Cledwyn Hughes, former Cabinet Minister and former Chairman of the PLP, a deeply religious Welsh Methodist. He had seemed shocked when I said in the meeting that I would never leave the Labour Party. He had questioned the word 'never'. Surely I put my religion before politics? I compromised, 'Well, not in the foreseeable future.' He told me over a drink that he was desperately worried about the party he loved and had served so long. Shirley Williams, whom he thought of as the obvious leader of any Social Democratic Party, had been pressing him very hard on Sunday night to join the new grouping. But he still lived among his old constituents; he could never look them in the face if he seceded. 'I suppose', he said, 'that all one can do is to pray.' I told him that in 1947 Father d'Arcy had told me once and for all not to go to spiritual advisers for political guidance. (I was contemplating resignation from the Attlee Cabinet over German dismantling.) Cledwyn had received the same advice from Methodist ministers. He was kind enough to say that my coming or going would make a real impression. But obviously his position is far more crucial. His accession to 'the Gang' would be a jewel beyond price. Somehow I don't think they will secure it.

To my immense surprise, he gave me his opinion that a well-organized combination of Liberals and Social Democrats could actually win a general election. The Liberals had the votes (five million or so) and the Social Democrats had the credible leaders. He admitted when pressed that the required organization might well not be forthcoming. Incidentally, he said two other things about Shirley. First, that she is a very strong woman. The *Daily Telegraph* has just referred to her as having built up a reputation for indecisiveness over the years. Margaret Thatcher once expressed to me genuine admiration for Shirley but implied that decisiveness was not her strength. Perhaps both things are true. Perhaps one makes a mistake in associating decisiveness and high principles. If one has principles at all, one principle may well be in conflict with another, which makes decision harder. Shirley is certainly very tough and courageous and immensely popular with the public. She is the only public woman in my experience whose untidyness seems to be a positive asset. Cledwyn added that Shirley has said to him, 'Anyone who joins the Council now would be expected to leave the Party if and when that was decided on.'

Thursday, 29 January 1981

Two p.m.: meeting of Labour peers. Six p.m.: meeting of PLP. General reflection afterwards that both groups are in some sense clubs. The Labour peers, in spite of their much increased numbers, are still a family. Leaders Eddie Shackleton, Malcolm Shepherd, Fred Peart and I and Chief Whips Frank Beswick and now, most ardently, Pat have worked hard to that end.

Elaine Burton, ex-MP, national sprint champion in 1920, spoke extremely well, but a shade too long. Expressed the disquiet felt by almost all present about Wembley and what led up to it. Finished by saying that she was joining the Council for Social Democracy, hoping to 'remain inside the party'. No one believes that this is possible. Many speakers tried to catch the eye of Fred Peart in the chair. Fred, handsome and able, is always kind to me. Harry Walston, selfless as always, explained his attempted initiative. Lord McCarthy referred to the great defectors of the past, the 'honour roll, Ramsay Mac, Mosley, etc., down to Reg Prentice'. I kept trying to 'get in' – unsuccessfully.

As time was running out, Fred announced: 'I was about to call Frank, but [to me] will you be here next week?' I said I would, if I was going to be called. I had just remarked to Donald Soper that 'not being called is a good mortification'. He replied, 'Yes, good for the soul.' Like other forms of suffering, it has to be accepted in the right spirit, which is not easy. Anyway, I shall be called next week, probably first. I shall appeal for a more positive line by the Labour peers generally. Collectively we are so terrified of raising our heads above the parapet, for fear of unspecified retribution.

Arrived early for the PLP meeting to find only one person there, Tony Benn. (Last time it was Harold Wilson and a very good talk we had too on that occasion.) Tony called to me in friendly fashion from the platform, 'Are you one of the signatories of the Walston letter?' I said that I had indeed agreed to the letter deploring the drift to the Left, but had made my position plainer in an article in *The Times* last Saturday: I would not be leaving the party. I added that I did not think as many as five active peers would be joining the Council for Social Democracy which would take them half-way out. He seemed a little disappointed. I gather that he wanted to refer to the defection in his subsequent remarks. (In the event he didn't.)

The meeting was low-key. Michael Foot, looking very old and changing his glasses repeatedly as he read, or didn't read, from a manuscript, announced that the Parliamentary Committee would be bringing a resolution before the PLP in pursuit of an amendment to the Wembley verdict. Everyone agreed to leave it there for the moment. Michael Foot read out a resolution passed at the NEC of the 'Mind you, I've said nothing' variety. Everyone agreed to work for everything good and loyal and socialistic. Tony Benn, looking more than ever like a keen young schoolmaster, somehow got himself called, though sitting on the platform. He blamed the media for even suggesting that he had tried to introduce an oath of allegiance. The dislike of the media, out of which many MPs make part of their living, is exploited remorselessly by any shrewd operator.

Tony made the point, new to me, that the Council are waiting until after the local elections, so that their adherents can win many seats on the Labour 'piggy-back' and then switch to the new party. He wound up effectively: 'They are using the Labour Party as an instrument for destroying the Labour Party.' He spoke with his usual preternatural calm. No one ventured to ask why Michael Foot had not made a public attempt on Saturday to sway the conference in the direction desired by himself and the PLP. He had reserved himself for the final oration.

Saturday, 31 January 1981

As usual at the weekend I jogged and walked over to see Chris and Elizabeth Maxwell. Chris is my old golfing partner, doctor and friend, who has been more or less housebound for fifteen years. He has acquired a serenity, almost a sanctity, during his long affliction. In the late afternoon I was taken over to Mayfield College for the annual Mass, dinner and speeches. My hosts were Plunkett House, which gave me a lucky opening. I told a story of Randal Plunkett, now Lord Dunsany, my first cousin, heir in so far as there is one to the canonized Saint Oliver. Randal attended a celebratory Mass. Though a Protestant he did not hesitate to go up to the altar rails for Communion. The local priest knew all about him and passed him by. Randal stayed on his knees. The next priest was less well-informed and gave him Communion. Randal stayed down and when the third priest came along got Communion for the second time. Afterwards someone said to him at the banquet, 'Bad luck, Randal, you must have been the only person here who couldn't get Communion.' 'On the contrary,' replied Randal, 'I am the only person here who got it twice.'

His father (Uncle Eddie) would have slapped his thigh and shouted 'HA!' with huge satisfaction. He once remarked of a Catholic lady of his acquaintance, 'For every spy the Kaiser has, Lady Saltoun has ten.'

Mayfield College must be 'rather unique', though that phrase was singled out for special opprobrium in the House of Lords debate on the English language last Wednesday. Originally a school run by an order of brothers, it is now under lay control, though still officially Catholic. Three hundred boys, only half of them Catholics, and at least twenty Chinese. Some of these are Catholics, but the others come for the discipline and the mathematics. The staff are also divided half and half between Catholics and non-Catholics. The very bright young master who motored me from Bernhurst told me that no one asked him about his religion when he was accepted as head of mathematics. Although some kind of agnostic, he has built up an excellent choir.

Sunday, 1 February 1981

I finish Julian of Norwich's *Revelations of Divine Love*, one of the relatively few mystical classics in the English language. The book is famous for two interrelated doctrines: 'All shall be well and all *shall* be well and all manner of things shall be well.' And 'Love was our Lord's meaning.' Julian is troubled (in so far as such a serene spirit can be troubled) by the conflict between the infinite mercy of God and the teaching of the Church that some of us at least go to Hell. Her editor, the Reverend Clifton Wolters, treats her as trembling here on the brink of heresy, but drawing back in time, in deference to official guidance. I cannot help feeling that she would be much relieved to find herself today among intellectual Catholics, including elevated clergy, who do not believe that any of us are eternally damned. For that reason, anong others, she is more relevant today than ever.

Thursday, 5 February 1981

The debate on the nationalized industries in the House of Lords yesterday passed off peacefully, our sharp criticisms being smothered in Conservative *bonhomie*. Frank Beswick, my parliamentary secretary many years ago when I was Minister of Civil Aviation, and more recently chairman of British Aero-Space, made an excellent speech. Plenty of bite without undue barking. I was honoured to be pressed to speak by Pat, on Monday. My contribution, offered out of loyalty to Frank, was a small, but distinct, success, with plenty of 'fun and games'.

A little debating break came my way. John Boyd-Carpenter, Tory ex-Cabinet Minister, had derided the idea of the nationalized industries as the 'commanding heights' of the economy (Nye Bevan's old phrase). He preferred to describe them as 'demanding depths'. No remark could have suited my purpose better. Part of our motion denounced the Conservatives for their everlasting sniping at the nationalized industries. I picked up John B-C's phrase and made the most of it. Possibly I overdid the point, but everyone seemed to enjoy a change from statistics. Peter Thorneycroft, chairman of the Conservative Party, sitting just opposite me entered into the spirit of jollity. John took it well, but when I met him next day remarked, 'You don't often take part in that sort of debate.' A gentle score.

Today the Labour peers assembled at 2.00 p.m. for continuance of last week's discussion about the future of the Party. After Elwyn-Jones, former Lord Chancellor, had opened rather non-committally but genially on behalf of the leadership, I was expecting to be called. But Fred Peart, our leader, announced, 'I understand that Jack Donaldson wishes to make a personal statement. Then Frank.' Jack Donaldson explained that he had been embarrassed by the publication of his name that morning among the hundred (selected) supporters of the Council of Social Democracy. He had agreed to his name being used, but had not expected to see it in print without some warning. Jack, a great friend of ours, as is Frankie his wife, and a man of brilliant if wayward intellect, is one of our front bench spokesmen and may have had a painful quarter of an hour with the Chief Whip. He finished by saying that he was in no way anxious to leave the party: he still hoped it wouldn't come to that. The party might decide to 'kick him out', which if it happened he would much regret.

I began my remarks with a sincere if obvious comment that I was relieved to hear that Jack was not leaving the party. I felt sure that the party would never kick him out. I then crudely laid down three propositions: (1) Thatcherism must be defeated at all costs; (2) the Party were undergoing what Elwyn-Jones had just described as a 'mood of madness'; (3) 90 per cent of us or more wanted to work *within* the party to reverse the present trend. I proceeded to argue in favour of some collective effort in that direction by Labour peers. Individually we would no doubt all do what we could through the media or in our localities or indeed in the House itself. But collectively I hoped that we would not be so frightened of attracting adverse publicity that we would do precisely nothing. I referred to our lack of emphasis on positive action as 'less than enterprising'. (I did not quote Esmond Warner's dictum to me, when giving me lunch at Brooks's two days earlier: 'As long as the Lords are getting forty-four quid a day they won't be causing any trouble to anyone.' Then, roaring with laughter, 'Old boy, they're only in it for the lolly.')

I called on our representative in the Shadow Cabinet, the Leader, the Chief Whip and Fred Lee, the peers' nominee, to put over our general standpoint with the utmost urgency. There are a handful of Labour peers who are much respected unilateralists. Fenner Brockway and Ritchie-Calder spoke in that sense. But the vast majority favour the Atlantic Pact, which involves at present reliance on nuclear weapons. On the EEC there would be much more difference of

opinion, though I imagine a good majority favours British membership. Nicky Kaldor hoped that the Social Democrats would leave the
party as soon as possible. We would then be able to leave the EEC
without further difficulty!

Later in the day I ran into Pat Llewelyn-Davies. 'Thank you', she
said in her cordial, though sometimes mischievous, way. I thought she
was referring to my speech of the day before, which later she praised.
But what she was really thanking me for was the line I had taken at
the party meeting which was 'most helpful'. But what had I said that
was of such value? That we must fight inside the party? Did she not
know that already? I got the impression that somehow my remarks
had strengthened her hand in the Shadow Cabinet. But against
whom?

Later again I met Jack Donaldson who had looked unhappy at the
meeting, which is rare with him. I expressed sympathy and praised
the dignity of his remarks. I remembered that he had said to me a few
days earlier, 'I shall be very much influenced by what Shirley does.'
I concluded from *his* hesitations that *she* was still very reluctant to
leave the Party. Jack was clearly not so close to Roy as usual. This was
significant coming from Jack, who has always admired Roy immensely. He keeps saying, 'Roy got me my peerage.' My claim to have
done something to help as Leader of the House at that time is dismissed, I dare say rightly. Obviously Roy, on returning to England,
had no future in the Labour Party. The same was by no means true of
the 'Gang of Three'. At the moment of writing it seems almost certain
that a new party of some kind will be started. But there still seems just
a chance, an outside chance, that Shirley Williams, their one great
potential asset, will hold back.

Sunday, 8 February 1981

Dinner last night at the Muggeridges – as enjoyable as always. There
was more theological expertise available than I expected, in Alec
Vidler, former Dean of King's, possibly Malcolm's greatest friend.
There was also Alan Fraser, a staunch Presbyterian lawyer who was
Malcolm's number two when the latter was Rector of Edinburgh
University.

I have just finished reading de Caussade in Kitty Muggeridge's
sensitive new translation. I had previously read his book under the
famous title *Abandonment to Divine Providence*. Kitty rechristened it *The*

Sacrament of the Present Moment. In her introduction she claims that the two titles between them sum up his whole spiritual doctrine. De Caussade himself announces, 'It is enough for us to know what we must do', which means discovering God's will for us at the present moment. This, he goes on, 'is the easiest thing in the world'. He adds that, 'There is no one in the world who cannot *easily* (my italics) attain to the highest degree of perfection.' I readily believe that at any and every moment there is a course of action or non-action which is God's will for us. But how on earth can we be sure what it is? Kitty, still soaked in de Caussade, does not find the question alarming. She argues in effect that if one gets the answer wrong, God will soon put matters right. Certainly there was plenty of that in de Caussade. Not only does he announce sublimely like Julian of Norwich that all *shall* be well, but insists that all *is* well (already). Alan Fraser, accustomed, it seemed, to this kind of debate in Edinburgh, intervened, 'You mean God can't lose', which Kitty did not dissent from at the moment. (I suppose that she might have added, 'We can't lose either.')

Alan and Alec recognize the danger of being too sure of our own guidance. I said that years ago my headmaster at Eton had recommended us to bring all our human powers to bear on a problem and then pray as hard as we knew how. After that we could leave the result in God's hands. But de Caussade is really going further when he says that everything that happens is in accordance with God's will. When that view is asserted nowadays one naturally asks, 'And what about the Nazi concentration camps?' That God *allowed* them to happen, Christians must believe. That he *wished* them to happen – no, no, no, no.

There is no doubt whatever that Malcolm and Kitty have a truly religious conviction that all will be well eventually, presumably in the next world. Incidentally, Kitty heads one of her sections, 'Pessimists are the Only Optimists', a phrase which also occurs in her translation of the text. Nothing could describe Malcolm more accurately. I must look at the earlier translation of de Caussade, to see whether it agrees with this rendering.

Monday, 9 February 1981

A *Times* opinion poll this morning purports to show that immense gains would be secured in an election by some kind of Liberal–Social Democratic alliance or merger. Still very sceptical myself.

I was joined in the train from Etchingham by Martin Jackson, a friend and neighbour from Hawkhurst, former Labour candidate and councillor, television journalist and now a member of a television syndicate, which has secured the concession for Southern Television. I tell him that this is the last time that he will travel second class. Martin, a good judge of things political, also takes a poor view of the prospects of the Centre Party or Alliance. His next-door neighbours played a large part in the Dick Taverne movement in Lincoln, a few years ago. It was highly successful for a time but then faded out. The strongest support came in fact from dissident Tories. The neighbours in question believe that the same thing will happen to the proposed Alliance.

The same kind of view was expressed by Alan Watkins, whom I ran into and lunched with at the Garrick, though he thought they might have some initial successes in the Midlands. I accepted a drink from him (sherry). I offered him one in return. This proved to be a glass of champagne, costing £2.25. He made atonement by producing a bottle of superlative claret for our luncheon. He is a connoisseur of wine.

He is writing a kind of modern version of Aubrey's lives. Tony Crosland and I are included. Tony remains a bit of a hero to him, though Alan was sometimes appalled by his rudeness. Tony once told me that I would have had much more influence on his generation if I had not been so arrogant towards the waiters in the George café at Oxford. From Tony, this was indeed expert praise. Sitting next to him in the Cabinet, I was always anxious to please him, but seldom if ever did. At the time of the devaluation discussions in 1966, he said to me, 'You are the only intellectual in the Cabinet who has voted against us' (the devaluationists), which wasn't quite true. I had been much influenced by Douglas Jay, President of the Board of Trade, who was as clever as any of them.

Alan is rightly rather proud of a recent article by him on Richard Ingrams, a devoted disciple of Malcolm, but a sharp critic of mine. We both agreed about Richard's peculiar talent, but deplored the anti-Semitism of *Private Eye*. Where could it have come from? Shrewsbury? Why should it? Except as a symptom of public school immaturity. Belloc? Richard's mother is a devout RC, his father was Anglican. The children were 'split' between the two religions, Richard being brought up a Protestant. But none of this explains the anti-Semitism. Bron Waugh, also an RC, talks that way occasionally, as did his father. But it is difficult to believe he means it.

Wednesday, 11 February 1981

Sat next at lunch to Sir David McNee, Chief Commissioner of the Metropolitan Police. David McNee was far less rigidly puritanical than his so-called image. He had a keen, if Scottish, sense of humour. Everyone thinks they have a sense of humour, but few people really do see the funny side of life. McNee, though a strong Presbyterian, is no teetotaller, nor is he a heavy drinker. Three of us had a bottle of wine between us. Last night, however, I dreamt that he and I had an argument which finished with his saying, 'The trouble is that I'm one over and you're one under.'

Thursday, 12 February 1981

Lunch at the Lords for Mike Fisher. We agree that as soon as I have next seen Myra I shall write to the Home Secretary asking for a personal interview. The idea at lunch was that I should go alone. But immediately afterwards I ran into John Hunt (of Everest fame, but also the first chairman of the Parole Board, until recently president of the Probation Officers' Association). He visited Myra years ago as Parole Board chairman when she first went to prison, and remarked afterwards, 'She has got such guts.' I told him that I would be seeing her two days later and would then be asking Whitelaw for an interview. He said, 'I would be glad to come with you.' Of course I accepted the offer with alacrity. What a man!

A word with Hugh Trevor-Roper, Lord Dacre, in the library. He is a director of *The Times*. I said, 'Hugh, how could you let that man [Rupert Murdoch] get your paper?' He replied, 'There was no alternative. At any rate, we put a hook through the nose of Leviathan.'

Two p.m.: Michael Foot addressed the Labour peers. They are so polite to any guest, especially the leader of the party, and to one another that their true reactions are well concealed. He was courtesy itself, with that God-given humour peeping through some ponderous verbiage. He began with the story of Trotsky inspecting the statues in the Kremlin on first arrival and remarking to them, 'You must be wondering what I am doing here.' Applied to himself among the Labour nobles, that went down well. But most of the time he just orated away, his answers getting longer and longer. At the end, the Irish saying would have been apposite, 'Mind you, I've said nothing.' His reply about the future of the Lords was typical, 'I've always

been an abolitionist.' (In unholy alliance with Enoch Powell he sabotaged the reform of 1968 which I had done much to initiate.) But he
added disarmingly, 'On the other hand, I consider that the Lords
were badly treated in not having their own proposals considered
before the Party drew up its plans on the last occasion. I will make
sure that that does not happen again.'

I asked him about the party attitude to the Atlantic Pact. He
answered with even more elusiveness than usual, 'The party has
recently passed resolutions in favour of unilateral disarmament,
multilateral disarmament, and the Atlantic Alliance. ... You may say
that my answer is confused, but this is a confused situation. ...' He
went on to warn us against excessive certainties and finished with a
denunciation of President Reagan. All were disarmed.

Having been given the gentlest of rides, Michael departed amidst
civil applause. Frank Beswick surprised me by rising to say that we
ought to thank him officially for coming. Ted Short, another stalwart,
went even further by saying that we ought to let it be known that our
gratitude to him for coming was unanimous. I and others protested.
So in the end it was all very inconclusive, though everyone persuaded
themselves that we had done some unspecified good by inviting him.
No doubt there will be more of the same fraternal spirit next Wednesday, when Michael and his wife Jill come to our annual binge.

Friday, 13 February 1981

Set off north to visit Joe Kagan in prison. I had become friendly with
him in the House of Lords and had sat next to him during his maiden
speech. The *Daily Express* asked whether I would be visiting him. I
replied, 'Certainly, if he would like to see me.' An invitation came
along promptly. I was met at Leeds by Liz Foreman, Joe Kagan's
secretary; five foot nine, slim, smart in black, with trendy steel-rimmed
glasses. Joe's daughter Jenny, aged fifteen, was with her. She motored
us to her motel to lunch, close to the open prison where Joe is resident.
I was with him for more than an hour. I expected Joe to be jaunty,
but was hardly prepared for his absorption in the life of the prison. He
was full of enthusiasm about the whole set-up. He was performing
some administrative task in the weaving shed and made it sound as
though he was running it. Having graduated in textiles at Leeds and
employed many weavers, he was in a good position to pass judgement
and gave the prison weaving a first-class certificate.

I asked him whether, at sixty-five, he found it trying to sleep in a dormitory. 'Far from it', he replied. He had never really got to know the working classes until now. He would not have missed the experience for anything. He was liberal with his tobacco and in this and other ways had apparently become a kind of father figure. He proudly showed me his shoes which had been blacked that morning by an ex-guardsman. My mind went back to my Territorial camp in 1939, which I had found most uncomfortable, though I was half Joe's present age. An elderly private had indeed blacked my boots, but charged me 7s 6d. The only anxiety expressed by Joe was that the conditions of life, plus the security, provided a much better existence than most of the men would find on release, about which they were distinctly nervous. He had a scheme under which prisoners would be allowed to continue working in the weaving shed, for example, after release while finding something better to go to. He had not worked it out, but his intention was patently genuine.

At times he seemed to forget that he was a prisoner. For no very clear reason, he persuaded a prison officer to join us for some part of the time. At one point he gestured the prison officer to a seat as though he were back in his office. He didn't talk a great deal about his case. He complained bitterly, as I expected, about the Inland Revenue authorities. But for them, he would now be providing 1,500 jobs. Some of his offences would not be crimes today, since Mrs Thatcher removed the exchange regulations. He was also accused of stealing from a business which he owned 100 per cent.

He expected to be released in June and would be taking his place in the House of Lords thereafter. I assumed that he would want to make a public statement about all sorts of things, but urged that this should be done to the Press before he spoke in the Lords. He is, I hope, as aware as I am that the one thing the Lords can't bear is embarrassment. If he wished to attack the Inland Revenue there, he should do it as impersonally as possible.

I told him his 'flight' would be the case against him more than anything else. He took the point, though I did not press him for a real answer at the moment. Douglas Houghton, his MP, who knew him extremely well, had told me at tea in the Lords the previous day that when the Revenue authorities raided his house and offices, Joe saw the whole horror of his incarceration by the Russians and Germans rising again before him. Can 'I must get away from them' be the explanation? I don't know whether he will ever be able to make that persuasive. He still insists that the Inland Revenue simply arrested his wife and son to blackmail him into pleas of guilty. It is obviously possible to take many different views of Joe Kagan. His admiring secretary told me that she didn't think that she would ever understand his mind. But he is, whatever else he may be, a fabulous survivor. As Beatrice Webb said of Sidney in the early days of their courtship, 'I like the man.' So, I know, does Elizabeth.

Saturday, 14 February 1981

I visited Myra for an hour this morning, arriving in a state of some trepidation. A letter received from her at the weekend painted a rather horrifying picture of her stay in the punsihment block; she had been refused permission to go into solitary confinement in a voluntary capacity. While waiting to see her I asked the young prison officer, Joan, whether Myra was still on punishment and was relieved to be told she was back to normal, if life in the women's wing at Durham deserves that adjective.

Myra when she appeared made me some coffee, a concession won recently, and told me the whole painful story. A great sense of prison nausea had come over her. She felt the need to shut herself away from prison life as far as possible. At the same time she longed to make her protest at the total refusal of the authorities up to now to hold out any hope to her, after fifteen and a half years in prison. She obtained solitary confinement, but by no means the solitary confinement she was looking for. She had to spend the day in a punishment cell with only a hard chair and later a table for company. No papers, no radio, visits cut down to a minimum. Her very good friend, Sarah Trevelyan, a young doctor, married to the famous delinquent Jimmy Boyle, had begged her to abandon the protest as damaging to her long-term interests. After a week she did so.

The issue was complicated by her need to secure permission at this time from the authorities if she were to read honours with the Open University, having already obtained a pass degree. In the end a kind of bargain was struck with the Governor that if she were allowed to read for honours she should pledge herself to finish the course. The permission of the Home Office involves a modest expenditure, tuition (mainly by correspondence, though she would see a tutor once a month), books, television, etc. She has now given the promise and is at the moment rather fearful lest the drama course prove too difficult.

It is not the literary side of it which dismays her. There is, however, a good deal about theatrical production and so on.

No one who knows her has any doubt that she is mentally capable of doing the work if she is not too emotionally disturbed. The Governor appears to have behaved quite sensibly. Life alone in her cell for any length of time would hardly be good for her and, if under punishment conditions, very damaging. When making 'the deal' the Governor of the prison had tried to argue, no doubt with good intentions, that after so many years prison ought to be 'getting easier'. (Rather like saying to someone in a wheelchair, 'You must be getting used to that old chair of yours.') She had retorted, 'No, harder', as would any candid prisoner not hopelessly institutionalized.

Later in the morning, I told the wing governor that I should have thought that after fifteen and a half years they could have stretched a point and allowed her to take a short rest from the communal life of the prison. He said that exemptions from work were freely granted to her and others on medical grounds. But she was explicitly making a protest and if she 'got away with it' (my words) other prisoners would soon follow her example. I told him that if she were still being punished I would kick up a fuss. But, as things were, I would refrain.

I gave Myra messages of love from Elizabeth. She brightened a bit when I told her that on Wednesday Elizabeth and I would be going to a play about the women's wing in Durham. (Myra calls it 'the submarine'; I usually refer to it as 'the living tomb'.) She was anxious for me to write and tell her about it, which of course I promised. I also tried to cheer her up with news that I would immediately be asking for an interview with the Home Secretary and that John Hunt, former chairman of the Parole Board, had volunteered to come with me. But she is deeply pessimistic about the decision of the Joint Committee concerning her consideration for parole in December. The Home Office committee will decide whether she can be *considered* for parole – a far cry, of course, from *getting* it. In the early autumn the prison authorities will begin to put together reports about her. I could not help exclaiming to the wing governor, 'What a farce it all is! The whole thing will be decided in terms of political expediency.' He mildly agreed that there would be nothing new to say about her.

I asked him whether it would do her more good or harm if she had a real nervous breakdown, which one of her friends was apparently having at the moment. She had told me earlier that she would never allow herself to have one because it would so upset her mother. She always tried to avoid telling her mother how depressed she was. The wing governor thought it might cut either way. It might make the authorities feel that a total collapse must be averted by a step towards parole. On the other hand, it might be treated as an example of her dangerous instability.

Of course there cannot be any logic or honesty in refusals of parole based on her actual condition. Home Office officials persuade themselves that it is their duty not to involve their minister in any unpopular decisions. They go further, in my experience, and argue (implicitly) that if he is so involved he will lose his head and put back the cause of penal reform. It is a shocking argument, which they would hardly dare to unfold in public. But they have one or two precedents to support their thesis. When George Blake escaped in 1965, Roy Jenkins set up the Mountbatten inquiry which laid an absurd stress on security, still operating. When Mrs Wing, governor of Holloway, took Myra for a walk, such walks had been authorized for twenty-five years. But from then, 1972, they stopped and have not been resumed.

Myra's home circumstances add further elements of gloom. Her sister died suddenly last year. Her sister's widower is suffering from a progressive spinal illness which makes work impossible. Her mother, an elderly woman, has some very poorly paid employment. Even with help from NACRO (the National Association for the Care and Resettlement of Offenders) they can only afford to visit her every three months. I promised to do what I could.

Altogether a sad visit, though not perhaps quite as bad as I feared. I think that her spirit, as distinct from her spirits, is beginning to rise in response to the challenge of the honours degree. I must use every faculty I possess to make an impression on Willie Whitelaw. I couldn't ask for a finer or more relevant ally than John Hunt.

Monday, 16 February 1981

I finished and sent off to the *Contemporary* my review of Dick Crossman's new volume of Diaries (1951–64). Dick had such transcendent gifts of expression in speech and writing, and he was so life-enhancing a personality, that one is left asking why his huge promise was unfulfilled. 'No judgement', was the verdict of Lord Attlee, a great friend of Dick's father, but in Dick's eyes persistently unfair to himself. 'Waspishly inaccurate at the net' was how Dick described Clem's tennis. Dick was, up to a point, but only up to a point, clear-sighted about himself. In these diaries he does not hesitate to describe the distrust felt towards him in the Parliamentary Labour Party, but he could never understand how he could be admired and distrusted at the same time, often by the same people, including myself. The phrase 'double Crossman' was cheap and nasty, but it could never have flourished if it did not contain a kernel of truth. It was widely supposed that if Dick said something today, he would say something different and perhaps contradictory tomorrow. Yet I am sure that he never deliberately deceived anyone.

Compared with Hugh Gaitskell, he was the essential hare to Hugh's tortoise. And the hare could never understand why the tortoise outstripped him in the chosen field of battle. I am told that when Bevin was asked in 1945 to nominate the two most promising Labour politicians, he nominated Dick in the first place and secondly myself. He gave each of us his opportunity and in his eyes each of us let him down. Dick over Palestine and I over Germany. Dick antagonized Attlee, for one reason or another. Clem always remained favourable to me, perhaps because my father had died at Gallipoli, where he himself had served so bravely.

My relationship with Dick was as unpredictable as was he himself. It is clear from his diaries, and no surprise to me, that he wanted me removed from the Cabinet in favour of Eddie Shackleton. But he ramains the most vivid of all my contemporaries in politics, and in the next world, which he declined to believe in, the most exciting to encounter.

Wednesday, 18 February 1981

Good news from Weidenfeld. They like the book that Anne McHardy and I have written about Ulster. It is a daring experiment. I am much relieved to hear that they are favourable. Our young editor, Sally, recently from Wadham, is highly intelligent. Her criticism that I have quoted other historians too copiously is absolutely right. But I am sure that the error can be corrected.

Labour peers' annual party. Elizabeth and I always enjoy this function hugely. This year the air of mutual congratulation is greater than ever, by reason of our *not* having ratted on the party in its hour of need. Pat was very gracious and said that she could have kissed me after I had announced at the party meeting that nothing would induce me to desert Labour. I said that it was never too late – so the rite was duly performed.

Michael Foot, our honoured guest, seemed genuinely reluctant to make a speech. He was induced to say a few words, in his usual happy vein. 'Many of my best friends are peers', he began. A jocular voice, 'All your best friends are peers.' Unless there is a hitch, Mrs Thatcher will soon be sending us a reinforcement of ten or so Labour peers, on Michael's nomination. Yet he keeps saying that he is still an 'abolitionist'.

Then on to a theatrical evening at the Oval Theatre, part of an artistic complex much patronized, it would seem, by students. Two short plays were performed. Both were written and acted by women who had been in prison, the first by Eva and Jenny, who had called on me at the Lords; the second dealt specifically with the women's wing in Durham Prison, where I had visited Myra a few days earlier. The boredom and artificiality of prison life were brought out effectively.

Thursday, 19 February 1981

Meeting at the House of Lords to discuss a proposed Bill to strengthen the laws against pornography. Dick Nugent and Tony Halsbury were the authors. I am happy to follow them in matters pornographic. They are not only strong Christians, but effective performers in the House of Lords.

A Private Member's Bill to deal with the limited area of indecent display is likely to pass into law. We debated at length whether to tack on to this Bill a provision to make *all* pornography illegal. When I had to leave the meeting this seemed unlikely, as liable to damage the prospects of the limited measure.

In the evening I distributed the prizes at the Prendergast School at Lewisham. The school, with nearly six hundred girls, is in process of changing from grammar to comprehensive and has a high academic reputation, which the young, vital and very pretty headmistress has no intention of allowing to decline. She was a Chamberlain by birth and a daughter of Elizabeth's first cousin, Dick. I predict a brilliant career for her. She told me hair-raising stories of threats to the staff in her last school. The headmaster was pursued with a gun. She was visited by two thuggish-looking men, who said that they had come to 'do' her because of the way she had treated one of their relatives. She informed them coolly that there was a policeman in the next room. (By some lucky chance, but perhaps not entirely by coincidence, there was.) The two thugs took to their heels.

I distributed a number of prizes to black girls and asked the headmistress why they seemed to be specially applauded. Did the other girls feel sorry for them? No, I was told, it's because they are such good athletes. I am not an observant person, but I had noticed their long, graceful limbs. 'The athletes and the naughty ones are always cheered the loudest.'

Friday, 20 February 1981

Elizabeth reports on her hour and a half yesterday with Harold Wilson. He had kindly agreed to see her about her projected book on *The Queen as Monarch*, for which George is offering a splendid advance. He looked tired but not at all ill; he felt much better since his three operations. The only time I have met him recently, when I sat beside him at a PLP meeting, he had gained in charm. He was always full of fun and benevolence, but there was too much bombast, which seems to have been melted away in suffering.

He has written four books which bear on Elizabeth's subject since 1970 and had inevitably not a lot to add that was new. He by no means accepted the view that recent changes had destroyed the Queen's discretion in choosing her prime minister. Situations were not difficult to envisage in which she would still have a delicate task to perform in discovering a prime minister who could command a majority in the Commons.

He was more outspoken about the present state of affairs in the Labour Party, though he expressed himself at times in monosyllables worthy of Attlee. The Council for Social Democracy? No future. Might Tony Benn become leader? No chance at all. He was just as firm in rejecting the possibility that a Labour government might leave NATO or the EEC. Might they abolish the House of Lords? 'They'll never win.' He meant that the Labour Party would never win an election on a left-wing ticket and was therefore unlikely to fight on one. He told Elizabeth that he would not be standing again for the House of Commons. No doubt he will come to the Lords, where he would find himself very much at home, with his general mateyness matching theirs.

Elizabeth will soon be approaching the other ex-prime ministers,

Macmillan, Home, Heath, Callaghan (and possibly Mrs Thatcher, who is said to bear a certain likeness to Elizabeth, though admittedly twenty years younger).

Saturday, 21 February 1981

A visit to Father Kevin Cronin, for many years the outstanding Principal of the St Mary's Catholic Teachers' Training College at Strawberry Hill, Horace Walpole's house. In that last connection he had come to know Jackie Kennedy, before she married. She was studying Horace Walpole. He introduced her to a Catholic priest in Dublin, with whom she developed a remarkable correspondence on spiritual matters in her search for faith. She had actually asked this priest to marry her and John Kennedy, but he thought that local talent would be more appropriate. Within twenty-four hours of the assassination she had written to him a heart-broken letter, saying that for the moment her belief in God was sadly shaken. But later she wrote to say that it had returned.

I myself have never had a spiritual director, but first (Father) Martin d'Arcy SJ and then (Father) Tom Corbishley SJ helped me on innumerable occasions. Father d'Arcy prepared me for my reception over a period of two years, but at the last moment he had to go to America on war work. Since then I have lacked a regular adviser, though my parish priests, Father Docherty in Hurst Green and Father De Zulueta in Chelsea, have been holy men by any criterion.

Lunch at St Mary's College, Strawberry Hill. I was assailed rather unexpectedly by one of the lecturers and his arresting wife on my attitude to the public schools. The dialogue followed the usual course. I said that I thought that the country would be better without them. They said, 'Why did you send four sons to Ampleforth?' I said I put their education above my theories, etc., etc. The sparkling lady adopted a new tack. 'Why did Shirley Williams take her daughter away from a school which went independent?' I said 'You can't win.' They agreed whole-heartedly. The little episode reminded me of the disaster that once befell my dear old friend Charles Snow in the Lords. Charles was defending the comprehensive system from the Government front bench in the Lords. I, as his Leader at the time, was sitting beside him. David Eccles, penetrating of mind, deeply religious in his later years, but at that time insensitive on occasion, interrupted, 'In that case why do you propose to send your son to Eton?' (Charles's son later won the first scholarship there.) Charles replied that he thought it best for him to meet the same kind of boys at school as he met in the holidays. This might be psychologically sound, but politically the one thing that could not be said. I had a ghastly awareness that Charles had indicated something of the kind to me the previous evening and I had raised no objection. The Conservatives fell on him. The Labour peers did not know where to look.

Later, after he had left the Government, he became one of the most popular members of the House and gave the best account yet provided of one large aspect of the life there. A most generous soul whom I was always happy to sit next to. I recognize myself in his book about the Lords as a genial purveyor of gossip about the Old Etonian peers. I was once at least mistaken for Charles. He was the same age, roughly the same size; both of us were bald, horn-rimmed, later gold-rimmed. Once I was asked at the Chichester Theatre Festival for an autograph. 'You are C.P. Snow, aren't you?', to which I replied without hesitation, 'Yes, of course', and duly signed: C.P. Snow.

Then on to Twickenham (England v. Scotland). Six tries were scored. England came from behind to win in the last ten minutes. I entered into the spirit as keenly as ever, but caught a nasty cold on the chilly benches. All the time I was thinking of Cardiff, where Ireland were beaten by nine points to eight by Wales, although they scored the only tries of the match. They clearly wilted in the last quarter. I shall be eager to see who, if anyone, is dropped when the team to play England is announced on Monday.

In the evening Elizabeth and I attended the annual dinner of the Cranbrook Labour Party. We were addressed by Jack Jones, described when he was General Secretary of the TGWU as the most powerful man in England. My attitude to him passed through three phases during the evening. I arrived full of intense suspicion, identifying him with long-standing left-wing associations and a reflection of many of the weaknesses that had overtaken the Labour Party. As we were going to the dinner, I asked myself what I have got in common with Jack Jones, except that we are both elderly men who have been members of the Labour Party for forty or more years. Then he spoke. By common consent, including mine, uncommonly well. He and Michael Foot have the compelling gift of expressing strong indignation without appearing bad-tempered. (I find that about as hard as combining joy and suffering, the prerogative of the saints.) There was just the right amount of anti-Thatcherism and some excellent cracks about

Roy Jenkins and the other defectors: 'Looking at the economy today is like looking through Alice's looking glass, or should I say through Roy Jenkins's brandy glass?' (Much happy laughter.) End of second phase.

Then I went up and spoke to him and his friendly wife who recalled our pleasant meeting at a Labour conference. After twenty minutes I had improved my opinion of Jack unmistakably. Admittedly I am always gratified when a big trade union official calls me by my Christian name and treats me as a comrade, after all these years in the party. Jack left on my mind an indelible impression of profound concern for his fellow humans. I should describe him as the most effective champion that the old people of this country possess. Nothing alters my opinion that far too much power in the Labour Party and in the nation lies in the hands of these trade union bosses, whose whole training equips them to think in sectional rather than in national terms. I told him sincerely that I was very sorry that his attempt to introduce workers' participation had not yet got anywhere. When I was a Cowley councillor (he remembered me from those days) I used to see thousands of men emerging from the Morris and Pressed Steel works. I used to say to myself a change in ownership, nationalization for example, won't make much difference to their lives, but participation would. He said that neither Harold W. nor James C. had been really interested in the subject, but their very small majority in the House of Commons provided some excuse.

Elizabeth said to me as we drove away, 'The Labour Party is always happiest when it has a good split on its hands.' She did not mean it quite seriously, but the remark contained an aspect of truth.

Tuesday, 24 February 1981

The papers tell us that Prince Charles's engagement to Lady Diana Spencer will be announced today. Elizabeth's book on the Queen Mother will be out in June; there will be just time to insert a statement that the engagement will give special pleasure to Prince Charles's grandmother. It all fits in very well with Elizabeth's conception of the Queen as a sublime exemplar of the family principle. We learn that Lady Diana's parents have a house next door to Sandringham and that her father was an equerry of King George VI. Elizabeth thinks of saying in her book that 'Lady Diana will fit into the royal family like a hand into a glove'. This, however, is too much of a cliché – can I think of another, better simile? I rack my brains hopelessly. She then comes up with this: 'She will fit in like a royal crest into its nest.' It is this which gives Elizabeth, in addition to all her academic qualities, the edge on other biographers.

William, Margaret and I gave lunch to Norman St John-Stevas at the Garrick. We hope to secure a book from him. A number of other publishers appear to be wooing him. We are hoping that somehow or other he would write something that revealed the sharp difference between his compassionate caring Conservatism and that of Mrs Thatcher. This seems to be unlikely. He talked of a 'rush towards the centre' in the Conservative Party. I asked him whether she was leading it. He said, 'No; following it, or she soon would be.' He saw himself as someone who had spoken out a few weeks too soon.

I had the feeling that he would naturally hope, as I would in his place, to re-emerge in the Cabinet under her or her successor. But he seemed to assume that she would remain PM, whatever the U-turn or S-turn. I put it to him that he had been apparently an unqualified admirer of hers – the blessed Margaret, and so forth. He claimed still to have a high respect for her qualities, but he conceded that her outlook was narrow.

Norman was astounded when he was dismissed from the Cabinet. He was not surprised at being moved, but thought that it would be Education. He was offered instead the derisory appointment of Minister of State in that department. I was amazed to hear that Margaret Thatcher had her private secretary with her when she performed this painful operation. Attlee was considered a good butcher, but he would have scorned the presence of an adjutant on such an occasion.

At the end of the lunch, the best chance of a book from Norman seemed to be a biography of Disraeli. In spite of Robert Blake's masterpiece, he was certain that there was plenty of room for a new interpretation. Norman was not uncritical of the food and the general ambience of the West Room, where ladies have to be entertained. I pointed out that he was a member of the Garrick, figuring largely in what I call the Top Table. It was rumoured recently that he had protested because his seat there was taken by another member. This story turned out to be all wrong. In reality, Norman took Charles Forte to a late supper in the back room and found that the seats reserved had been given away. He made, I am sure, a spirited fuss. Eventually they were allowed to have a meal in semi-darkness in the deserted front room, which is not used for these late suppers. To make matters worse, the avocado pears were cold and hard. Charles, who is said to take his chef with him when he deems it necessary, no doubt wished he had done so on this occasion. He is so kind that I am sure he was as upset for Norman as Norman was for him.

Wednesday, 25 February 1981

Footnote to yesterday's lunch with Norman. Since our lunch yesterday Elizabeth and I received the following letter from him: 'I am so grateful to you for sending me that telegram at a time of difficulty. I am just getting to the end of the 800 letters in reply! Since I was hunted out the whole of government policy seems to have collapsed – cause and effect?'

Lunch for Bill and Jean Procter. Bill has been production manager of S & J through many vicissitudes, going back well beyond my time. Norah [Baroness] Phillips who joined us at lunch described them afterwards as lovely people. She is the sprightliest of all the women peers and a number of them are full of sparkle. Alma Birk, for example, has become a fine debater. No one in the Lords has developed more strikingly. Norah is the widow of Morgan Phillips, for many years General Secretary of the Labour Party. Not long ago she became Lord Lieutenant of Greater London and is hence the senior Lord Lieutenant. She has a great deal to do with the Palace and hopes that her place is assured for the royal wedding. Elizabeth and I were (admittedly to my surprise) not asked to the wedding of Princess Anne. I being a Knight of the Garter to which order Prince Charles belongs, we might have a chance this time.

No doubt it depends partly on whether it is a State or private wedding. Partly also on where it takes place. Most people seem to be assuming that it will be in Westminster Abbey. But Elizabeth sat next at dinner last night to the Dean of Westminster, Edward Carpenter. He said that they 'had heard nothing' which makes them fear that it will be in St Paul's. The latter holds an extra four hundred. Our chances of squeezing in would then be improved. Elizabeth has a considerable *tendresse* for Reverend Carpenter. She shares his left-wing views and can sympathize with, without sharing, his unilateralism. He told her that he had been to many royal religious occasions and 'never seen a thing'. He spoke enthusiastically about the Christianity of the royal family, though adding the comment 'more matins than sacramental'.

Friday, 27 February 1981

A day of encounters with extremes of happiness and unhappiness. In the morning I saw two painfully unhappy women. In the afternoon one very angry and unhappy man. The evening I spent with as happy a gathering as you could find anywhere.

At 10 a.m. I visited a Romany lady in Holloway Prison. She is serving a ten-month sentence for (allegedly) extracting £1,600 from a West Indian by fortune-telling. I am absolutely sure that it was a case of mistaken identity; it is quite obvious that she was in Scotland at the time. The poor woman was absolutely stricken. She kept protesting her innocence. When I assured her that I believed her she leant forward and kissed my hands. Her husband took me to the prison in his car and told me to mention his pet name for her: Kaprushka – little turtle. This had a magical effect, though she still kept bursting into tears.

For once I felt that the benefit of my visit was not purely psychological. She is a diabetic but did not seem to be having the right diet in Holloway. I obtained the interest of the Governor, herself a doctor who knows me quite well from the days when I used to visit Myra. I am sure that on the medical side she will now be well looked after, but I have never come across a more blatant miscarriage of justice.

Back at my office I was called on by a lady who through no fault of her own made me feel desperately inadequate. She had had, it seems, five convictions for shop-lifting with two more charges hanging over her. She assured me that she had always been innocent and had brought masses of documents to prove it, but I simply had not got the time to deal with her case properly. I promised to speak to her solicitor and told her that I would be happy to see her on another occasion. Happy is not quite the word, but I do feel desperately sorry for her. She seems to have no one in the whole wide world to help her.

In the afternoon I visited Ian Brady at Wormwood Scrubs, as I have been doing these twelve years. He was in a thoroughly bad temper and indeed he had something to be in a bad temper about. I have been long of the opinion, which on the whole has been shared by him, that Broadmoor would be the best place for him. Not long ago I discussed the question with the psychiatrist who visits him in the prison hospital. The latter seemed to concur. When, however, I wrote to Lord Belstead, the Minister at the Home Office, I eventually received a negative reply. I had requested that the psychiatrist's opinion should be obtained. John Belstead replied that the principal medical officer at Wormwood Scrubs did not consider this necessary. I sent the Belstead answer to Ian Brady as permitted. Ian tells me that the principal medical officer has no objection to the views of the psychiatrist being obtained, so who is fooling whom?

I will take up the matter through Birnberg, Ian's solicitor, with renewed irritation. Ian, as I say, was in a thoroughly bad temper and indicated not obscurely that I had not exerted myself sufficiently. We were soon for the moment more angry with each other than with the authorities. I must write and apologize to him. Considering that he has been in prison fifteen years, I really ought to make more allowances.

Down to Bernhurst in time for the cricket dinner, a sweet medicine for jangled nerves. Cricket certainly induces much mutual happiness and many irresistible anecdotes. I came to the dinner as president of the club for many years; I always used to bring a team against the village, and many years before that, as a small boy, achieved a hat-trick with a trio of 'sneaks'. Kitty and Malcolm Muggeridge came as honoured guests. Malcolm, called on for a few words, began by announcing that he was probably the only man in England who has never played cricket. I am reminded of Tim Healey, Governor-General of the Irish Free State, beginning a speech at a dinner of Irish sportsmen for Prince Ranjitsinhji, with the words, 'The only game I ever played was one of marbles.' But Malcolm gave the expected pleasure, quoting Gibbon on the connection of sport with the Decline and Fall of the Roman Empire. He expressed concern that there was now too much buying and selling of players. 'What price', he demanded, 'would you place on Lord Longford if you wanted to dispose of him?' Malcolm as usual was able to impose his own picture of reality on his audience. In fact, there is no buying and selling of cricketers in the sense he had in mind. He was no doubt thinking of football, but it was by common consent a delightful speech.

Saturday, 28 February 1981

I have become rather self-indulgent in my reading of St Francis de Sales's *Love of God*. I keep dipping into it. This morning I am left wondering whether I love the *will* of God sufficiently. St Francis seems to assume that this should come naturally to all of us. The answer of course must be a thunderous NO. How then can I love it more?

Obviously by loving Him more, but what are the approaches available to someone as far removed as I am from mystical experience? Through nature? Through people? Through Christ? 'I have loved O Lord the beauty of your house' is one of Elizabeth's favourite passages. But my appreciation of nature, though I am not altogether insensitive, is so defective that I seem unlikely to make much headway along that road.

I respond to what seems to me the Divine in all sorts of people but it would be an affectation to pretend that the strength of my belief in an all-powerful and all-loving God is increased by the first three visits described in this diary yesterday. So many people seem to have had and still to be having so harsh a deal irrespective of any action within their power. I put this to my son Paddy, who replied with agreeable candour, 'Your trouble is that you lack a Catholic theological training. Your religion is simply Father d'Arcy grafted on to the Gospels. Now I had a first-class Catholic theological training in my formative years at Ampleforth.' All right, I said, then how do you explain the misery and degradation in which so many live if God is indeed all-powerful and all-loving? The condition of each one, he replied, must be seen against the background of eternity and the bliss which will one day be theirs. It was no doubt a correct theological answer which would have satisfied great spiritual writers down the ages.

But can I not come to love of God through love of Christ? At Bernhurst we have a church a few hundred yards from our house with a statue of Christ on the Cross on the tower above it. I go over there increasingly and there and elsewhere try to realize not just with my intellect but with my heart what the Passion of Christ should mean to us. In that way I try to love Him and, one day perhaps, God through Him.

Sunday, 1 March 1981

James and Bice Fawcett and George Martelli for the weekend. It is rare for us to have non-family house guests. George lost his beautiful wife Ann recently, after prolonged Parkinson's disease. The address at her funeral in Dorset by the parish priest was the best I can remember, culminating in the triumphant exclamation, 'The Church was her life!' George says Ann was heart-broken at the modernist trend in the Church. Cardinal Hume was a great friend. Ann used to write him letters, imploring him to stop the rot. He would reply affectionately but vaguely. George gloomily forecast that on present trends our

Church will soon be indistinguishable from the Church of England. Basil Hume is a holy man, but, thinks George, has been subjected to intolerable pressures.

The Martellis are our oldest friends, though we have seen them too seldom. Bice is closer to Elizabeth than anyone else outside the family. James is arguably what was once said of Peter Jay, 'the cleverest man in England'. Double First, of course; Fellow of All Souls, Professor of International Law; president for many years of the European Commission for Human Rights. His reading in bed is cosmogony and the higher mathematics. A great brain, but sweet and diffident.

Monday, 2 March 1981

Jack and Frankie Donaldson came to lunch at Bernhurst yesterday. A load of delightful political gossip. One or two facts or semi-facts emerged. Jack will be leaving the Labour Party along with the Gang when their defection is announced this week. He expects about ten peers to leave at the same time. This is a good many fewer than the number forecast in *The Times* and *Guardian* on Saturday, but more than I told Tony Benn was likely. Jack has obviously experienced a good deal of agony about the decision to leave. Though the best and most self-sacrificing of husbands, he is politically speaking strongly influenced by (a) Shirley Williams whom, in fact, he will follow into the 'wilderness'; (b) Pat Llewellyn-Davies, who has exerted strong pressure on him to stay in the party. Now that the die is cast, he looks much happier.

He retains an attachment to Denis Healey, who served under him during the war, and cherishes a dream or illusion that if things go wrong for Denis and the party he (Denis) will join the Social Democrats, possibly becoming their leader. All this is a bit fantastic, but it is rather typical of Jack, brilliant and lovable, reluctant to accept what seemed to me the harsh realities.

Today at lunch at the Garrick I had an amusing time with William Rees-Mogg and Robin Day. William Rees-Mogg has bet Robin Day a magnum of champagne that the Social Democrats plus the Liberals will be the strongest single party after the election. I joined a wise colleague at the table in betting William Rees-Mogg that they would not. William is wonderfully urbane; agrees that this combination would have to win more than two hundred seats in the new Parliament, but goes on doggedly saying that he believes this will happen.

After he left, Robin Day and I agreed that it was quite incredible that someone so shrewd and balanced should deceive himself to this extent through some strange process of wishful thinking.

Wednesday, 4 March 1981

Ash Wednesday. What if anything do I intend to offer as a Lenten sacrifice this year? I have tried many times to give up drink, or drinking before seven o'clock. At seventy-five, still leading what people tell me is too active a life and afflicted at the moment with a heavy cold, I shall try something different this time. In theory, it ought to be easy to get to Mass more, but drawing generous expenses from the Lords I don't like to leave too early. I have decided on an extra half-hour's religious or quasi-religious reading. (I have done half an hour for many years.) This Lent I want to work at the idea of the Cross. If only I could *feel* as well as believe in Christ's sacrifice! But there is also an intellectual issue. Apart from strengthening our faith, what difference does the idea of the Cross make to a distinctive Christian ethic?

Dinner at Grillions. Twelve present, the ideal number. While waiting for dinner I was rung up by Arthur Bryant, our dear secretary, prince of octogenarian authors. Arthur had flu and asked me to act as secretary, which meant nominating the chairman. Quintin was an obvious choice. He offered to hand over the chair to me. I assured him that the role of secretary was more acceptable. He was in capital form, as always at these dinners. Some of the members, through training in the diplomatic service, need pulling out of themselves by an invigorating presence like his. He asked me, not for the first time, to sit next to him. Soon he was referring to his depressed condition. No one questions the depth of his sorrow over the tragic loss of Mary, but we are told that the saints combine joy and sorrow and he seems to share that quality with them.

He told us this fine story about Winston Churchill. Churchill had recently retired from the premiership when Quintin, newly appointed First Lord, went to see him. 'His mind', said Quintin, 'was like a vast mountain range wreathed in mist. Every now and then the mist would lift, the sun would shine brilliantly, and a glorious vista would be exposed to view. Then the mist would descend again.' Churchill had this to say about British defence and nuclear warfare: 'The Russians must be convinced that we possess a power of impregnable retaliation. They must know that even after we are dead we shall be able to destroy them from our graves.' Only a man of genius, said I, could have found those words. Yes, said Quintin, he was a genius which you and I will never be, though we are two very talented men.

I should have mentioned earlier that I sat for a while in the gallery of the House of Commons and heard David Owen make the most remarkable, the most gripping speech on defence that I have heard there or elsewhere for many years. I told this to Pat who retorted, 'Yes, he is very clever, but he looks like Lucifer.' Elizabeth, who has come to admire him greatly, admits that he has a Mephistophelean look. Young, tall, lean and handsome, he reminds me of Tom Mosley in his young days. There is something, however, about the way David Owen's eyebrows come together that might be improved by cosmetic treatment.

Thursday, 5 March 1981

This afternoon, Eddy Richardson took me to see his father, Charles, in Wandsworth Prison. Charles has served thirteen of his twenty-five years' sentence and been refused parole several times. He could stand it no longer, and walked out of an open prison last summer. He spent six months on the run. Later he was recaptured by accident. He was picked up with a group of suspects, though the police had no idea who he was with his beard and glasses. His solicitor rang up to enquire after his welfare; the police suddenly realized that they had caught Charles Richardson. I visited him often when he was in Maidstone Prison, and became very fond of him.

I was pleasantly surprised to find Charles looking so much better. He had had 'a whale of a time' while a fugitive, visiting Holland, Paris, where he was interviewed by the British newspapers and TV, and Spain, where his mother came to see him. Later he returned home to Camberwell where he moved about with complete freedom. He taught me something with this observation: 'When in prison, you depend on pleasant memories, if possible recent ones.' He had acquired the latter during his 'holiday'. Surely there are lessons here about legitimate holidays for long-term prisoners.

A book is being written about Charles's case, the so-called torture trial. He told me that I had always 'laughed' when he tried to explain to me that his crimes were nothing like as horrible as depicted. I wouldn't like to think that I had ever laughed at anyone in prison, but he is acute enough to realize that I thought that he was overstating his argument. He has always insisted that (1) no one was permanently injured; (2) those who were allegedly tortured were professional criminals who had betrayed him in business. Soon afterwards they were themselves convicted of serious crimes. 'In my situation,' he used to say to me, 'you would have gone to the police, but in my world we were brought up to fend for ourselves.' However, he now accepts the normal values of society.

Charles is sure that I will be impressed by the book, which is being written by a high-class journalist. I said that I would be happy to assist the author if required. Not that I know much about the original case, but I have already spoken up for Charles in the columns of *The Times*, and in the House of Lords. Charles's article in *The Times* was attacked by Bernard Levin, who is usually brave and enlightened about prisoners. He denounced the absence of any apparent remorse, but most people who know much about prisoners are aware of the complexity of this issue. Those who are ignorant of prisoners think it simple.

At the moment, my auxiliary religious reading is Dante's *Purgatory* in Dorothy Sayers's translation. In her introduction, I came across this: 'Dante has grasped the great essential of penal reform, namely the prime necessity of persuading the culprit to accept judgment. If a man is once convinced of his own guilt, and that he is sentenced by a just tribunal, *all* punishment of whatever kind is remedial, since it lies with him to make it so; if he is not so convinced, then *all* punishment, however enlightened, remains merely vindictive, since he sees it so, and will not make it otherwise.' But that is altogether too facile. A man or woman may be convinced of their own guilt at the beginning of their sentence. But when they are detained for years and years in confinement, and in some cases given no hope, the resentment overrides the remorse, as it would with ninety-nine of us out of a hundred. Shane O'Doherty, ex-IRA, deeply religious before he went to prison, and again today, may prove an exception to this rule. I hope and pray that he is not put to the test.

Saturday, 7 March 1981

Elizabeth and I lunched with Harford and Robbie [Montgomery Hyde] at Tenterden. Harford has written many worthwhile books. On Carson and, of wider relevance today, on Oscar Wilde he is the leading authority. He was a Conservative member for an Ulster constituency for ten years, but though a Conservative was found too

Liberal for their tastes. The other guests were Professor Pat Grosskurth and her fiancé, an insurance man of handsome aspect. The professor is a very pretty young-looking Canadian who has just written a definitive book on Havelock Ellis, very well reviewed but selling disappointingly in England. (That is no doubt due to the decline in library purchases at the moment.) Her friendship with Elizabeth had a curious beginning – an unfavourable review by her of Elizabeth's book on Byron – but they are now fast friends.

Returning to Havelock Ellis, Elizabeth and I recall him as compulsory reading in enlightened undergraduate circles in the 1920s. I gather that he is quite out of fashion there and elsewhere at the present time. One must concede that for good or ill he has made a permanent difference to the study and discussion of sex. His conclusions (free love, etc.) are anathema to me. But if asked whether I support freedom of discussion, I mean serious discussion, I have to vote in favour.

Dinner with the Muggeridges. Fun, as always. A striking talk with Kitty Muggeridge about aging. She and Malcolm are slightly older than Elizabeth and me. As the years pass, she thinks less and less of this world and more and more of the world to come. When she was seven she used to want to die (and be covered with leaves) before her brothers. She couldn't bear to live without them. She agrees that today this would be a selfish wish. It would mean leaving Malcolm alone. Neither Elizabeth nor I can imagine him existing without her. Still the supernatural world seems to her more and more the real one. She points to the chairs and sofas in her drawing room and says, 'They are losing their texture, they are becoming pale reflections of the spiritual reality.' I said to her, 'But you take great interest in the future, your children and your grandchildren.' (She crosses the Atlantic to catch sight of the latter.) She says, 'I feel that small children are very close to me, they have just come from the world I am shortly going to.' There is a faint unconscious ring here of the last words of Socrates.

I told her that I was in a bit of a dilemma. Should I be continuing so actively in public affairs and social action or should I emulate her by 'making my soul'? Obviously her first duty in her own life is to look after Malcolm. This means pursuing a life which in fact leads her nearer and nearer to the supernatural. I can't believe that this can be quite right for me at the moment. I cannot believe that Elizabeth would wish it for me. Nevertheless I feel that Kitty is living on a higher plane.

Monday, 9 March 1981

Elizabeth and I came up to London last night to dine with Antonia and Harold. A persistent cough, the residue of a fluey cold, has pulled me down a bit lately. But after a champagne introduction we were soon chatting away happily. Elizabeth has given up drinking for Lent, except at parties. Last night counts for the latter purpose. She could become a total abstainer without difficulty. Whereas I....

Harold is not in the conventional sense a conversationalist. He thinks, indeed almost hesitates, before he speaks, whereas the rest of our family do the opposite. He has beautiful manners and a genuine interest in his fellow-humans (if he likes them or is intrigued by them), which makes him an excellent listener. When he tells a story, he is actor-producer-author in one. His best anecdote last night went like this:

Harold presents himself at the Soviet Embassy with a letter protesting about the treatment of dissidents. A huge porter opens the door guardedly.

Harold: I wish to see the Ambassador.

Porter: Ambassador not here.

Harold: I wish to see the Ambassador.

Porter: Ambassador not here.

This goes on for some time. Finally, the porter: 'Ambassador may be there', pointing across Kensington Palace Gardens to the residency. Harold goes across and rings a bell at the residency. He is greeted by a small and friendly secretary. But the end of the conversation is the same: 'Ambassador may be there', pointing across the road to the embassy. So in the end Harold had to send the letter by post. All this told with the famous Pinteresque pauses that have helped to make his fame and fortune.

Antonia had just written in two days a 3,000-word article on the princesses of Wales. After hard bargaining she had been paid $10,000. One of the editors is crossing the Atlantic to collect the document. Antonia is naturally elated. She says to me, 'I know you like to think that your children are earning a lot of money.' This is not true, as it happens, though I like them to be secure, and to be happy.

Elizabeth takes a maternal interest in the politics of Antonia and Harold. He was a Labour supporter until the last election. Now he is inclined to be unilateralist, which throws him back towards the Left. Elizabeth expresses rather more unilateralist sympathy to him than she does to me, possibly to keep him on the right (i.e. the left) side of politics. Antonia, in Elizabeth's view, is strictly non-party. 'I don't think that she admires any contemporary politicians.' Her heroes and heroines belong to history.

Tea at the Lords. I told Dora Gaitskell of the dream I had had last night. In the dream she and I were attending Hugh's funeral in Washington. There was a vast concourse. We found it impossible to get in. Finally she seized an attendant by the arm. 'You must let me in,' she cried. 'I am what it's all about.'

She felt sure that telepathy was at work between her and me. She was still seething with indignation over Michael Foot's review of Dick Crossman's new volume of Diaries (1951–64). I agree that the review was utterly unfair. Michael argued that Dick's scathing criticism of Hugh Gaitskell was based on the sound understanding of one Wyke-hamist by another, but that his much milder criticism of Nye Bevan betrayed Dick's ignorance of Welsh proletarian genius.

Dora and Michael are alike in one respect – they arouse immense affection in all who know them well. Of the two, I know Dora very much better. But Michael charms me whenever I meet him.

A few minutes later another dear friend, Norah Phillips, outwardly at least a much less emotional person than Dora, was talking about the horrible things that Dick had written about her late husband Morgan. The remarks about Hugh are, on the whole, persistently disparaging. The relatively small number about Morgan would clearly be actionable, if Morgan were alive. What infuriates Norah is that journalists, and she has many journalistic friends, seem inclined to believe Dick's version. She and I and most of those who knew Dick would not regard him as a witness of literal truth. But will his versions get accepted by history?

I ask Elizabeth how far a diarist like Greville had affected historical opinion. She replied to some extent undoubtedly, e.g. his description of the frumpery of the young Queen Victoria's court. The thought of Dick's diaries conjures up a comparison with Evelyn Waugh's *Diaries* and *Letters*. Evelyn put in quite a lot about myself, none of it wounding, but some of it nonsensical, such as my alleged suggestion that Princess Margaret should be made Queen of a United Ireland. One difference seems to be this: Evelyn put down what amused him or he thought would amuse his correspondents. Dick persuaded himself that he was writing accurate history. But he was too much of an artist, though not quite on the plane of Evelyn, and too much involved in the controversies he was discussing to provide an objective narrative.

Tuesday, 10 March 1981

I listened from the gallery to the last part of Geoffrey Howe's budget speech and the beginnings of Michael Foot's reply. The latter was feline in the best parliamentary tradition. Howe's presentation was the deadest I can remember on such an occasion. He ploughs remorselessly on with the Labour benches happily deriding him and the Tories looking embarrassed. Later in the day I asked an influential Conservative back-bencher what he thought. 'It gives no one any hope,' he replied cheerfully. I gathered that he was talking more about the manner than the matter. Hugh said that the Conservatives were still hoping for an upturn in the economy this summer.

Wednesday, 11 March 1981

An absorbing talk with Hugh Trevor-Roper about the Murdoch acquisition of *The Times* and *The Sunday Times*. Hugh had, arguably, the best academic career of any undergraduate in this century. Raymond Asquith and Ronnie Knox were regarded in the Christ Church Common Room as rival candidates. We had many happy arguments about it in the old days. And what about another candidate – Quintin? Hugh belongs to a new phenomenon – the group of outstanding Tory academics who have joined us in the House of Lords. They include Robert Blake, Max Beloff, John Vaizey and Hugh Thomas. In my early days in the House of Lords they would have been considered a contradiction in terms. Now they shine brightly.

I reminded him that he had claimed earlier that they had 'put a hook through the nose of Leviathan'. It was, alas, he admitted now, a paper hook. He and his colleagues had no control over the editor's appointment of his staff which was the decisive factor.

Thursday, 12 March 1981

Lunch at the Lords for my West Indian friend, Ashton Gibson, eccentric (but I am the last person to complain of eccentrics), original, creative. Some years ago he started in Brixton the Melting Pot, a centre for young blacks, which has done splendid work and won recognition from the Government. I was a patron from the beginning. Ashton, however, fell out with his colleagues and moved to Hackney where he has started 'West Indian Concern'. Once again, I am a patron and lunched there on Tuesday. Mostly with voluntary labour they have made it look spick and span. Money is a sore problem as always. Ashton is thinking unceasingly on how to improve the education given to the young blacks at the beginning of life. Under the handicap of their way of speaking they easily fall behind. When they leave school they have the additional handicap of colour prejudice. Ashton is somewhat timeless like many West Indians. Before now, he has arrived an hour late for lunch. Today he arrived an hour early. But he is full of insights, and understands the colour issue better than anyone I know. To his dying day he will labour on behalf of the West Indian community.

A routine meeting of the Labour peers. We were asked for suggestions as to suitable speakers. I put forward the name of Arthur Scargill, not on the grounds that he would be of benefit to us, but we would be of benefit to him. This proposal was not taken very seriously. Fred Peart told me afterwards that he thought that it would expand Scargill's ego, assumed to be quite large already. I described him at the meeting as the most dangerous man in the country, left of centre. I suppose that if I met him I would find him quite a good chap.

Saturday, 14 March 1981

At last someone has said it. Fred Emery in the first feature article in *The Times* raises the question of whether or not Mrs Thatcher will survive. He says that there are three obvious possibilities – either the 'wets' will resign or they will be sacked or she will modify her line. It was beginning to be assumed that the third course would be taken, but it seems less certain now.

Last night I attended a dinner for the Knights of St Gregory at the Café Royal. I am profoundly honoured to hold the Grand Cross of the Order. Only two others in Britain possess it, though the Duke of Norfolk belongs to an order which is, I believe, senior to that of St Gregory. Last night Miles Norfolk seemed to judge the audience perfectly. I am not quite sure whether his frequent use of the word 'bloody' went down as well with the matrons as with their husbands, though they all chuckled away.

The dinner was expensive (£13 a head, apart from drinks). I was rather absurdly put out by the cost of the wine. I habitually assume that if one is placed at the top table the wine is supplied free. Not so on this occasion. I found myself buying a bottle of wine for myself and my two lady companions. The price was reasonable but I was unprepared. This was at the Café Royal, a Trust House Forte establishment. At the moment my revered patron Charles is trying to acquire the Savoy Hotel group and is being described rightly as the acme of efficiency. Certainly he has brought home to us in Sidgwick and Jackson the absolute duty of making a profit on every transaction. But unless you have a long-established back-list, you will never make a financial success of publishing without obtaining a good supply of best-sellers, which means running financial risks. I hope that Charles, when he becomes chairman of Sidgwick and Jackson, will be ready to take the same risks in publishing that he has taken with such immense success in catering.

Monday, 16 March 1981

I was pleased to hear this morning from Willie Whitelaw that he will be very ready to see John Hunt and myself about Myra Hindley, though not for the next fortnight. As it happens, Elizabeth and I are going to dinner with the Permanent Under Secretary at the Home Office, Sir Brian Cubbon, on Saturday week. I cherish a slight hope that there might be an opportunity of having a few words with him at that time, but I shall be very tactful about raising it.

Looking through my letter to the Home Secretary, I feel tempted to add a comment on the problem of helping both Myra and Ian, whom she repudiated fairly soon after I got to know her. It would be easier for me to put the whole blame on him if I had not got his interests to consider also. If I say that he is a Broadmoor case, that does not mean that I think he ought to be there for ever. I believe that he can be healed, but it might take a long time and will not occur in prison.

Wednesday, 18 March 1981

Lunch for Harold [Pinter] at the Lords. He is a remarkable listener and was obviously drinking everything in. I can't help, stupidly, imagining the kind of play that he would write about their lordships.

Jack Donaldson joined us. It rather startled Harold that Jack, recently
a Minister for the Arts, had never heard of Simon Gray, but he was
impressed, if a little surprised, by Jack's vitality. His glorious moment
arrived when I asked him to guess the vintage and the year of the port
we were drinking. He had indicated a preference for vintage port.
He guessed Dow 1961. It turned out to be Dow 1963, but all of us
from the restaurant manager downwards were amazed that he got so
close.

After lunch I introduced him to a peer who had been in prison. He
reported to Antonia that I had said, 'He doesn't speak often but we
are very proud of him.' I think that what I said, no doubt with pride
in my voice, was this: 'We've got all sorts here.' Then to the new Duke
of Portland and, among others, to Heather Brigstock, the headmistress
of St Paul's which Rebecca and Flora attended. Harold was suitably
impressed when we were suddenly called on to make way for the Lord
Chancellor, and Quintin strode forward leaning on a stick but trav-
elling at a good pace preceded and followed by acolytes. I was reminded of an occasion when Neil Marten MP approached Quintin in
full rig. Quintin greeted him exuberantly with the single word 'Neil'.
An American lady accompanying Marten fell on her knees. The
beauty of the Lords is that 99 per cent of the time relaxation and
informality are complete, but at certain moments the iron discipline
could hardly be exceeded in the Brigade of Guards.

Thursday, 19 March 1981

Ten-thirty: reported at the offices of United Newspapers, 22 Tudor
Street, for journey to Bill Barnetson's funeral and cremation in the
country. Lunch beforehand close by and tea afterwards at the Bar-
netsons' home. Back to the Lords by 6 p.m. I was flattered and honoured to be asked to Bill's private funeral. There was only room for
seventy. The others present had nearly all worked with Bill in the
world of newspapers, or lately television. Bill till recently was chairman of *The Observer*, who were well-represented – David Astor, Arnold
Goodman, Conor Cruise O'Brien, the present editor Donald Trelford,
and others.

David took me back to London in his car. I sat on the front seat.
Conor, till recently editor-in-chief of *The Observer*, and David, editor
for twenty-seven years, sat at the back. Possibly I did not realize soon
enough that they wanted to talk about *The Observer* crisis but were too

polite to say so. Eventually I dozed off but could not help hearing most of their discussion. In any case, David had already 'put me in the picture'. He is the most sensitive of friends.

Thinking over the day I realized that I had passed it in an atmosphere of love. The spirit of Bill Barnetson lives on. There was no depression visible though his private secretaries could hardly restrain their tears. Bill had been of sustained, imaginative assistance to our family over the Catherine Pakenham Award. This award for the best young woman journalist of the year was organized following our daughter's death in a motor accident in 1969. Catherine had just begun to make her way in journalism. More widely, Bill had spread a message of friendliness and hope throughout his many enterprises. Everyone present cherished some permanent memory.

Saturday, 21 March 1981

Very busy this weekend preparing speeches: (a) for the Lords on Thursday when I am opening the debate on mental after-care; (b) for the conference sponsored by Lord Denning at Windsor next weekend on victims. With the first I have had every assistance, especially from MIND and the Richmond Fellowship. The second effort would be impossible without Michael Whitaker, who was the inspiration behind our Report in 1978 and my Private Member's Bill in 1979. The first has been accomplished by lunchtime today; the second, a trickier task, will no doubt get managed somehow.

I am also writing a 1,200-word review of Malcolm's Diaries for the *Listener*. I don't want it to be too palpably a panegyric, but I would hate to say anything that hurt him. I have always understood that he permanently damaged one of his closest friendships by a review that caused quite unintentional annoyance. Later, I rang up Malcolm and asked whether he would like to see the review before it appeared. He said that he would far rather see it in print. I understand his feelings. It spoils a Christmas stocking if you see it overnight.

Sunday, 22 March 1981

A long interview with Shirley Williams in *The Observer*. Elizabeth and I felt very drawn to her, though she finished with the routine suggestion that all present difficulties, including her departure from the Labour Party, were somehow due to Mrs Thatcher. She conceded that she had not spent enough time with her husband and maybe that was the reason for her marriage break-up. But she surmised that he wanted in any case a 'more traditional kind of wife'. She was brought up, it seems, to think of a woman's career as quite as important as a man's. Having known her mother and father well, I can understand what she means. Vera Brittain, in the eyes of the world, was much more 'successful' than George Catlin, a very nice, highly-gifted man consistently underrated. Bernard Williams is about as successful as any man still youngish could be; a professor of moral philosophy and now Provost of King's College, Cambridge.

I remember visiting Shirley ten years ago when she was Minister of State at the House of Lords. As I went out I ran into Bernard, leading their small daughter by the hand, just like a faithful wife visiting a ministerial husband. He shot me one of his brilliant smiles. But I couldn't help reflecting that he might not appreciate that role indefinitely unless he were a saint, which on the law of averages was not probable.

What, I may be asked, about Elizabeth? The equal, or more so, of any of these. The short answer is that she is different. She could have entered Parliament without question in 1945, but gave up her constituency in the interests of myself and the children. The family came before the career.

Monday, 23 March 1981

Great excitement in S & J as the *Mail* starts to serialize Chapman Pincher's book, *Their Trade is Treachery*. The most sensational of its many exposures is the clear indication that Sir Roger Hollis, the deceased head of MI5, was for many years an active Russian spy. William took extraordinary precautions to make sure that copies of the book did not reach the shops until the last moment. He had bet me a bottle of sherry that the secret would be kept – I bought a bottle at a local Victoria Wine shop and presented it to him on reaching the office. William is rightly jubilant, but not devoid of understandable anxiety. The Cabinet Office is unsuccessfully trying to obtain a copy of the book from him. Someone outside politics like him is less impressed by the Cabinet Office than someone like myself would be.

Wednesday, 25 March 1981

Lunch at the Garrick. I find myself surrounded by actors. A leading member of the committee told me recently that they were having the greatest difficulty in keeping down the number of lawyers. The theatrical presence should cheer them up. Have just been asked to speak at the Cambridge Union and to oppose a motion which denies the existence of the Soviet menace. Glad to be given the incentive to get up the subject again. I can't rely for ever on my experiences at the Council of Foreign Ministers, 1947, etc.

Delighted and surprised to hear that I have won first place in the ballot for short debates. I am a natural pessimist in regard to all lotteries. My motion is a very broad one, calling for 'more equality'. Hugh Gaitskell always used to say that socialism was about equality. That has always been a large part of its message for me, though the ideal of a society motivated by public service rather than personal profit has always gone along with it. The Bishop of London, a much-esteemed friend and a strong influence in the House, tells me that he would like to deliver his swan-song in this debate. He wants to bring in his pet theme of national service for youth. I say 'OK, but please give us some spiritual guidance.'

Thursday, 26 March 1981

A full day. In the history books, I suppose the launching of the Social Democrats will be the event recorded. But today's news has been, as they say in the City, discounted well in advance. The Gang of Four have appeared before the media many times already. It is impossible to judge from the first reactions how things will look a year from now.

The Labour peers had an interesting talk from Roy Hattersley. He does not look like the ordinary idea of an intellectual. Even after all this jogging he has a bulky air. He spoke, however, pleasantly and well, showing himself perfectly well aware that most of us were very unhappy about the left-wing trend. He soon won a measure of happy laughter by referring to Roy Jenkins as a literate Alf Robens, but he begged us in general not to be beastly to the defectors. Shirley was still a socialist at heart, they had been our comrades until recently and, he implied, might be again. Roy's desperate attempts to be loyal to Michael Foot landed him in some tortured gymnastics. I asked him, 'Are you aware that many of us here, and many more outside, do not believe that there can be a compromise between multilateralism and unilateralism without fudging the issue?' Ted Short and Michael Stewart developed the same point sharply. Roy said in effect that the Labour Party policy might take a turn which would make it impossible for him to serve in a Labour government. A man I would gladly follow.

The great excitement in the office has of course been the Pincher book, serialized since Monday in the *Mail*, since Tuesday in *The Times* and published today. I sat on the edge of my bench (below the gangway on the opposition side) while Quintin repeated Margaret Thatcher's statement. I had the sense to keep my mouth shut pending Harry Pincher's reply, though I would have felt bound to intervene if the publishers had been criticized. The immediate reaction in the Lords was pompous and patriotic; to me at least, more pompous than patriotic. But they are a sophisticated crowd and they won't be easily hoodwinked. Then I dashed off to the Waldorf Hotel for Harry Pincher's press conference.

Our pornography report press conference in 1972 was larger and our Beveridge Report press conference in 1942 larger still, but there was a good crowd and much television. I was slightly anxious lest Harry should be shaken by the Prime Minister's animadversions. I underestimated my man. He expressed himself to me privately and then to the press conference as delighted with the Prime Minister's statement. Where she had gone wrong, it was because she had not had time to read the book and had been misled by her advisers. I am genuinely happy that S & J have scored so heavily in publishing terms. As a director, I share responsibility for the publication, but I cannot put out of my mind the pain caused to the Hollis's. Though they must have known of these things some time ago. From this point of view, I am rather glad that I am no longer chairman.

Saturday, 28 March 1981

Arrived back at Bernhurst from Cumberland Lodge, Windsor Great Park, where I was speaking at the conference on victims. Cumberland Lodge is a royal house rebuilt after a fire one hundred years ago and lent to my late friend, Amy Buller, for student conferences. The Queen Mother's house is just over the fence. The whole ambience was much appreciated by the students, nearly all black graduates.

Main speeches were made this morning by Michael Ogden, chairman of the Criminal Injuries Compensation Board, and myself, very much assisted by Michael Whitaker. When I came to speak I was able to describe Ogden's speech as brilliant, which in its own way it was. I described him as a real expert, but I went on to say that under our democratic system experts like him had to accept a system foisted on them by mere politicians like myself. I myself would not claim to be an expert, but I doubted if there was a member of either House who was more expert than I was.

I warned Michael Ogden that the All-Party Penal Affairs Group had recently recommended an extension of the scheme beyond victims of *violence*. He did not seem to mind the prospect, though doubting whether there would be much change in the near future. I asked Mrs Ogden whether she found great ignorance among their friends about the CICB. She more or less said Yes, but suggested that a more attractive name would secure more attention. I repeated in my speech a suggestion in our 1978 Report that there should be a minister for victims who could publicize the cause more effectively than could be expected of a quango chairman. Michael Ogden told me that one of the Home Office ministers was nominally responsible for victims; he agreed that his role could be made much more explicit. I was rather relieved that I had come through the conference without hostility; so I think was Michael Ogden, who may have expected me to be offensive. So appeared to be his wife. The students manifestly enjoyed the brisk exchanges.

Sunday, 29 March 1981

Last night we went to dinner with Sir Brian and Lady Cubbon, in their rather romantic converted farmhouse near Tonbridge. Brian Cubbon, Permanent Under Secretary at the Home Office, is a dominant person in the penal world, alike for official and personal reasons. He greeted us at the door looking younger and slimmer than I remembered (when he was head of the Northern Ireland Office he was seriously injured when the British Ambassador was murdered). He and his wife are intensely vital. She does not claim to be an intellectual, but teaches art in a Tonbridge school and misses nothing.

The other guests were the Chancellor of the Exchequer, Sir Geoffrey Howe, and his wife Elspeth, and Lord Hunt and Lady Hunt, the former till recently Secretary of the Cabinet, the latter the sister of

Cardinal Hume. I cannot remember when we were last asked into such an 'inner establishment' society.

The word 'owlish' might have been coined to describe Geoffrey Howe, but behind every owl there is a robin trying to get out. His delivery of his budget speech was incredibly flat and dreary. But socially he is pleasant to talk to. He turned out to be, surprisingly, of Welsh extraction. I have never seen anyone look more English or less Welsh. If he were not Chancellor he would make less impression than his wife, an ardent spirit dedicated beyond all else to equal rights for women. I asked her where women were still treated unjustly. She replied at once in the pay received for part-time employment. Howe conveys an impression of possessing reserves of strength. He told Elizabeth that he had done quite a lot of journalism himself and knew enough about it not to take it seriously (including, I suppose, the many references to the dullness of his delivery).

I had a short conversation with the Chancellor before dinner. He emphasized that the Prime Minister and himself needed ten years for their policies to bear fruit and were thinking in those terms. I agreed from my experience of banking that businessmen were better placed to take long views. Politicians were at the mercy of a fickle electorate. He seems to be a natural optimist, which is just as well for any Chancellor of the Exchequer these days. He had no doubt that the coming of the Social Democrats would benefit the Tories and help them to get their ten-year mandate. His own party would lose nothing of any value, the Social Democrats would make no headway in the main Labour areas. The Labour Party would be losing some of their brightest and best.

Hunt, like Howe, conveys an impression of great solidity. He is more obviously genial. Cubbon, like the other two, is clearly a man of strong character. Between them they illustrate the point that strength need not depend on assertiveness. The evening passed like a flash, everyone enjoyed themselves, but discretion was an ever-present, if intangible factor, as I have always found it in social contact with high officials. When the men were left alone after dinner I, having dined well, addressed myself to our host, 'Do you really mean to prosecute our favourite author, Chapman Pincher?' (Brian, under the Prime Minister and the Home Secretary, is responsible for MI5.) The three eminent gentlemen are accustomed to not batting an eyelid, but the conversation was swiftly shifted on to general aspects of the security service.

Tuesday, 31 March 1981

Six to eight-thirty p.m.: debate in the House of Lords on my motion demanding a much more adequate system of mental after-care. A very satisfactory day. The Minister in his reply spent a long time setting out the whole story of what the DHSS are now achieving. But he is such a sweet man that I could easily forgive him. When he announced that the Government welcomed the Inquiry I was proposing to set up, I could even have hugged him.

My own speech was not as well delivered as I could have wished. My manuscript was not in the condition in which Gwen would have allowed it to go forward. But I was conscious of the sympathy of the House throughout.

There were twelve speakers in all and a general consensus that the whole subject has been grossly neglected. John Maud [Lord Redcliffe-Maud] sat in the House throughout the debate and wrote me the kind of note afterwards that makes every effort of this sort abundantly worth while. Now I have to collect the money for the Inquiry. I write at once to General Brown of the Dulverton Trust and await his reply with trepidation. Favourable or unfavourable, we shall press on.

Wednesday, 1 April 1981

Lunch at the Garrick. I sat down at the top table, as usually now, unless it is empty when I enter the Club. A middle-aged member, a prison visitor at Wormwood Scrubs for many years, is training to be a probation officer. I am almost speechless with admiration. Donald Sinden, the illustrious actor, was opposite me. He told me that the great difference between the elocution of actors and that of ordinary mortals is that actors learn to pronounce their final consonants (in other words they do not talk of huntin', shootin', fishin'). A good actor, he tells me, despises a microphone. When his company acted in New York they were equipped with microphones, but insisted on their being switched off.

At 6 p.m. our religious group at the House of Lords. I was asked to open the discussion on the text selected by myself: 'Anyone who wishes to be a follower of Mine must leave self behind; he must take up his cross and come with Me.' I said that I was clear about the infinite inspiration of the example of Christ's sacrifice on the Cross. I was also more or less clear about the acceptance of involuntary suffering which this text insisted on. But should we seek voluntary suffering? There was a good deal of uncertainty about this, in which I fully share. But I think that all of us come away somewhat enriched by these inconclusive little séances.

Tonight we watched one of Malcolm's resurrected programmes with his up-to-date comments. I can't imagine anyone describing Lourdes more effectively. No one could have brought out more powerfully the faith of the pilgrims. His genius comes almost visibly to life in personal interviews such as these. But when he is tackled, as in this case, about the alleged contradictions in his hostility to television, he almost visibly loses interest. I wonder if Shakespeare felt this way about acting.

Thursday, 2 April 1981

Some nice things said at the peers' meeting and elsewhere about our debate on mental after-care. Pat asked me to say a few words about my forthcoming debate on equality. I said, looking round significantly, that equality was one of the two things that united us, a variegated crew. The other was the search for a society based on the motive of public service rather than private greed.

Pat tells me that she is off to China, in charge of a parliamentary deputation arranged by the universally respected Hervey Rhodes KG. She is accustomed, it seems, to dress his serious wounds – a legacy of the first war. She tells me incidentally that she had delivered many babies in the African bush. 'Is there anything you can't do?' I exclaimed. She says, 'I am not original' (by the standard, I suppose, of her husband, Professor of Architecture Victor Rothschild, and the other 'Apostles' generally), 'I am just practical.' Jean Davies, most practical champion of ex-prisoners, said to me: 'You're academic; I'm just practical.' Is there here a legitimate distinction between the sexes? A successful man is accustomed to other people doing things for him, beginning with the housework. Women do the things themselves and secretly take pride in this form of superiority. Is this true of Elizabeth? She only once had a full-time secretary and then was reduced to sending her to amuse herself by doing her own shopping. I asked Gwen whether she had any comment to make on my comments. She smiled discreetly.

Saturday, 4 April 1981

Returned to Bernherst after a flying visit with Elizabeth to stay with a distinguished and wonderfully well-preserved lady of eighty-five. She was born Mary Charteris but was actually the daughter of Wilfrid Scawen Blunt, Elizabeth's hero. Her country house, several hundred years old with modern additions and far-reaching view, provided the romantic background which Elizabeth was looking for. Our hostess showed her a number of Blunt's letters which thrilled her intensely. From my angle it was a snapshot of a life I seldom impinge on.

Another guest was Raymond Carr, Warden of St Anthony's, a great friend of Thomas's whom he made a Research Fellow. An extraordinary life story: Raymond describes his family as having been rural working-class. It sounds to me as if they were yeomen, as Raymond grew up driving a horse plough. He won a scholarship to some kind of county school and then to Southampton University. But the examiner there, with singular generosity and perception, told him he was too good for Southampton. So he proceeded to win a scholarship to Christ Church from where he won a fellowship at All Souls and made many aristocratic friends. Eventually he married into the aristocracy.

He has written two highly acclaimed treatises – one on Spain and the other on hunting. His early experiences with the horse plough started him on the right tack. He is now writing a book on Puerto Rico; he tells me that very soon there will be more Spanish-speaking Americans than there are Negroes. Already the census forms have to be printed in American and Spanish. The status of the Spanish immigrants is lower than that of the blacks.

On the way home I was recognized several times, as tends to happen even though I am not so much in the public eye. One very good-looking, moustachioed, youngish man buttonholed me at Cheltenham station with the words, 'You are the gaol person.' He was on leave from some high-paid work abroad as a civil engineer and spent last weekend in a police cell on the charge of being drunk and disorderly. His views on the police are unprintable, but even on his own account he must be quite an awkward customer. 'The policeman said to me, "I have a good mind to run you in." I said, "If you want to arrest me you will have to find something to arrest me about." He said, "I'll soon do that." I said, "I'll save you the trouble" and smacked him on the cheek.' He was duly taken into custody, not allowed to see a solicitor, and properly roughed up. I began to feel sorry for him but could not agree to his suggestion that we should travel together to London. I did have a lot of work to do. All the same, a real Christian might have done more for a worried man.

Back at Bernhurst I received a letter marked 'Fan Mail' from Leslie [A. L.] Rowse, whom Arthur Bryant regards as the best historian in England. Indeed, I think he regards him as the best historian we have ever had. Leslie had just read and appreciated my third volume of autobiography published in 1974 and was proposing to read the first two volumes. I will quote what he says about Ian Brady, whom I had quoted from extensively in *The Grain of Wheat*: 'What a remarkable brain Brady has – I am forced to agree with much that he says. He might well find purpose in life if only he would write – become a writer. As Dostoevsky did after his imprisonment.' I recall that when my book originally appeared Philip Toynbee wrote that Ian Brady must be a 'remarkable man' and clearly understood Tolstoy and Dostoevsky on the subject of suffering better than I did. I agree that Ian has a fine, untutored intelligence, but his mixture of arrogance and diffidence has prevented him taking, for example, an Open University course in prison where Myra has taken one degree and is proceeding to another.

I should like to encourage Ian by showing him Leslie's letter, but fear that it will inflate his ego. I must find a way of conveying the message. I am truly astounded that Leslie should even have begun reading my book, let alone admired it, and my writing too for that matter. He quotes something that I said in the book, though I have long since forgotten why I said it. 'Try as we can we cannot control our own destiny.' He comments, 'Not always true. I have proceeded on the opposite line. Tried hard and largely succeeded in controlling mine.' But he implies that my life has been as fruitful as his. And yet I have always thought of him as conceited though utterly brilliant. I must make haste to ask him to lunch in the House of Lords and meanwhile must return to Shakespeare.

Monday, 6 April 1981

I went off this morning to St Thomas's Hospital to have my swollen knee drained. My old friend, Dr Mac of Hurst Green, had called it housemaid's knee. The bright young doctor at St Thomas's said that strictly speaking it was clergyman's knee. Housemaids get their knee trouble from leaning forward, clergymen kneel in an upright position, so that their swelling is lower down. While awaiting my turn to be drained, I was accosted by a friendly drug addict with his young wife, admittedly 'stoned'. He sat down beside me and asked, 'What's your trouble, Lord Longford?' I pulled up my trouser leg and showed him my swollen knee. 'Ah!' he commented sagely, 'Myra Hindley has been kicking you! Give her my love; she must be a pleasant girl.'

Old labels die hard. The nurses recognized me as Lord Longford. There was a cry for Mr Pakenham; they assured me that it wasn't me. Of course it turned out to be.

Thursday, 9 April 1981

Labour peers' meeting. Address by Joe Gormley, surely the most lovable figure in public life, wonderfully sensible and calm. He stressed the physical and economical realities in the mining industry which all politicians and trade union leaders must come to terms with. I told him that we all much admired him, but were anxious about events after his retirement. He said serenely that he would be happy to be followed by 'the Yorkshireman', meaning Scargill. He would find the job a great education.

4 p.m.: crucial meeting at the Home Office with Willie Whitelaw about Myra, accompanied by the noble John Hunt. I told Elizabeth before leaving home in the morning that I would follow up the arguments in my letter to Willie. When it came to the point, horror of horrors, I couldn't lay my hands on the letter. It was locked away somewhere. Gwen only comes on Tuesdays and there was no reply from her telephone. So I had to work out my line afresh, which turned out for the best as it happened. Man proposes. . . .

Willie greeted us at the door of his office with the expected warmth. 'Frank – John – ' his tone was almost ecstatic, but I shall always insist that he is a *vrai* and not a *faux bonhomme*. I was relieved to find that he was alone except for his secretary, who seemed civilized and friendly. Those who advised me against bringing a deputation were 100 per cent right.

I plunged straight in. 'May I speak for three minutes, please?' Willie smiled assent. My habit of fast talking is an oratorical defect in front of large audiences, but in this situation, as sometimes on television, it came in handy. I argued: (1) anyone who had been in prison for fifteen years ought certainly to be *considered* for parole unless there were some extraordinary circumstances to prevent it; (2) there was no such circumstance in the case of Myra who was admittedly 'not dangerous'; (3) the responsibility for the decision was unavoidably Willie's.

The third point was a vital submission. The Home Office have shuffled the buck round and round on previous occasions (this and that committee, the Parole Board, etc.). Willie grasped the nettle immediately. He accepted full responsibility without prevarication. He mentioned incidentally that someone had said that he was being left two hot potatoes, Mary Bell and Myra. So far the release of Mary Bell, he said, had not led to trouble.

At the end of quite a long interview, forty-five minutes, he said that he was *not* prepared to interfere with the arrangements under which she would come before the Home Office Parole Board Committee in December. They would have to decide whether she would be allowed to go before a local review board, i.e. enter the parole process. But he would give very careful attention to what we had said to him.

John was invaluable and I thought rather subtle. He said that in the early stages of her imprisonment he had seen her as chairman of the Parole Board. (Later chairmen of the Parole Board don't see prisoners as he did.) After talking to the prison governors, he had felt, even then, that she was not dangerous to society, but there might well be a danger to herself if she were released. He pointed out that if the committee decided in December that she could be considered, she was not likely to be free until 1983. That, eighteen years, would be in his opinion enough. He said all this very gently, but weightily. Before we left I put in a word about the argument that in her own interests it might not be safe to release her. Surely no Home Secretary could seriously defend retaining her in prison against her fervent wishes because she couldn't be protected outside. Willie appeared to agree.

When I say that John was subtle, I mean that by mentioning as the main reason for not releasing her at one time an argument that could not stand up today he left the case for release all the stronger. As we went away Willie said to me in his guarded fashion, 'I think you have some grounds for encouragement.' I said to Willie, 'What do I say to her and anyone else who asks?' He replied, 'You can only report that I am not altering the existing arrangement.' 'But,' I persisted, 'you don't mind me saying that I have confidence in your humanity?' To that he had no objection. A good man, as I have always thought since I saw him on television giving tea to the wives of the Derry internees.

Later I said to John that I hoped that he would be happy in the Social Democratic Party. He rather surprised me by saying that the one thing he felt about passionately was Proportional Representation. Of course, it's the one *new* thing they've got, except in so far as it's already espoused by the Liberals. He went on to say, 'I'm sorry you are not joining us.' I said, 'After the honourable positions I have been awarded in Labour governments it would not be decent, apart from policy considerations.' He said, 'No, I understand. You can't desert the sinking ship.' I was too grateful to him for what he had done that afternoon to continue the argument.

Friday, 10 April 1981

Lance Thirkell, who is doing a grand job as director of the New Bridge for ex-prisoners, looked in with a lot of letters for me to sign. He tells me that he is one of the organizers of the SDP in Kensington and Chelsea. Last night he went to their inaugural meeting. A very reasonable attendance, two hundred or so, but almost all middle-class. David Owen addressed them. He spoke well. He always does. I have heard him in recent months at Brighton, Blackpool, Wembley and from the gallery in the House of Commons. He has always been first class, with plenty of controlled fire, but Lance told me that when it came to questions his performance was unhappy. He seems to make no effort to enter into the minds of the questioners. He just went on haranguing them. His reputation for arrogance when Foreign Minister may not have been altogether unjustified. Shirley is reputed as saying that the Gang of Four are enjoying their collective leadership. Her suggestion that the dangers of assassination are reduced must be regarded as facetious. No doubt the general public would much prefer her as leader, but until she can get back into the House of Commons, which looks anything but easy, they will have to make a virtue of necessity.

Afternoon visit to Ian Brady. After my last visit a letter of apology from me to him crossed one from him to me. I was determined that the same thing should not happen this time, but I must say that this afternoon he was pretty tough.

Ian has a keen sense of humour, which can make his face look very attractive and shows itself at the corners of his mouth, but there was no sign of it on this occasion. When we came away the assistant governor said to me, 'You were very patient.' I will give myself a beta mark. A woman, almost any woman, could have got through to him better than I did.

Since Leslie Rowse said flattering things about Ian in his letter I began to say to Ian, 'I don't know whether you know of historian A. L. Rowse.' He replied sharply that he knew that he was an extreme conservative. My attempt to convey Leslie's good opinion was strangled at birth.

I shall of course keep pegging away. If I had been in prison fifteen years I expect that I would be just as difficult to deal with, if with less aggression and more self-pity.

Saturday, 11 April 1981

Last night the news came through that Bobby Sands had won the by-election at Fermanagh, South Tyrone. I must admit to being relieved that the winner was not Harry West. Not that the latter is unpleasant. Far from it, in my experience, just a decent old bigot, not bright enough to know he's a bigot. A victory for Unionism at this juncture could only have encouraged hard-line Protestants, even though Paisley was not directly involved here.

And a victory for Sands? After the assassination of Henry Wilson in 1922 De Valera said, 'I cannot condone, but I must not pretend not to understand.' People are entitled to call Sands a terrorist, but whether he lives or dies no one can call him a villain, a label well adapted to many members of the IRA and UDA. I find some consolation in the fact that people in Britain will be forced to think a little harder instead of averting their gaze, but however hard one looks a solution still seems far off. The *Guardian* leader is very good, calling yet once more for a three-cornered approach to the whole issue: Britain, Ulster, the Irish Republic. I hope that Anne and I will be able to say something which has some small influence along these lines when our book comes out in the autumn.

My Lenten religious reading is an hour a day instead of the usual half-hour. I am spending a lot of time just now on the works of the present Pope. I have been reading or re-reading addresses he gave in Ireland and America (I heard those at Phoenix Park and Knock). In the meanwhile I hear from our very tall and very engaging bishop that there is a reasonable chance that the Pope will be able to see me at least 'towards the end of the year'. I would dearly like to interview him, however briefly, and hopefully write about him afterwards. The

Bishop of Arundel and Brighton writes as follows: 'I will approach Bishop Martin, head of the Papal household, again at the end of the summer and try to obtain a definite date for the audience.' I somehow feel that our bishop, who was head of the English College in Rome, will pull this off.

Whether he is able to see me or not, I think of him as a stupendous man. His charity simply flowed out from him to the vast crowds of which I was a member, and with it goes his superb intellect. He is theologian, philosopher, and all the rest. Harold and Antonia think of him as poet and actor. I imagine millions of manual workers throughout the world feel that he is one of them. I suppose that any pope is better briefed on the problems of the world than any other human being, but even apart from the requirements of his spiritual life, it is only a pope of rare intellect who can absorb much of this vast supply of information. The present Pope appears to be such a one. Any Catholic who tries to form any view at all on world problems and combine it with any degree of worship has urgent reasons for trying to see things through his eyes.

Sunday, 12 April 1981

Gospel reading Matthew Chapters 19–21. Passage to ponder Chapter 19, verses 20–21. The rich young man, 'I have kept all the commandments. Where do I still fall short?' Jesus, 'If you wish to go the whole way, go, sell all you possess and give it to the poor.' My alibi? This is not a feasible course of action for an elderly married man, the young man was presumably a bachelor. But there must be an equivalent sacrifice available to married oldies. Give up the search for fame? But one does not confer any benefit on anyone else by that sacrifice. Redouble efforts, perhaps, to help outcasts and the disadvantaged?

I felt a bit senile this morning at Mass. My knee, housemaid's or clergyman's, is still not right. I report to St Thomas's again tomorrow. Dear Father Docherty told us a cautionary tale at Mass about a young woman who avoided the stations of the Cross because they hurt her knees. I apologized to him afterwards for not kneeling. He replied gently, 'I was talking of young people.' I still cling to the idea that I am fitter than the average septuagenarian, but more than one creak is developing. Considering my mother's arthritis and my father's sciatica, I have so far been lucky. Elizabeth puts it down to my copper bracelet.

No doubt a well-disposed Martian would reserve his main anxiety today for the news from and about Poland, but there has been a lull there the last few days and Poland has temporarily disappeared from the British headlines. The horror stories of the massed riots in Brixton come home to me with special force because of my association with the Melting Pot. One or two black men whom I much respect are obviously appalled at the set-back to race relations. I feel much sympathy, however, for David McNee, Chief Commissioner of the Metropolitan Police, a fine Christian to whom I helped give lunch recently for publishing purposes.

How on earth can the relations of the police with the young blacks be improved? It is sadly like Northern Ireland where few Catholics are prepared to join the police force. At the Melting Pot party last Christmas, I saw at first hand the excellent relationship with the specially appointed police liaison officers, but there was sharp criticism of the police in general. Somehow the ordinary police must get to know the ordinary young blacks and vice versa.

I am relieved, temporarily at least, to read today that the chance of Bobby Sands being expelled from Parliament is diminishing. Strange to reflect that soon after I wrote my *Peace By Ordeal* (1935) and joined the Labour Party in 1936 Hugh Dalton, a genuine friend to many young Socialist politicians, suggested my standing as a Labour candidate in that very constituency. Of course, I would never have got in – even four years later when I became a Catholic. I cannot see myself doing well on hunger strike. When it came to martyrdom my spirit might be willing, but my flesh would assuredly be weak.

I am glad that I said not long ago in the Lords, 'There is an element of nobility in anyone who dies for a cause, even a bad cause.' I consider asking a question (there is not much time left before Easter) about the difference, which must be small by now, between the demands of the hunger strike prisoners and the Government's last offer. When I saw Shane O'Doherty in Gartree Prison, he didn't appear to be dressed in prison garb. It would be tragic if one or more prisoners died for an almost non-existent difference, but I hesitate to take any step that a friend like Eamon O'Kennedy (the Irish Ambassador) would think harmful.

A good deal of publicity, one way or another, about Shirley and her book out tomorrow. Everyone continues to agree that she is enormously popular. Will she remain so if she has to take decisions in office? The chance of that is fairly remote at the moment. I see her as a young female version of Stanley Baldwin with a flair for pleasing public opinion, God-given and beyond analysis. Her views appear to be very 'Nuffield College', well informed and fashionable in conference circles, but it is not necessary to have original ideas to be quite a successful leader.

Wednesday, 15 April 1981

Foyle's lunch for Malcolm's Diaries. An exhilarating crowd of communicators were mobilized at the top table. On arrival I was asked what I thought was Malcolm's most irritating quality. I brushed the question aside, as itself irritating. I soon discovered, however, that Malcolm had answered it himself with gusto, naming his tendency to belittle prominent persons. I did not know he was aware of this little weakness. Thereupon I nominated his claim that he never reads newspapers, while always knowing everything that's contained in them. Richard Ingrams, corduroy-jacketed and larger than I remembered him, supplemented this thought. 'He claims he never sees *Private Eye*, but he's always read it from cover to cover.' Sat next on one side to Kitty, wearing Malcolm's laurels as modestly as ever, and on the other to Alan Taylor's third wife. Elizabeth and I were very fond of his first one, Margaret. The new Mrs Taylor is Hungarian, petite, with steel-rimmed glasses, attractive to me with my penchant for women who wear spectacles. She is highly intelligent, has written several books including one on the Anglo-German naval agreement of 1935. After that her present work, *The British Husband*, meaning Alan, should be 'child's play'.

Malcolm's speech was the best I have ever heard from him, at first hand or otherwise. He described the world he had known as inclining him to the belief that it was one big theatre of absurdity and yet he loved the absurd inmates. His happy expectation of death goes hand in hand with an enjoyment of life that sweeps everyone away. It is hard to remember that he was once widely resented.

Thursday, 16 April 1981

Down to Bernhurst for Easter. I saw Enoch Powell as I was leaving
the House of Lords. He greeted me with that strange, ironical, rather
charming look of his. His mouth creased at the corners rather like Ian
Brady's in one of the latter's genial moods. 'Good evening, my lord,'
bowing. I asked him, 'What are you going to do on Good Friday?' 'I
am going to Ulster. On Easter Day I am attending Mass which should
satisfy all my constituents. But in fact a large number of them won't
count it a Mass.' (And I should have thought that the rest would have
disliked him calling it a Mass.) I said I supposed that it was a High
Anglican ceremony (rather a surprising event in Northern Ireland).
'A Catholic Mass, my lord,' he replied with great satisfaction.

I have just read his reviews of Patrick Cosgrave's short life of Rab
Butler. Powell and McLeod, as we all remember, declined to serve
under Home in 1963. Somehow I get the feeling now that this was a
protest of the professional classes against the aristocracy. I know that
Butler's ancestry was immensely distinguished, but in the world of
academic life and public service I am left reflecting that in this century
the Conservative Party have been led by six aristocrats – Salisbury,
Balfour, Churchill, Eden, Macmillan and Home; by three substantial
businessmen – Bonar Law, Baldwin and Chamberlain; and by two
products of small business – Margaret Thatcher and Ted Heath. No
product of the professional classes, whereas the Labour Party have
had Attlee and Gaitskell. Powell implies that the concept of public
service was common to Butler, McLeod and himself and that none of
them, possibly for that reason, forced his way to the top of the greasy
pole.

Good Friday, 17 April 1981

Elizabeth took me this morning to see our dear old friend Mrs Hollis.
For many years she and her husband ran the Hurst Green village
school which Michael and Kevin attended when they were small boys.
She was and remains a great character, but now in her late eighties is
resident in a private nursing home for old people. She had had, I
believe, a stroke and at times was difficult to converse with, but at
other moments she demonstrated that she knew what was going
on. She asked after Antonia and her husband Mr Pinter. Did

we like him? We both said Yes, very much, at which she laughed merrily. Her sense of humour was quite unimpaired. I hope that if I have a stroke and am spared so long I shall be equally fortunate.

Easter morning, Sunday, 19 April 1981

A pause at Bernhurst. From the British standpoint, inevitably parochial, the world headlines have paused likewise. Events in Poland must, I suppose, prove more significant than those in any other single country. But El Salvador and a dozen other countries may prove me wrong. In the United Kingdom Bobby Sands is said to be 'sinking' and has certainly received the last rites. A television friend of Kevin's down here for Easter tells me that there is an impression that the British Government will make a final effort to avert a martyrdom. Meanwhile the three Dublin MPs will, I suppose, urge him to desist from his hunger strike. Naturally I take a special interest in Dev's granddaughter. By the end of his life Dev was so utterly opposed to violence that I am sure that he would not have wanted Bobby Sands to fast to death. The horrific events at Brixton and the Scarman Inquiry leave me feeling guilty that I have not made contact with the Melting Pot since the eruption. I must, however feebly, see what I can do when I get back to London.

Our family's literary activities have been absorbing quite a lot of our attention. On Wednesday night we attended a poetry reading in the Old Chelsea Town Hall; among others Judith [Kazantzis] read some of her poems and Harold Pinter read some of John Donne's. The whole exercise in aid of the Nuclear Disarmament Campaign. I was never CND and am not a nuclear disarmer now, but poets must be allowed to feel the full horror of nuclear warfare even more than ordinary mortals. Nor do we look to them for prudent statesmanship.

Judith and her striking daughter Miranda came to lunch. I told her that I had been struck by the depth of her feeling and the famous pauses in Harold Pinter's elocution. He was once credited with inventing the theatre of silence. She told me at supper after the poetry reading he asked her, 'What do you mean by feminism?' She neatly side-stepped with the question, 'Is there any feminism in your plays?' Harold, noted for his guardedness in reply to this kind of question, answered, 'You might find it in *The Homecoming*. There is a woman there who stands up for herself against the men and competes on their own terms.'

Last night we watched on television a film called *The Good Soldier*. All two hours of it directed by Kevin Billington. The critics have been full of enthusiasm for his direction. His career has not worked out as seemed likely when he married Rachel. The direction of British films has proved something of a cul-de-sac, but he has made an excellent living out of 'commercials', and whenever he gets a chance in the theatre or on television he shows an immense talent which I hope will not ultimately be wasted.

Elizabeth and I have read the manuscript of a thriller by Kevin [Pakenham]. We both agree that it starts laboriously but finishes powerfully and should certainly be published. He must drastically pare down or eliminate the economic discussions, but I feel that there is a big possibility for him in this role. The invention is excellent and the drama moves to a fine climax.

On Easter morning one inevitably asks oneself whether one has made a good or not so good Lent. The answer must be not so good. But I am glad to have read the Pope's *The Sign of Contradiction* and his addresses in Ireland and America. Also Peter Nichols's book *The Pope's Divisions* about the Church today. Monsignor Bartlett, shrewd and spiritual, recommended it to me as Lenten reading.

The Pope's almost fanatical emphasis on human rights carried away Nichols as it carries away me when I re-read his addresses. It goes interestingly with what is called his conservative thinking, e.g. in regard to birth control, etc. In *The Sign of Contradiction* the most conservative doctrine is the restatement of the belief in a personal Devil which no intellectual priest has propounded to me for many years. I suppose also the Mariolatry might have been called old-fashioned a few years ago. But Nichols says that it is in harmony with the new tide sweeping through the Church in the charismatic move-ment. The truth is that the Pope can never be placed in any pigeon-hole. I suppose he could be called a product of Polish Catholicism but no world leader can be talked of as a 'product'. What line is he taking at the moment about the Polish situation? I have not the faintest idea and nor has anyone else I speak to. As I pause, during the Easter period, I look back on the three and a half months of 1981; I will not attempt an estimate of spiritual progress, if any; very much 'if any'. The most satisfying event for me was the debate I initiated on mental after-care. Not just because of what happened that day but because it seems to encourage hopes of a valuable inquiry.

Tuesday, 21 April 1981

An hour and a half in the evening at the Melting Pot, Brixton. I was shown the recent damage, most of which occurred a few hundred yards from the Melting Pot offices. The psychological effect strikes me as more significant than the physical. The leaders of the Melting Pot, responsible citizens, left me in no doubt about the bad relationship, the ever worsening relationship, with the police, particularly the younger police who had been drafted in recently. I found it hard to credit the statement that a thousand plain-clothes officers had been drafted in during the last few months, but a white lady who owns a cinema in the most affected street assured me that this was so. It may well be that the sequence has been (1) increasing unemployment, especially among young blacks; (2) increasing crime; (3) increasing introduction of young police officers determined to make their presence felt; (4) escalation of mutual hostility. Against this background a trivial incident was enough to start two days of rioting.

No one disputed Mrs Thatcher's claim that the problem could not be solved by money, though of course the absence of jobs had vicious consequences. But her recent utterances caused real pain. The chairman of the Melting Pot had come to England in 1943 to join the Air Force. He is a much-respected local citizen but he still feels that West Indians are not treated as genuinely British. It seems that the police quite often address them as 'niggers'. As I went away I asked myself whether Irish immigrants would feel this kind of grievance. I thought not.

The Melting Pot leaders still pin some hopes on Willie Whitelaw. He visited the Melting Pot twice when he was Shadow Home Secretary, but they have not met him since. I agree with them that he would be capable of understanding their feelings as would few if any of his colleagues.

Thursday, 23 April 1981

Three p.m. train to Northallerton *en route* to Durham to see Myra. Suddenly (and uniquely in my experience in a train) a cry rang out: 'Wanted, a doctor urgently.' A tall, dark, strikingly good-looking young man sprang to his feet, picked up a bag and moved rapidly down the corridor. Soon afterwards he returned to say in reply to questions, 'She had only been very sick.' Meanwhile the ice had been broken between myself and the very sympathetic and slim young woman opposite who proved to be his wife. She asked me if I was 'Lord Pakenham – I mean Longford?' I said, 'Yes.' She told me she had much enjoyed Elizabeth's *Wellington*. I gather she teaches history at the polytechnic in Newcastle where her husband practises medicine.

She is engaged on a thesis on 'The Effect of the Nazi–Soviet Pact on the British Left'. (What specialized subjects supervisors impose on their students!) Christopher Hill, a Communist till, I think, the Hungarian Revolution, by now ex-Master of Balliol, had told her that at a Labour meeting in Oxford in 1939 he had supported the Pact, and I had opposed him. G. D. H. Cole, chairman of the regular gatherings of left-wing dons, known as 'the Pink Panther Lunch Club', had apparently made peace. I had completely forgotten the incident, but the brief encounter was quite a coincidence. I suggested that she write to Philip Toynbee, the first Communist President of the Union. She said that she had already read his published account of how he left the Communist Party on the morrow of the Pact. By another coincidence I was reading in the train at that very moment Philip's new book about his spiritual odyssey.

She and her husband and I talked happily about the Labour Party until I got out at Northallerton. She has become a unilateralist, but she would have been first-class material for the Social Democrats. I gathered from her, however, that in the north-east people like her would be very unlikely to join them.

A fifty-mile drive to the Inglebys, a Christian household but with no nonsense about teetotalism. The Pro-Chancellor of Leeds University came to dinner. It was indeed good news that Edward Boyle, Vice-Chancellor of the university, had for the moment made an unlooked-for recovery. Elizabeth and I have known and loved him since he was a little boy in Hurst Green. His weight when we last saw him had come down from seventeen stone to nine. I was in no way surprised to hear that he had done a great job as Vice-Chancellor. His health prospect must, alas, remain precarious.

Friday, 24 April 1981

Woke up to see a snow-storm. Feared I would never get to Northallerton, let alone Durham. But someone bravely drove me through the blizzard. Myra was looking positively cheerful. The tragedy and the melancholy at least for the moment in abeyance, with all her sights set on November. Her work for the Open University honours degree is stretching her to the full.

I gave her a careful account of the meeting of John Hunt and myself with Willie Whitelaw. As always, there was the ghastly problem of how far to raise the hopes of a prisoner. Survival during the long years of life imprisonment depends on hope of some kind. The authorities on the spot realize this; not so their distant masters. 'Ireland has been cheated of all her hopes, and yet she still hopes,' said a famous patriot. The wing governor, whose comments are crucial for any reports about her, was very cordial about Myra. 'I've got a lot of time for Myra, she has been an excellent prisoner here. Apart from her degree [in which they take legitimate pride] she has always done well in the workshop and participated in all the events. She won a recent prize in the Easter festivities. I admire her self-discipline and the way she has kept herself in shape.' While I was talking to Myra the other thirty-odd inmates passed by the window and waved in friendly fashion. But she has only one intellectual companion, I gather, who is also doing an Open University degree although in the social sciences. She much likes her tutor but sees him only once in six weeks.

I am horrified to hear that the Gillespie girls, Ann and Eileen, convicted for peripheral IRA connections mainly because they assisted the escape to Ireland of their brother, have again been refused parole though they have only two more years to serve and they have already done seven. I see this as a mean way of asserting an anti-IRA toughness.

Met Elizabeth at King's Cross and travelled down with her to stay with Esmond Warner and the beautiful Ilia near Cambridge. Esmond, son of the famous Sir 'Plum' after whom is named the stand at Lord's, is my oldest friend from the days of C. M. Wells's house at Eton. School chess champion, bridge international, an immense success as a bookseller, launching out from Bowes & Bowes in Cambridge. Raconteur extraordinary. Marina [Warner], also beautiful and a rising literary star, arrived in the morning. I feared that when Esmond retired from W. H. Smith he would feel sadly lost. On the contrary, he seems to be happier than he has ever been. As honorary librarian of Brookes's he is in London every week and his capacity to obtain and enlarge on gossip grows by the hour. He knows exactly which Cambridge dons are seeking peerages and which colleagues are putting spokes in their wheels. Rab [Butler] fascinates him. His fund of Rabisms is unlimited.

Saturday, 25 April 1981

Lunch with Jack Plumb, Master of Christ's, which dear old Charles Snow immortalized in *The Masters*. Jack, though I like him very much, is really Elizabeth's friend. They served together for years on the National Portrait Gallery committee. The bait that drew us was the news that Princess Margaret would be present. We both felt that this was bound to be valuable to Elizabeth's book. Elizabeth in fact got a quarter of an hour with Princess Margaret before we went in to lunch. She found her most amusing – my own experience in two earlier conversations. She felt that she obtained some useful background. Princess Margaret told Elizabeth with some regret, I gather, that she had not been well educated. The Queen, as is well known, was taught history by the famous Eton master C.H.K. Marten. He had a well-known trick of addressing his form as 'gentlemen'. Whether or not out of nervousness, he addressed the Queen in the same way. On one occasion he bit his handkerchief. This must surely be attributed to nerves. When the Queen finished with him, Margaret, four years younger, claimed that it was her turn; but education at that time was not thought necessary in her case, which seems very short-sighted in retrospect. Princess Margaret has completely recovered her looks and figure.

Before, during or after lunch I chatted to at least four ladies. I discussed married priests with the very companionable wife of the Bishop of St Albans. I am strongly in favour of them. He had voted for them in the Synod. I had a pleasantly controversial set-to about crime and punishment with a rather arresting young woman, widow of David Beatty, now married to the son of Tony Nutting. I sat next to the exquisite Vanessa Thomas, daughter of Gladwyn Jebb and once the girl-friend of our Thomas. I also talked to the wife of a famous sculptor who asked me, 'Do you write books like your daughter?' I said, 'Do you mean like my wife?' She quickly apologized. I asked her what she did. It turned out that her pictures had recently been exhibited in America, England and Germany. I quickly apologized.

It is quite fun finding out these these things about people at lunches, but on the whole I would rather be told first, otherwise so much time is wasted. As always, when I go to a university lunch or dinner I marvel at the ability of the dons and their wives to eat and drink so much without apparent damage, but in fact nearly all the visitors came from afar. One duchess, four peers, one bishop, etc. Jack certainly knows how to make his guests happy.

Mrs Nutting asked George Weidenfeld about his joining the Social Democratic Party. Who was his leader in the House of Lords? For the only time in my recollection, George was at a loss. After a time he hazarded a guess that he was Bert someone (Herbert Bowden, former Chief Labour Whip, now Lord Aylestone). After lunch Harold Lever firmly rejected any idea of leaving the Labour Party, though he said that he disagreed with almost everything they stood for at the moment and was sharply critical of the National Executive. Pat, however, he said, had told him that he could say anything he liked about the Labour Party in the House of Lords as long as he didn't leave it. He agreed with me that each one of us had only one life and must find the best way of making our own contribution. Asked about the economic prospect, he replied, 'I look forward to a sluggish recovery.'

Wednesday, 29 April 1981

A biggish day. My main event was my short (two and a half hours) House of Lords debate on the need for more equality. It came well up to my expectations, though with little Press coverage next morning. Nowadays more people know about a speech of mine in the Lords, and indeed hear my voice on the radio, than learn about it through the newspapers.

I had intended to speak for twenty minutes; I am proud to think that I kept to fifteen, which meant leaving out jokes and embellishments. I submitted three propositions: (1) a society marked by a high degree of equality, other things being equal, is morally superior to one which is marked by a high degree of inequality; (2) our present British society is marked by a high degree of inequality; (3) we should, therefore, redouble our efforts to make our society more equal if this can be done without damage to other values. The real controversy arose over the question whether in fact greater equality could be obtained without other values being damaged. I argued that while this was indeed possible, respect for the continuity of the family, along with liberty and economic gorwth, must be maintained.

Dora [Gaitskell], who was very keen to speak, had bad gout in the foot during the previous night and was kept away. At eighty she is still a dynamo, in spite of serious cataract. Amazing to think that she didn't come to England until she was five. She is very dear to Elizabeth and me Dora, reading the debate, told me that she thought all the speeches were good, except Janet Young's. She is a tremendous partisan; it was something of a compliment to Janet, who does a wonderful job for the Government, that Dora even expected to find her speech acceptable. I think Dora must have overlooked the speech of Lord Harris of High Cross who is an extreme right-wing economist. He made no bones about wanting not more but much less equality.

Certainly I was loyally supported by Labour colleagues with Michael Stewart winding up for our side. My friendship with him and Mary grows ever warmer. He is one of the few ex-ministers whose departure from the Labour Party, if it came, would indicate that something was fundamentally wrong. Janet Young's speech, winding up for the Government, was, as always in her case, agreeable and shrewd. She argued in effect that poverty had been much diminished. She implied that there had been a good deal of levelling but she left it an open question whether she and the Government wanted more or less equality. As I said when I wound up the debate, 'I defy anyone to say whether she wishes to see more or less equality', but I went on to point out that the present Government have in fact stood for a policy of more inequality and that Janet Young's speech, therefore, bore no relation to their actual purposes.

My general reflection about the debate is that it will always be extremely difficult to convince one's own side, let alone the other, that any particular course of action will increase equality. But unless we cling to this clue in our economic and social policy we shall drift hither and thither without a compass.

After the debate I dashed down to Brighton to speak to a bi-annual meeting of the flourishing Forum Club. Several hundred present. I spoke for the best part of an hour on 'The State of the Nation' covering politics, economics, social policy, the lot. I was questioned intelligently and widely. I felt that my feeblest answer related to young hooligans, but perhaps that is because I am still so uncertain in my mind as to how we ought to deal with them or help them, even after all these years at New Horizon and several months on the sub-committee of the All-Party Penal Affairs Committee. I came away quite uncertain about the political composition of the audience, a credit, it may be thought, to all concerned. The secretary of the club, who had retired after forty years in Unilevers, took me home to a family gathering where three generations argued far into the night.

Friday, 1 May 1981

Went at twelve o'clock to St Paul's for the memorial service for Bill Barnetson. A splendid turnout. Not surprisingly, for Bill had endless interests and made friends wherever he made contacts. Arnold Goodman, who delivered the address, did well to refer to Bill as a man with an unrivalled gift for helping people out of difficulties (the same could be said for Arnold himself), but Arnold's speech was far from characteristic. He speaks habitually without notes. This time he stuck inevitably but remorselessly to a script. For a long time in the House of Lords I was the fastest speaker. There came a moment, however, when the shorthand writers told me that Lord Goodman left me standing. 'You speak your paragraphs as fast as he does, but you pause between them; he goes straight on without needing to draw breath.' St Paul's, alas, is the worst place in the world for rapid speaking. Those who know it best, i.e. the clergy, pause between every sentence. Arnold's speech, deeply felt though it was, lacked his usual impact.

Visit to the Oxford Union. I find an invitation to speak there irresistible. I only once regretted my presence when the first speaker on my side was Jeremy Thorpe. In spite of, or because of, his case, which was then coming on, he was accorded such an overwhelming reception that I realized I was redundant. I am aware by now that the summer attendances are poor. Yesterday was no exception. The best time is late October when freshmen are still being allowed in free.

The motion was 'That current support for the Arts is ineffective'. On the opposite side to me were real big guns: Roy Shaw, Secretary-General of the Arts Council, and Arnold Goodman, an epoch-making chairman of the Council in addition to his other glories. In debating terms my own speech went well. I hit some easy targets to gratifying applause and laughter. But in the end I was completely eclipsed by Arnold and not in any way I expected. I was a little fearful that he might make a fool of me, though that would never be his purpose. He began by suggesting that I did not go often to the National Theatre. I hopped up and said that I often went to the plays there (more or less true) but the last time I went to that place was in connection with this debate. I was left in no doubt about their bitter criticism of the Government and the Arts Council over the inadequate subsidy.

When Arnold got going he gave a detailed and moving account of the part played by the Arts Council in promoting the arts in Britain in recent years. He finished by announcing that the arts in Britain today were flourishing. His far-ranging knowledge and still more his patent love of the arts went to the making of a *tour de force*. He had one big advantage over me (apart from superior knowledge of the arts, with the possible exception of literature), in his total supremacy in the world of arts administration. The Union has become very much his home ground. There was a time when I would have been very much the Oxford man and he (a Cantab) the outsider. But last night I was actually asked by a young admirer, 'Have you had any connection with Oxford before this evening?' Arnold, now Master of 'Univ', was introduced to us before the debate began as the trustee who had financially saved the Union. Harold Macmillan seems to have helped him somewhat. How like Arnold to have achieved such a position in a strange environment so rapidly.

It is easy, but false, to sneer at him for automatically making himself indispensable. The truth is that wherever he goes he radiates a benevolence which I myself exhibit at best intermittently. We both got on very well with the undergraduates at dinner, but this was very much my old scene. I should feel uneasy in many areas where he would be thoroughly at home. In a sense he resembles an unpaid universal solicitor with every human being he meets as his client.

To repeat myself, I had nothing to reproach myself with over my own performance. Harold had introduced me to the General Manager of the National Theatre, who put me on to a speech delivered by Roy Shaw at the National Theatre in January 1981. In that speech he sharply criticized the cuts imposed by the Thatcher Government and indeed the whole trend of their Arts policy. At that time Norman St John-Stevas was his one great hope. There was plenty of room for poking fun here, all the more as Norman, who had been President of the Union at Cambridge, just failed to 'make it' at Oxford.

Roy Shaw, a much bigger man physically than I had expected, made a straight-forward defence of his stewardship as Director-General. He argued that the motion did not say that support for the Arts was *inadequate*, which might be true, but *ineffective*, which must mean that it was inefficiently administered. This line was a bit too ingenious to convince the audience. If Arnold had not followed me I would have felt that we were well on top.

Through some odd misunderstanding Roy began his speech on *our* side of the dispatch box which I had never seen happen at the Union. Naturally I made the obvious debating use of the error. Roy told me afterwards that ironically enough he had been rebuked that very afternoon by the new (down-graded) Minister for the Arts, Paul Channon, for just the kind of criticism of Government policy which I had been offering in the debate. I more than once congratulated him on his courage in standing up to the Government. He assured me, as he had assured Paul Channon, that he intended to continue doing so.

Hammond Innes spoke first of the guests on our side of the motion. As he said himself, he was no public debater, but as the author of thirty successful books and the possessor of a well-delineated personality, he held the attention well. Of the four undergraduate speakers (all rising rather than risen) the two on our side made a big impression on me.

My young lady colleague not only spoke incisively but rose with complete assurance more than once to intervene when Roy Shaw and Arnold were speaking. The young man on our side, tall, dark, thin, sensitive-looking, told me that if ever a girl was on the way to becoming a super-woman, this was she. Though still in her first year she is already a hockey blue and is likely to add blues for cricket and athletics. She also excels at swimming and rows in her female college eight. She is expected to obtain a First in Classics Honour Mods and of course become President of the Union. Stanley Baldwin once wrote of the Eton and Harrow match, 'There are the boys eternal, and there too are the little sisters, most loyal of comrades in weal and woe.' In the Oxford Union, the little sisters have long since shaken off their subsidiary status.

The young man himself was interesting in a different way. Like the President, he is at New College where he won an open history scholarship. Something he said led me to ask him whether he had been at a State school. He said, 'No, Eton.' It transpired that his father is now headmaster of Eton, but he entered the school some years before that happened. Like myself, he had not been in Pop, though I assume that he was in sixth form. He assured me that if elected to Pop he would not have accepted, a very different attitude to mine at his age. We both agreed that Pop ought to be abolished. He has not yet made up his mind about leaving the Labour Party and joing the Social Democrats, though it seems likely that he will take this step. I was assured by my neighbours at dinner, one Labour, one Conservative, that the new party was making no headway in Oxford. I was told that you had to be called either Taverne or Williams to hold office. Shirley may be receiving a different report from her daughter.

Tuesday, 5 May 1981

Mary Craig gave me lunch. People aften ask me whether I like the book she wrote about me. I say sincerely that it was very flattering and unexpected to have a book written about me at all and there are some very reassuring things said about me anonymously, one of them, I believe, by Richard Ingrams who at that time was so savage about me in public. Some of the anecdotes are ridiculous, for example that I blundered into my aunt, Lady Dunsany's bed and slept there all night. I am not sure where she was supposed to have got to.

Mary has had four children, two fine, vigorous young men, one who died at the age of ten without ever recognizing her, and one an absolutely sweet mongol. Her book *Blessings*, which deals with suffering in the light of her own experience, has travelled round the world and brought consolation to many hearts. She is now revising her hastily written but vivid little book about the present Pope. She has many friends among liberal Catholic priests, one of whom at least has left the priesthood to marry. But I am glad that she is still a profound admirer of the Pope, though by no means uncritical of his conservatism. I also revere him as no other pope I have read about, even Pope John XXIII. That does not prevent me being unrepentantly in favour of women priests. I am sure that we shall see them in time, though not I fear in my lifetime.

Wednesday, 6 May 1981

Three fifteen: went to see John Belstead, minister responsible for prisons under the Home Secretary, about Sean O'Doherty. Sean is the ex-IRA prisoner doing a life sentence for his share in letter-bombing. I see him as pre-eminently the true penitent, an opinion shared by the Bishop of Derry, whose choirboy he was in earlier days, and Cardinal Hume, who has visited him more than once in the Scrubs. With much difficulty he secured permission to approach his victims and offer his apologies, but he is still a Category A prisoner (i.e. treated as specially dangerous). Not long ago he was transferred from Wormwood Scrubs to Gartree, which is very inaccessible and where the Open University facilities are much inferior. The latter point was the subject of my visit to John Belstead. I am not sure whether an improvement will be effected.

I was *absolutely horrified* to be told that the glowing reports about him which the authorities in Wormwood Scrubs always made were in no way borne out by their reports to the Home Office. I protested vehemently at the clear implication that Sean's repudiation of the IRA was bogus and that he had been pulling the wool over the eyes of his well-wishers.

Then to a meeting of the Christian Prison Fellowship Trustees. This inspiring movement started when Martin Ingleby introduced me to Michael Allison MP and his wife Sylvia Mary, both dedicated evangelical Christians. The Christian Prison Fellowship sprang from my first conversation with them. In two years it has moved ahead faster than I would have thought possible. Sylvia Mary won over the Chaplain General, a crucial happening. Michael Allison looked strained, as well he might. He is the Minister of State for Northern Ireland responsible under the Secretary of State for prisoners. He and Sylvia Mary were in Belfast last weekend and were returning when our meeting ended. The death of Bobby Sands between their two visits, and the possible death of other hunger strikers, weighed cruelly on him, indeed on both. All of us offered prayers for them.

Thursday, 7 May 1981

Yesterday evening to Grillions, Quintin in the chair – immensely ebullient though hobbling on two sticks and bearing marks of suffering. When he departed he took my overcoat by mistake, leaving his own. For a few hours this morning I was wearing a Lord Chancellor's outer garment. It contained no articles of any kind. Mine is invariably full of trivia. Some talk before dinner with Arthur Bryant. I told him that to my amazement and delight I had had a fan letter from Leslie Rowse. Arthur had told me that Leslie was the greatest living British historian. Did he think that he was the greatest we had ever had? Arthur replied, 'I don't think that any British historian ever possessed so complete a mastery of a period as has Leslie of the Elizabethan age.' I asked how he compared his own work with Leslie's.

Arthur is completing a twelve-volume British History by concentrating for the first time on this same Elizabethan period. Arthur said, 'I am a narrative historian, as is Elizabeth, Leslie is altogether more academic.'

Two or three pleasant little happenings during the day. I was telephoned by the secretary of Roy Dotrice, who is doing a two-hour one-man impersonation of Abraham Lincoln at the Fortune Theatre. He says that he owes more to my short book on Lincoln, published 1973, than to any of the other books. When I last heard there were over five thousand. Would I like tickets for the show? You bet I would. Elizabeth and I will be going next Thursday and taking with us William Armstrong and his striking wife Clare, an old Oxford friend of Judith's.

At the end of the morning I lunched at the Garrick. Roy Shaw rose from his seat and came across to greet me, 'You were very witty and urbane and kind to me.' I returned the compliment. I said that if the news about the termination of the Old Vic company had been published before the debate, some of us might have been tempted to use it against the Arts Council. I suppose, however, that it was a consequence of government cuts, 'and of the ineptitude of those running the company', said someone else present.

Friday, 8 May 1981

Sally (of Weidenfeld's) took me to Anne's house in Highbury for a penultimate discussion before our book on Ulster goes to the printers. Anne, who is pregnant with her second baby while still working at the *Guardian*, has been indisposed. I told her at the end that she looked better than she did at the beginning of the morning. She said, 'That's the adrenalin', a word usually associated with anger. We never become acrimonious, but we are both capable of digging our toes in. The only real argument we had today was about the proper treatment of Jack Lynch. Our present text seemed to me to push him off the stage with scant honour. Anne was not very much impressed when I told her that De Valera had once called him to me 'a holy man', but she agreed that she could not help responding to his charming voice. In the end we found a compromise which did not tamper with her recollection of the facts, but did make reference to the international respect accorded him.

Monday, 11 May 1981

Elizabeth and I went to dinner last night with Vanessa and Hugh Thomas (now Lord Thomas, one of the new group of Conservative professors in the House of Lords). The guest of honour was Arthur Schlesinger, slight of build, but only short when seen with his statuesque wife – not present on this occasion. They are both warm, friendly personalities. Arthur is a kind of American Isaiah Berlin, in the sense of being equally at home in Harvard and Oxford, though at present he teaches in New York. His devotion to the Kennedy family has been carried far beyond the line of prudence. His book on Bobby Kennedy was as eloquent as ever, but unashamedly eulogistic. He is finishing the last of his books on Roosevelt, which are more satisfactory because more dispassionate.

With the coming of Reagan, Arthur is politically out in the cold, but he was as good company as ever. Reagan was, in his opinion, mainly interested in domestic questions. His simplistic belief in market forces resembled that of Mrs Thatcher, but he was far more relaxed and far readier to delegate. Arthur thinks well of the Reagan team, with reservations about Haig.

Arthur considers that if the market philosophy of Reagan succeeds, they will be in power for a long, long time. If it fails, Teddy Kennedy might still be recalled by the American public, Chappaquiddick notwithstanding. I asked him how he rated Teddy Kennedy and he replied, 'A man was once asked, "How's your wife?" and answered, "It depends who you are comparing her with." ' He paid tribute to Teddy's progressive record in the Senate. I told him that his collective speeches which we published were very impressive – perhaps Arthur wrote them?

Also present at the dinner was a young Foreign Office man just finishing as Peter Carrington's private secretary. Aged forty-one, dark, thin, rather fierce-looking, in appearance not unlike David Owen, whom he served as private secretary before Carrington. He did not need me to tell him that David Owen had been very unpopular in Foreign Office circles, but referred approvingly to his courage. He thought that David O. would do better to concentrate on domestic questions if he wanted to reach the peak in British politics. I myself believe that he will be a significant figure for many years, but never reach the top of the greasy pole.

We discussed Peter Carrington. I told him that in my first six years in the Lords I had not noticed his existence. More fool me! He is an extreme example of a late developer. (Hugh Gaitskell was another.) Given his energy and his excellent, though not exactly memorable, style of speaking, what had he got that 'the rest of us' hadn't? He said that Carrington got on well with everybody and could put up, if necessary, with a lot of rudeness, e.g. from Mugabe during the Rhodesia conference. Perhaps a certain Etonian arrogance comes in useful here. He thought that Carrington's experience enabled him to take unpleasant situations very calmly. Carrington was a wonderful man for keeping up a front in all circumstances which gave others, presumably the officials, a chance to develop policy.

I thought that Carrington was developing into a great man, at any rate a big one, though he is not large physically. My new Foreign Office friend dwelt at some length on the absence of big men in any walk of life today, including the diplomatic service. To succeed, one had to learn to conform, a sure guarantee of mediocrity. I said, 'What about Carrington?' He pointed out that, except in the war, he had never had to conform, like a Member of the House of Commons.

Just before he left I told Arthur that Richard Nixon had asked Elizabeth and me to dinner with him at his house in New York. He said, 'In that case, you must look us up first. We live next door.' I asked him whether they met. He replied, 'No way.' I was rather shocked. I am sure that Nixon, in these latter days, would never refuse to meet anyone. But there is an arrogance about East Coast liberalism which seems to affect even Arthur, the kindest of men. Hugh defended him on the grounds that Nixon's damage to the American constitution seemed to him unforgivable.

Very good progress in regard to the Mental After-Care Inquiry. Lord Richardson, the eminent physician, who spoke so well in the debate, had tea with me and, after saying how much he and his wife liked my book on St Francis, showed himself most anxious to assist the inquiry. This could be crucial, because although he is not a psychiatrist he will be able to obtain high-class psychiatric representation.

Then on to Elly Jansen, where the news was indeed heartening. She is quite ready to provide the facilities for the inquiry. I would be the chairman, but it would be carried out under the auspices of the Richmond Fellowship and would bear their name, not mine. I always regretted that our Pornography Inquiry produced what was called the Longford Report, though that was insisted on by the committee.

Now I must push ahead with mobilizing the committee, with the idea of a first meeting at the beginning of June. Elizabeth and I used to have a category of 'wonderful women'. Elly ranks high in any such selection.

Then to dinner with Rachel for her thirty-ninth birthday. She looked stunning, in a long white satin dress. Elizabeth tells me that you can buy such dresses second-hand. I had admittedly thought that I might be called on for a few words and had prepared a neat little address on these lines: 'The Beatitudes in the Sermon on the Mount can be translated in various ways. You can use the word "happy" or the word "fortunate" or the word "blessed". Rachel is happy in her disposition, fortunate in her literary talent, blessed in the love of her husband and children.' This charming little speech was never delivered, or within a thousand miles of being delivered.

Peter Jay came in after dinner. I was much impressed by his lack of side. It is years now since he was first called 'the cleverest man in England', and if you became ambassador to Washington at the age of forty and were, in any case, much taller than ordinary human beings, it would be difficult not to become Olympian. But when we left the party at about midnight he was sitting on the floor and I felt that he was young and unpompous at heart. Naturally there was talk of breakfast television. I tried to be civil and said, 'I suppose that people will learn to change their habits.' He said, 'Fifteen per cent view it in America, and if only half that number view it here we shall be very successful.' I really think, though I did not say, that the whole thing is a bit beneath him, assuming as I do that he is, or could be, a leader of the nation. A big man sighed for by my Foreign Office friend the night before.

He told Elizabeth about a distressing problem. His wife for various reasons prefers to live in America. He intends to live here, and indeed must do so, for the purposes of his television adventure. His two daughters wish to live here, his son in America, though I gather he is very fond of Peter. So, as always, grandeur and misery are not separated for long.

Elizabeth had a fascinating talk with a young Treasury official, very close to Mrs Thatcher. He says that one of her most attractive qualities is her passionate loyalty to her own staff, which does not surprise me, but it is nice to know. She is really interested in science. She spent five hours going round a nuclear plant, which the young official found a very trying experience. She is the only top person in his recollection who has this almost obsessional interest in practical scientific detail. Her reading for pleasure also tends to be scientific, which leaves the implication, possibly unfair, that she is not strong on the cultural side.

He also told Elizabeth that she was anxious to shed her image of the iron lady, though he doubted whether she would ever succeed in doing so. In this connection I should mention that in the afternoon I ran into Michael Allison, back from Northern Ireland. I have for some time felt that I ought to be doing *something*, however feeble, towards persuading the Government to soften their attitude towards the hunger strikers. When I met Michael, I blurted out, 'I think that I ought to tell you that I am critical of the unbending attitude of the Government. I do not like to say so in public, for fear of encouraging the hunger strikers to continue. But it would be cowardly to conceal my thoughts.' I asked him whether he had looked carefully into the way the matter had been handled by the Dublin Government. He said, 'They have got a much smaller problem and they have fudged the issue.' I said, 'Why don't you try and fudge it a bit yourselves?' He alluded to the pressures from the Protestant side. I said that I did not envy him his role; that, after all, Michael is a great Christian, deeply involved in the Christian Prison Fellowship, and I had hoped for something more imaginative from him. I told him that I attributed the hard line ultimately to Mrs Thatcher, whom I admired in many respects. She suffered, I thought, from her obsession with not giving way once she had taken up a position. He said that she was very busy with lots of other things. But I am sure that ultimately the authorities take their guidance in this matter from her.

We had a little further conversation about the UDA and the reasons for not making them illegal. He puts them on the same level as the Provisional Sinn Fein who are not illegal. But I doubt if that attitude can be maintained. I felt like Victor Gollancz, denouncing me when I was Minister of State for Germany, for taking a stand over the dismantling policy during 1947-8. I would much rather see Michael there than not there, but at the moment he is a pawn of higher powers, politically speaking.

Wednesday, 13 May 1981

I attended the discussion group at New Horizon. Half a dozen of our 'visitors' recently came to the Lords and heard me speak, which may have added spice to the political free-for-all. A lot of intelligent talk, uncoordinated inevitably. I asked them what they thought about the motion at the Cambridge Union that evening, 'That the Soviet Union is not a significant menace to the West', which I was opposing. Most of them thought that the Soviet Union was indeed a menace. I am quite glad to think of that as a normal working-class reaction, though well aware that most members of all classes prefer to avoid the issue.

To Cambridge by the 5.36 for the debate just mentioned. I travelled down with Nora Beloff, an excellent gossip as befits an old political correspondent of *The Observer*. She used to forecast my political demise at regular intervals. I always assumed that she got it from Dick [Crossman]. Now she travels frequently to Russia, Yugoslavia, etc., and writes expertly on Eastern Europe.

Nora has recently seen Roy Jenkins, who has now made up his mind after much reflection that Britain should 'withdraw' from Northern Ireland. (Withdrawal can mean more things than one.) Roy wants the British Government to announce that they will be withdrawing after two years, giving the majority and the minority that amount of time to sort out their problems. This coming in the same week as Tony Benn has publicly demanded withdrawal is highly significant, though it is unthinkable that the two should have acted in any kind of concert. It is impossible not to associate these demands for withdrawal with the deaths of Bobby Sands and Francis Hughes and the world-wide criticism of British policy.

Nora, as a diplomatic correspondent and writer, is particularly concerned about the effect on Britain's prestige, whatever that may mean. I told her that I didn't think that the British man in the street cared an awful lot what foreigners thought about us. We both agreed, however, that public opinion was now moving towards an 'exit'.

This was confirmed later before and after the debate. Our opponents, both left-wing Labour, were Alf Roberts, large, jocular, outward-going, and Ernie Ross, small, intense, unsmiling, transparently sincere, indeed fanatical. I had run into Peter Shore at lunch in the Gay Hussar and asked him about Roberts and Ross. He said, 'You are bound to like Alf Roberts, whatever you have read about his goings-on in Afghanistan and Berlin.' About Ernie Ross he was restrained. His championship of the PLO did not seem to appeal to him. In the event I liked them both very much.

I was no doubt softened by the friendliness of these two young lefties towards their 'veteran peer' (my description in the *Guardian* this morning). The years roll back and I recognize them as the kind of young men Elizabeth and I worked with so hopefully and happily in the 1930s, when we ourselves were young left-wing socialists. Roberts might not be altogether serious-minded, though he has a good record as a social worker. He said at one point during the debate, 'I don't know much about foreign affairs. But I'll go anywhere to see what's going on. I visited the CIA as the guest of the Americans!' This helps to explain his strange antics in Berlin. But he, and still more obviously Ernie, are dedicated to an altogether different society from the present one. I do not get the same feeling about the present leaders of the party, but after all Elizabeth and I have also changed. Ernie Ross admittedly disarmed me by saying as we shook hands before dinner: 'Are you on the same side of the motion as we are?' He seemed surprised to find that I wasn't.

He, and I think Roberts, with whom I had less conversation, are convinced that support for withdrawal from Northern Ireland is gaining ground rapidly in the party. Ross, an active supporter of Tony Benn, is also convinced that Benn will beat Denis Healey for the deputy leadership. Ernie Ross said of Benn, 'The media make him out a bogey man. When you meet him you find he is a very nice fellow.' Still unsmiling he went on, 'It is the same with you, the media make you out a do-gooding Lord', which he obviously regarded as a horrible allegation.

So to the debate itself. The undergraduates were quite good, the best, not surprisingly, being the tall, dark, nice-looking son of Patrick Jenkin, Minister of Health. All sorts of statistics were selectively quoted to prove that the Russians were or were not getting ahead. When it came to my turn, I synthesized the guidance of my Foreign Office expert, Nixon's *Real War*, including the introduction to the paperback, and Alan Chalfont's brief remarks to me in the House of Lords. I had done a good deal of other reading. I submitted that two years ago it looked as though the Russians would be able to dictate surrender terms by 1985. Now it seemed as though we would be in quite as strong a position by that date – but only because of the new initiative of President Reagan, supported by our own Prime Minister. I still think that is quite a good summary, but a few carefully chosen figures might have strengthened my air of authority.

Roberts's speech was described by the president as eloquent. In a homely sense that was true. He made happy play with his visit to Afghanistan ('I am the only one who has been there'), and with the way it had been distorted by the media (Berlin was not so much as mentioned), and derided, which is not too difficult, some of the nuclear options propounded. He smiled throughout his own speech and indeed continued to smile during mine. Many years ago Elizabeth told me that I must 'smile more'. I had tried without much success to live up to an ideal so brilliantly illustrated by the Queen Mother. For good or for ill, Alf Roberts never stopped smiling and Ernie Ross never began.

Ernie trotted out a list of alleged Soviet objectives, all most laudable. Someone beside me murmured, 'Now I *know* he's a Communist', which indeed I was told next day by a Conservative minister. Later, he interrupted my speech at interminable length but once again disarmed me with a remark, 'Lord Longford is part of history!'

I have spoken better, e.g. at the Oxford Union recently, though we won the debate at Cambridge. I made effective use of a quotation from Denis Healey's speech in the Commons last week. He reaffirmed the Labour Party's firm support for the Atlantic Pact, etc. I described the two Labour MPs as totally unrepresentative of the party. In view of our current divisions, I might have had trouble with an old-timer like Ian Mikardo, but in the circumstances the point went well. In response to Roberts I said in my turn, 'I am the only one who sat with Bevin and Molotov in the Council of Foreign Ministers, 1947.' Few, if any, of the audience were alive at that time. I could speak from ministerial experience of Russian aggression after the war in Poland and elsewhere which culminated in the attempt to starve out Berlin. I was all for continued dialogue with the Russians, a dialogue which must be based on strength, yet disarmament and peace must be the ultimate purpose of foreign policy, now and throughout their lives. I came away exhilarated not by my own attempts at eloquence but by the contact on quite a deep level with such intelligent young people so serious about the issues which would affect the lives of everyone on the planet.

I learnt at dinner of the attempted assassination of the Pope. The shock was so numbing that it was not until I retired to bed that the full horror came home to me. I had spent much of Holy Week studying and reflecting on his words and actions and personality.

Thursday, 14 May 1981

Elizabeth and I to lunch with Pam and Michael Hartwell for their daughter Harriet's wedding on Saturday, or rather to meet her bridegroom's Argentinian parents. A very strong martini cocktail was handed to me on arrival. Michael and I were soon discussing the extraordinary happenings at Collins, still the premier publishers in my eyes in spite of losses incurred since the death of the renowned Billy. Ian Chapman, who has just replaced Jan Collins as chairman, I would single out as the outstanding figure in British publishing at the moment. George [Weidenfeld] forms a category of his own. Whether Chapman will be able to beat off the take-over bid from Murdoch remains to be seen. My great friend there is Pierre [Lady Collins], who has built up the magnificent Fontana religious series and has promoted Malcolm with much shrewdness and sensitivity.

The cocktail may have been responsible, but before long I was denouncing Mrs Thatcher's handling of the Sands issue to an impressive-looking gentleman who turned out to be Nicholas Ridley, Minister of State in the Foreign Office.

He claimed superior knowledge on the strength of seeing the Foreign Office papers. As a former Minister of State (or its equivalent thirty years ago) I disputed the amount of wisdom to be obtained from such documents. But I would never have said any of this if I had known whom it was I was talking to to start with. I was suitably apologetic and as a peace-offering sought his guidance on the situation in El Salvador, which is part of his Foreign Office responsibility. He seemed reasonably hopeful about the possibility of an election and its likely outcome.

At lunch I sat next to Ridley's wife, a woman highly *simpatica*. I renewed my apologies through her to her husband. She responded by asking me what I thought about it all. I told her that I admired Mrs Thatcher in many ways and had been vigorously defending her attitude towards Russia the night before, but I thought that she was at her worst in dealing with an issue such as that of Bobby Sands where the emotions of her opponents were so strongly aroused. I told Mrs Ridley that I had seen enough of the IRA in prison to understand what I would not otherwise have realized, that they regard themselves as an army. This seemed to give her an instant comprehension. An unusual woman.

House of Lords from lunch till dinner. Two single-sentence interventions by me. Neither premeditated, but both carefully formulated while others were speaking. A lot of anger was being worked up at question time against the BBC's alleged softness towards the IRA. I rose to ask the Minister to join in condemning the many atrocities of the UDA, mentioning that I had myself condemned the IRA in the House, more than most noble lords. I think I did it about right, but nerves are on edge just now. I must not forget that ordinary Englishmen, even peers, want to think well of their country.

My second intervention required some artfulness. There was quite a dramatic finish to the long-drawn-out struggle over Barbara Wootton's Affinities Bill, which would have permitted one to marry one's stepdaughter, etc. Terry Boston, from our front bench, presented an unqualified case for the Bill in spite of it being a free vote. The House was already anxious for a division – a speech on my part would have been counter-productive. The moment Terry finished I rose to ask, 'Does the noble Lord agree that some members of his flock are totally opposed to the line of persuasion he has just unfolded?' He replied neatly and civilly, 'The noble Lord has just proved that he is well able to speak for himself.' In Hansard the word 'flock' has been put in inverted commas. Curious where phrases come from. 'Unfolding a line of persuasion' – I had never thought of using such a combination of words. The defeat for Barbara, aged eighty-four, revered by all and most of all by me, was painful, but as I said to the Bishop of London as we left, I hope that it is not triumphalist to be pleased with a Christian victory. He assured me that it wasn't.

Dinner for Elizabeth, William and Clare Armstrong at the Gay Hussar followed by a visit to Roy Dotrice's one-man show, *Mr Lincoln*, as his personal guests. He was exactly like my idea of Abraham Lincoln. Without change of make-up, except during the interval, he conveyed the idea of Lincoln aging by sheer artistry. Lincoln was of course only fifty-six when he was assassinated. We went round to see Roy Dotrice afterwards. He repeated his sense of the debt owed to my book, in particular to my interpretation of Mary Lincoln and Lincoln's feeling for her. It was sad for him and for us that the English interest in Lincoln seems so limited. There has been hardly any writing about him here. The audience last night was pretty thin. On the other hand, Roy was amazed that he, an Englishman born in the Channel Islands, should be accepted so enthusiastically as Mr Lincoln in America. The amount of research he has done was edifying. Someone had pointed out the different way that Lincoln holds his right hand and his left hand in the Lincoln Memorial. Dotrice had discovered that the sculptor had a deaf and dumb son and that in sign language Lincoln's right hand clenched would represent A and his left hand open L. All four of us were equally enthusiastic about the performance.

Friday, 15 May 1981

Indecent Displays Bill. The Pornography Report had recommended a three-pronged attack on pornography: the milder forms should not be displayed in public, the harder forms should not be sold at all; the exploitation of performers should be rendered a criminal offence (some steps have been taken in the last direction). The present Bill deals only with display. I described it as a small step forward. Mary Whitehouse, with whom I had coffee just before the debate, doubts whether it is even that. Everyone supported it except for Douglas Houghton, who like Barbara Wootton is approaching the middle eighties. He and she are the last of the great old-fashioned humanists. Not that everyone is now turning into a Christian, far from it, but Barbara and Douglas, born in the 1890s, bring to bear a kind of Victorian solemnity which young agnostics and atheists cannot rival.

I did not speak for long. After some hesitation I told an oft-repeated story: 'A taxi driver dropped me at my flat and said to me, "Excuse my asking your name. I know you are Lord Porn, but what's your other name?"' The *Guardian* quotes it this morning, as does *The Times*, which adds 'laughter'. I suppose that a successful joke cannot be repeated too often. But I avoid the eye of noble lords who must have heard this one more than once already. The Christian front are exceptionally lucky in our leader on all these issues, Dick Nugent (Lord Nugent of Guildford), probably the most popular member of the House, whose smile (returning to that subject) is as appealing as that of the Queen Mother.

Lunch at the Garrick. I sat next to a distinguished professor of music who told me that for many years he had been secretary of the organization responsible for musical examinations (outside the universities). He was much heartened by the immense improvement in the musical consciousness of the population. I asked him whether the music to which he had given his life had any connection with pop music. He replied, 'None whatever.' Yet at this moment S & J are negotiating for a book by a disc-jockey who is said to have twenty million listeners. Certainly in the barber's yesterday, when I was getting one of my rare haircuts, I discovered that Radio One music with commentary by this disc-jockey is piped to them literally all day. I wonder whether there is a little more of a connection between the high music and the low music than is admitted by my learned and charming friend.

Tuesday, 19 May 1981

Eleven a.m.: visit to Professor Wing at the Institute of Psychiatry, Denmark Hill. A most encouraging encounter. Dr Wing, slight of build, unmistakably a live wire, very easy to talk to as befits a psychiatrist, is positively eager to play a full part in our Mental Health Inquiry. He tells me that the crucial people in the Ministry are most sympathetic. We agreed on a provisional list of names. I am hoping that our first meeting will take place on or about 9 June.

Lunch at Weirs in Old Compton Street as guest of Mike Shaw, who has succeeded Graham Watson at Curtis Brown, and taken over our family business. Mike as live a wire in his own way as Professor Wing. I told him that my way of life made it much more attractive to write a short book rather than a long one. *Abraham Lincoln* and *Humility* had been perfect long-vacation exercises. I had suggested to Elizabeth that I might try something on the Pope and she had approved the idea. There would be a flood of biographies, but I had in mind something which centred on his teaching. Mike was most enthusiastic, but insisted that it must be written before the end of the year, so that it could come out in time for the visit to England.

A long letter from Roy who is in Exeter Prison. Roy can by now be properly considered as an old friend if only because I have visited him in Dartmoor, Exeter, Parkhurst and Maidstone Prisons. When I was sitting down to write a book about prisoners I asked Roy to explain how he could come and have tea with me at the House of Lords and immediately afterwards set about opening other people's cars. I was very reluctant to let him pay for lunch at one of my favourite restaurants and would have been more reluctant still if I had known where his funds came from.

Roy is genuinely gifted and has recently been invited to Strasbourg in connectiion with a case he is bringing against the Home Office. I asked him why he has this compulsion when he hàs the makings of much better things. He replies: 'If I could answer that question then I wouldn't do it.'

A cousin of Elizabeth's, who is happy to style herself a lesbian, had asked me to address her group, a flourishing affair, with at least three hundred members. My subject was 'Outcasts', on which I have spoken and indeed preached to general audiences. I myself havę been described (by Alan Brien) as 'the outcasts' outcast', so I suppose that I have a certain standing in the discussion. I told them that when writing a book on St Francis of Assisi I had selected homosexuals, male and female, as an important category of outcasts. I knew more about male homosexuals than lesbian. I was told by my best friend in my house at Eton that 75 per cent of the boys had had homosexual experience. I said I hadn't noticed it, to which he replied, 'That's because you are somewhat unobservant and also rather repressed.'

A good free-for-all followed. I was assured at the end that they thought I was 'marvellous'. But there are so many reasons why that might have been said that I hesitate to record it, even in my own diary. I am sure that there were a hundred versions of human love represented among the hundred people or so present; sex may have played a predominant part in many of the relationships, not perhaps in others. Putting it crudely, they were women who preferred to be with women. More than one told me that they were married, indeed still happily married with children.

Several poignant life stories were told me during the evening. I am sure that there are many others available. The sweet lady who entertained me munificently at dinner, along with Elizabeth's very pretty cousin, told me that after the war she fell in with a man who had been a prisoner of war for several years. He was aware that she was a lesbian, but said to her, 'I am a lonely person; I think that you also are lonely. I believe that we could have a lovely marriage, in which sex didn't enter.' They were happily married for twenty-four years until he died, from which time she has lived with women – or did she say with one woman? Recently she was asked to appear on television, but if she had done so she would almost certainly have lost her job. As she explained to the club, she had to decline. This supported my argument that lesbians are still outcasts. The question of how they ought to be treated was left open, though I insisted that because I said that lesbian sex was wrong that did not mean that I thought I was a better person than they were.

Wednesday, 20 May 1981

This morning a black young woman called Christine (not her name) who works in S & J asked to see me. She is having a baby at the end of July. I asked about the gentleman responsible. She told me that she would never see him, she hoped, again. When he heard she was pregnant he demanded that she have an abortion. In her own words, 'I was not going to kill my baby, because I had got into this situation.'

He beat her up and left her unconscious. Two good samaritans took her to the hospital. A doctor is arranging for the birth itself, but she is much concerned as to where she will live afterwards.

I rang the emergency department of the Housing Authority. The official at the other end was a mixture of pomposity and practical kindness. I told him that we liked Christine very much and that she was a very nice girl. He said that that was of no relevance. He himself knew and liked her but that was not relevant either. Having got that off his chest, he showed himself ready to make sure she was accommodated.

I am sorry to have to mention an example of black violence, but I came across plenty of white violence in the course of my 'criminal' activities. Michael Davies and his still glamorous wife, Sandra, came to tea at the Lords with a shocking tale. Michael, Sandra and I have been linked in friendship for a quarter of a century since he was unjustly condemned to death and nearly executed for the Clapham Common murder. He gives me more credit for saving his life than I deserve (I think Cardinal Griffin was the main influence). But I certainly stuck to him well and helped him to emerge from prison after seven years – a kind of drawn battle with the authorities.

Their daughter, recently divorced, was walking out with her child, aged two and a half, when she was brutally mugged by five black youths. She crept into her flat nearby, but was so shattered that she could not communicate with anyone for three or four days. Eventually she made contact with Michael and Sandra, who took her into their house. Soon afterwards her flat in Brixton was broken into and all her property stolen.

Michael is desperately trying to get her accommodation in a part of the country where Lambeth has an overspill. The bureaucrats are being anything but helpful. Meanwhile she is paying £17 a week for her ransacked and unusable flat and told that if she gives it up her chance of getting alternative accommodation will vanish. Naturally I say that I will do anything I can. Michael, who broke his back some years ago when window-cleaning, bears up bravely and in Sandra he has a wife in a thousand. They have recently started a wine bar in Horsham, where dinner can be obtained for £5 a head, which is beginning to flourish. The last time Michael took Sandra to dinner in London it cost £34.

Thursday, 21 May 1981

I sat next to Rupert Nevill at dinner. Rupert is Prince Philip's principal adviser, his wife Micky is said to be the best friend of the Queen. No one who does not understand Micky and Rupert Nevill, and I do not know them as well as I could wish to, can begin to assess the merits of the British aristocracy. I would describe them both as very *good* people, though they are thoroughly involved in society and would not easily be labelled as do-gooders. If, as I believe, the Queen is exceptionally virtuous, it is not surprising that her best friends should be of the same disposition. We were completely *ad idem* in our admiration for the Queen as monarch and person.

I told Rupert that when I was Colonial Secretary for a short while in 1966 I had had lunch with her alone to discuss her coming visit to the West Indies (I had two gin and tonics in the ante-room before going in to the Presence). She had shown an impressive grasp of the facts and issues involved. Rupert told me that everyone who had seen her in the years since then has noted this same mastery. By now she knows the world scene better than any minister, which does not of course imply that she could run the country, which she has not been trained for. Jim Callaghan, a close neighbour of Rupert's in the country, has told him that when Prime Minister he never went in to see the Queen without learning something from her. Harold Wilson and other prime ministers have testified to this effect.

Naturally, we talked a good deal about Prince Philip. I acknowledged his fine brain. He would have certainly sailed into any cabinet if he had gone into politics. I recalled the dinner at Buckingham Palace with him in the chair to discuss penal reform. I had sat next to Dickie Mountbatten about ten weeks before he was murdered. Prince Philip had readily held his own in an unfamiliar area with representative experts. He gave an excellent lecture soon afterwards on penal matters, but what had we heard from him since? Rupert said that he worked enormously hard, frequently till two in the morning, but agreed to discuss with him the possibility of a major speech in the New Year. Incidentally, he told me that Prince Philip, though he had been a very keen polo player, had a certain disdain for hunting. His present passion was driving a four-in-hand. He insisted on using carriage horses in order that these admirable animals should not be wasted.

This put him at a certain disadvantage in the highest class of competition, but there was much about the sport that appealed to him, not least the element of danger. Is it possible that real men like Prince Philip and Prince Charles accept the homage which we all have to pay them with a certain reluctance?

Sunday, 24 May 1981

Flew on Friday afternoon to Northern Ireland, returning yesterday evening in time for dinner at Bernhurst. I was attending the wedding of Eleanor Jordon, a remarkable member of our New Horizon team. Her parents are large Protestant farmers; the family indeed owns a whole string of farms near Lurgan, forty miles south-west of Belfast. Lurgan means to me the Deeney family (Catholic). Twelve years ago, on resigning from the Labour Cabinet, I agreed with Hodders to write a book on Ulster, which I abandoned at that time, though it led indirectly to my joint undertaking with Anne. Obtaining the services of Finoulla Deeney, a recent graduate of the National University, as personal assistant and chauffeur, I toured the province widely, staying more than once with Dr Deeney, a leading physician in that area, and his wife Ann.

This time I was again the guest of the Deeneys. Donald as restlessly dynamic, talkative, amusing and shrewd as ever, and as elegant. Most of the men and women at the wedding were broad of shoulder with Ulster faces. The Ulster representative in London once said that I had such a face myself. Ann looked slender and almost Parisian in contrast, though in fact she comes from Donegal. Eleanor's fiancé is working in the same field as she is. He is tall and thin while in physique she is a child of Ulster. In the depressing situations which sometimes envelop New Horizon, she never fails to exhibit a radiant benevolence. A passage in a book of Hugh Walpole's about a certain duchess comes back to me: 'She is a great woman but she is all heart. She longs to be loved.' On her wedding day, Eleanor looked sublimely confident, as if she had found what she was seeking.

A number of their friends had flown over for the wedding. Donald Deeney met Vaughan of New Horizon and myself at the airport, taking me to their house for dinner, afterwards to the Jordons nearby for further refreshments. Next morning we turned up half an hour early by mistake for the wedding at 12.30. Punctuality is a recognized virtue or otherwise in Ulster, but not usually associated with the southern Irish. The leading Catholics on this occasion set a good example to their Protestant neighbours. The church, described by the vicar to me as the largest Church of Ireland parish church in Ireland, was well filled. The atmosphere was relaxed and confident. Many of them must have passed as we did through streets with quite a few black flags for Bobby Sands, but politics might have been a thousand miles away. One of the bridesmaids suffered from a painful limp. She is a voluntary worker at New Horizon who had come over to do honour to Eleanor. With no trace of depression or self-pity and a rather lovely face, she was a fitting companion for Eleanor on such an occasion.

The Jordons are special people. He was president of the Northern Ireland Farmers, with rugby football coming next to the family and farming as his passion. His son, whose breadth of shoulder was re-markable even in that company, hopes to play for Ulster and even Ireland. When some of the Protestant workers on his farm objected to his employing a Catholic, he stood his ground. Now all the employees, on that farm at least, are Catholics. His brother, with whom I had a long talk the previous evening, is of the same ilk. If Ulstermen in general were like these Jordons and Deeneys, there would be 'no problem'.

At the reception I argued with a number of Unionists; one of them introduced me jocularly to another as a 'viper in our bosom'. Some of them had been quite prominent in official Unionist politics. No one had a good word to say for Paisley, but one remarked to me, 'There are some men here who would vote for Paisley, but wouldn't own up to it.' For the most part they gave me the impression of political (though not commercial or personal) helplessness. They seem very disconnected with England, even where they had served in the forces and had English wives. My inclination towards an independent Ulster was strengthened. Somehow when you are there nowadays it seems the inevitable outcome. But could these excellent Protestants, patently religious as far as I could judge, be trusted to treat the Catholics properly? (Incidentally, I was told that there has been a large increase in all kinds of Protestant church attendance recently.) Donald Deeney should be the best of witnesses here. The town of Lurgan is 60/40 Protestant/Catholic. For many years the Protestants exploited their position to the full and took all the seats in the city council (plus the municipal employment). Donald himself broke through and with the coming of PR the Catholics got a better representation. Donald was the first Catholic to be elected captain of the Golf Club. He became master of a non-sectarian pack of hounds. He is wary of offering general propositions. The Deeneys and Jordons are great friends, but Donald would, I think, assume that by one means or another the minority must be especially protected.

Did I come away with any constructive thoughts about the future of Northern Ireland? The local elections had just brought Paisley great gains at the expense of the non-sectarian Alliance Party, though Finoulla's Protestant husband, David Cook, recently Lord Mayor of Belfast, and one of her brothers had been returned on the Alliance ticket. Most of the Unionists I talked to, as I say, seemed rather helpless, but one local Unionist pundit, recently a mayor, offered me a ray of hope. 'Put your money on the table,' he kept repeating. 'Put your money on the table, and the deal will be on.' This *could* mean that an independent Ulster could be established with sufficient safeguards for the Catholics, if the right financial bargain could be struck. But Catholic safeguards by now must mean some kind of Catholic representation. *The Observer* pleasantly surprised me this morning by returning forcibly to the idea of power-sharing. I look up to Conor Cruise O'Brien, but I have deplored his influence over *The Observer* while he was editor-in-chief. Has he departed by now?

On the way back in the aeroplane I fell in with a journalist who has spent a week in Belfast, studying for the *Sunday Mirror* the appalling effect of the 'troubles' on Catholic children in the militant areas. I knew the sad story already more or less, but three things I learnt from him more clearly. That the children who make the petrol bombs begin at seven; that scores of them have already been killed – I only read about one every now and then; that the plastic bullets are huge objects. He fished one out of his bag to show me. In general terms I have no reply to those who say that the army must protect themselves. At present all the young people had to do is to build barricades in the certain knowledge that the army will arrive to pull them down, whereupon the petrol bombing starts. Great fun at the time, but my journalistic friend describes the tragic 'elderly' faces of the children to whom this has become a way of life. All this is remote from the Lurgan wedding reception and indeed, as the journalist stressed to me, from life in the centre of Belfast, not much more than a mile distant. A tragic world overlaps a normal one; an indomitable spirit shines through both.

John Silkin is to stand for the deputy leadership of the Labour Party. What has John got that Denis and Tony haven't? He is certainly more sensitive than either of them, he has a better sense of humour about himself. He once told me that he would like to see written on his tombstone, 'He forgave everyone, even himself'. I can't see Denis or Tony asking for such an inscription. I scratch my head and try and think what they might ask for. Denis, perhaps, something in German, Luther's *Ich kann nicht anders*. Tony, if he was candid, would prefer *Vox populi, vox Dei*, but then he might reflect that his image would require something in simple English. He would probably wish for something from the Levellers about the 'Greatest he'. But John is certainly not being put forward on grounds such as these. For the moment he is said to represent the Democratic Left. Now we have Social Democrats, Democratic Socialists, Democratic Unionists in Northern Ireland, and Democratic Lefties. The word retains its position of advantage in the political vocabulary, but what effect will John's intervention have? I take it for granted that he will come bottom of the three, although it is apparently intended by his Tribunite colleagues that this is a way of checking Tony. I can't help feeling that Denis would be better off without him.

Tuesday, 26 May 1981

Our guests for the weekend were Harold, Antonia and Antonia's Benjamin and Orlando. Kevin and Ruth had three of their sprightly television friends staying in Backstairs (the back half of the house, converted into a separate establishment). One of them, Denny, a young woman with a dazzling smile, is expecting a baby in August and seems to have been persuaded by the media that at thirty-three it is somewhat dangerous for her to begin. I told her that Elizabeth had five children after thirty-three. Kevin, her host, was born when Elizabeth was forty-one. Denny seemed somewhat reassured.

What an astonishing success Antonia has by now achieved. For a long time her beauty and the quickness of her wit were recognized, but not the sheer strength of her brain. This could be denied no longer after *Mary Queen of Scots*. She lay intellectually fallow during her late teens, but then I did precisely the same at Eton.

I am not going to be caught distinguishing between the literary talents of my children; Antonia and Thomas the historians, Judith the poet, Rachel the novelist and television playright. In Paddy's case the gift of expression is revealed in advocacy, in Michael's in compelling dispatches, in Kevin's in highly technical economic exposition. It is difficult to know which of them, taking speech and writing together, is the most articulate. All this is derived from Elizabeth no doubt, except that odd kink of Kevin's. I don't think Catherine would have suffered in any comparison.

Kevin has been hard at work on the telephone organizing a City 'cell' of the SDP. His initial colleagues are impressive-sounding young merchant bankers. I say, 'All right for the pin-stripe area, but what about the grass roots?' One of them, reputedly very close to Roy Jenkins, arranged a planning session in Oxford and invited Roger Opie, once my pupil, later Kevin's tutor in economics. Roger, sparkling in person and on television, would go close to the top if he entered Parliament. His wife Norma, once my secretary, now a teacher, would be the perfect politician's lady. Roger, on Kevin's account, came to the meeting and announced at the end that it was all a load of rubbish, but that he had not enjoyed a political meeting so much for years. As he left they shouted at him, 'You enjoyed it so much because you talked without stopping for two hours.'

The SDP in Oxford have a ready-made candidate in Evan Luard, a former MP of the city, only just beaten at the last election; quiet and thoughtful. Kevin doubts whether he has sufficient charisma. Roger, who is supposed to have his own eye on the Labour candidature, has plenty of that. Kevin says that he is very far to the Left. Well, so was I when I was chosen Labour candidate in 1939. It's true that when the time came I was beaten, but the seat is far more winnable for Labour these days.

I am unquestionably flattered to have received a letter from two academic gentlemen at the University of Manchester Institute of Science and Technology saying that I have been selected, after consultations with thirty editors, as one of forty-two individuals who are identified as 'key change agents' in our society. I spoke to them on the telephone and learnt that Terry Wogan was strongly supported as a candidate, though they do not regard him as a reformer in their sense.

Wednesday, 27 May 1981

Spent the day in Sussex; Elizabeth, always happiest at Bernhurst, is not returning to London until next week. The House of Lords is having its Whitsun holiday. This afternoon I walked over to see Father Docherty, our holy priest, who is retiring after two cataract operations and prolonged and painful chest trouble. The distance to the convent where he lives is about seven miles, but through a misunderstood direction I made it into ten. I was glad to find that I could complete the distance without distress, but when on my arrival Father James offered me tea or whisky, I had no doubt about my answer.

We argued for a while about women priests. I have seen all too much of male prejudice against women in banking and, before they arrived, in the House of Lords, where they have been an unqualified success. I am unhesitatingly 'for', Father is just as strongly 'against', but his loyalty to the Church is total. If the change came about, though there is little prospect of it in his lifetime or mine, he would throw in everything behind it. He is very popular in Catholic and non-Catholic circles, not least with nuns. I asked him what the latter thought about women priests. He replied, 'Those who would like to be priests are the last ones who ever should be.'

Friday, 29 May 1981

Farewell lunch at the Old Dutch at £3 a head for Christine and Caroline who are leaving Sidgwick and Jackson today. I sat with half a dozen junior staff (female). I came to the conclusion that I am not good at talking interestingly to the young. Elizabeth says it is because I dislike any idea of being a guru. But I think I am rather good at listening to them. It would be strange if I weren't. I love hearing their life stories and some at least of their dreams.

This afternoon I visited Ian Brady at Wormwood Scrubs. He reproached me at some length for not having yet been to see Lord Belstead at the Home Office about a transfer to Broadmoor. I defended myself on the grounds that my partner in this enterprise is Ian's solicitor, Ben Birnberg, and he is still in correspondence with the Home Office. Moreover, Ian wrote to me a week ago to say that Lord Avebury had been to see him and was anxious to take up his case. It seems essential that his three allies should co-ordinate their approach. There were some strong points to be made in his favour. Ten years ago, Reggie Maudling, the Home Secretary, tried to get him into Broadmoor but was thwarted by Keith Joseph, then Minister of Health. The Home Office psychiatrist who visits Ian regularly and whom I have met appears to be favourable, but the Home Office at the moment are preventing us from drawing on his evidence. I admit to a feeling of guilt at not having pushed things along faster. I wish that Ian and I could get back to our old discussions of Tolstoy and Dostoevsky, but I cannot blame him for trying to make the fullest use of me for business purposes. His true gifts are wasted.

Monday, 1 June 1981

Twelve noon: S & J party for Bob Willis, the handsome, 6ft 6in England fast bowler, whose book on the cricket revolution of the 1970s is being published today. The book itself, expertly ghosted, is full of frank comments, showing some distaste for the Australian approach to the game and the damage done by commercialism generally. It presents an unflattering picture of Ian Botham, at the moment of writing the much-criticized England captain.

The *Daily Mirror* rang up yesterday to ask whether the book was going to be held up pending Botham's trial for assault. I assured them that there was no question of it. Certainly Willis showed no signs of embarrassment.

I knew that he had three operations on his left knee and ventured to show him a scar still visible after my cartilage operation of 1925. He easily outdid me, pulling up his trouser leg and revealing a horrifying patchwork. The photographer spotted a wonderful picture, but I rapidly lowered my trouser leg to avoid comparison with the wounded hero.

Lunch for Jon Snow at the Garrick. What a staggering life he has led these last few years – all over the danger spots of Asia, Africa, Central America and now, after a lapse of four years, Northern Ireland! He told me that he saw little change there on the surface, but he had come away convinced that British withdrawal was bound to happen sooner or later. He said that that was the opinion of everyone he spoke to during his fortnight there, including the security people. There seemed to be general agreement that the policies attempted since 1969 had failed. Jon felt sure, as I do, that if any kind of independent Ulster were established a United Ireland would follow before long.

Jon had met Paisley. He had once helped him over a journey from London, but had not expected to be remembered. (Jon is 6ft 5in, and not easily overlooked.) Paisley, 'every inch the politician', greeted him enthusiastically; by chance they travelled back together next day. Paisley said nothing which could be quoted against him, but Jon felt pretty sure that he too was thinking in terms of a British withdrawal. Confirmation of this came to Jon from a close friend of Paisley's.

Jon has reluctantly had to postpone the book he was doing for us. He would wish to make it controversial, in other words not suppress his opinions; his chiefs in television consider that in that case his usefulness would be diminished. Apparently Tory MPs have already protested about his softness towards El Salvador guerrillas and towards Marxist aggression generally. I can't pretend to be altogether surprised. Jon and I are very close to one another in our attitude to Labour policy in Britain, though he has always had a *tendresse* for Tony Benn. But he simply cannot see the Soviet menace as I do. We asked ourselves whether this was partly due to the generation gap.

Eight p.m.: ward meeting of Chelsea Labour Party. Elizabeth and I are subscribing members, but I haven't attended a meeting for years. Jane Ewart-Biggs, whose peerage gives widespread pleasure, is a regular attender. She had warned me about extreme tendencies but, disappointingly perhaps, there was no excitement of any kind. The audience were middle-class, well-educated, public-spirited, courteous. It was impossible without previous information to guess what they stood for in the Party turmoil. The lady on my right, who recalled that Judith and Alec, now a brilliant arbitrator, had first met in the Chelsea Labour Party, hoped that I would come next week and vote for Healey against Benn. I would if I could, but alas I can't. I assume, but not from anything I saw last night, that Healey will be outvoted.

The charming young man on my left, who stood me half a pint before the meeting, told me with some satisfaction that Healey and Len Murray had been hissed and booed at the huge rally in Trafalgar Square on Sunday before the unemployed marchers. (I had read nothing of this in the Press, so I doubt if it was general.) A. J. Balfour, regarded as the wittiest prime minister after Disraeli, though not by me, was once asked by someone who knew he was a Christian, 'Don't you consider Christianity and journalism the two curses of civilization?' He replied coolly, 'Christianity of course, but why journalism?'

Slightly more seriously I might have asked my young friend, 'Healey of course, but why Murray?'

He complained that they had totally failed to give the lead against Thatcherism that the party was looking for. (What about Michael Foot, our popular leader?) I read him a little lecture on the dangers of trying to overthrow Mrs Thatcher's Government by extra-parliamentary activity. That road led straight to a Fascist counter-revolution, etc. He remained friendly but unimpressed. No one could possibly describe a young Socialist of this kind as sinister, yet he and many others like him could be won for sinister developments. I genuinely respect and personally like the moderate leaders of the party from Denis Healey downwards, but the party will steadily slip away from them if they cannot provide more evidence of a vision of a new society.

Wednesday, 3 June 1981

Given lunch by a penetrating young lecturer, who is one of the pair organizing the report on the 'agents of change'. He told me another fifteen or so of the names who had not yet accepted. The politicians were Mrs Thatcher, Keith Joseph, Enoch Powell, Tony Benn and Shirley Williams. I am not sure whether I belong to this category. Glancing at the names, I ask myself, indeed I was asked by him, what we had in common. I suggested that *we all felt sure we were right*, though in regard to the beloved, 'indecisive' Shirley this must be interpreted liberally. He agreed, and went on to ask me, 'Why do you think you are always right?' I replied, 'I don't always think I am right. I am very seldom sure of it, but on the whole I have taken up neglected causes where one could hardly be wrong in demanding some action at any rate.' (Ireland in the thirties, Germany in the forties, pornography in the seventies, victims a little later, and prisoners at all times.)

Thursday, 4 June 1981

Grillions last night. Alec Home in the chair. What a serene face he has! It does one good to look at him across the table. Not an intellectual giant, even by political standards which are not all that exalted, but a sharp, clear, witty mind and the character that impresses all who meet him. At Eton he was two years senior to me and the grandest boy in the school. Outstanding at games, though now he looks so slight, president of Pop. I was in a different house and I would never have dared to accost him. I remember how surprised I was when he married our revered headmaster's daughter. I would have assumed that his bride would have been the Diana Spencer of her time. Their marriage has offered the world a model of Christian happiness.

Arthur Bryant on my left; he is always funnier than I expect. I told him that Elizabeth had decided that Tony Benn was a puritan – like Cromwell. I had agreed that he was a puritan but not like Cromwell. He is always holding forth about the Levellers. Arthur seemed to agree with me. Cromwell, he said laughing mischievously, was much more like Baldwin, whom Arthur knew intimately. 'Surely,' I said, 'Baldwin would never have carried out the massacres at Wexford and Drogheda?' Arthur, laughing now hilariously, said, 'Oh, yes, he would have done anything to the Irish.' The only time Baldwin discussed Ireland with me, aged twenty-five, was on a walk at Hatfield. He lent me *The Victory of Sinn Fein* by O'Hegarty, which he compared to Thucydides. If that was his main source, no wonder he was unenlightened about Ireland. Mrs Baldwin, a stout lady, told me how she put the North and South delegates at their ease during the boundary negotiations in 1925. She put one lot (I am not such which) on her right and the other on her left at lunch. 'I want you', she said, 'to imagine that I am the Irish boundary, but I am too well covered to be a bone of contention.' The result was disastrous for the Irish Free State. Half a century later, Conor Cruise is calling for a re-partition.

My best talk of the evening was with an ex-Conservative minister, company chairman, etc., indubitably high-minded, a real insider, with a private line to every sort of person in business and politics, no possible axe to grind. He considers that the present economic policy is quite disastrous. This is not only his opinion but the opinion of business in general. Any sane policy must provide for steady growth. A policy based like the present one on stagnation is bound to prove fatal.

Turning to politicians, I asked him where we could find the 'rescuing genius' (Churchill in the world crisis, describing the collapse of Germany in 1918, pointed out the absence of a 'rescuing genius'). He surprised me by saying emphatically, 'Margaret'. 'Margaret', he went on to say, 'means to stay where she is', i.e. at Number 10 Downing Street. She is far too intelligent not to change her policy dramatically if that becomes clearly necessary for the survival of herself and the nation. 'Who', I persisted, 'will stand at her side to carry through the new policy?' He again had no hesitation. 'Ted Heath,' he replied. 'In what capacity?' 'Chancellor of the Exchequer.' Ted had been really ill but was now much better. Relations between him and Margaret had been ludicrously strained, but Ted was basically 'a big man of world stature'. Well, I said to myself, if anyone could bring about this surprising combination it would be my friend.

Friday, 5 June 1981

Yesterday evening I addressed the parents' guild of Latymer Upper School, formerly grant-aided but now independent. I spoke on 'Outcasts' and as usual enjoyed question time more than my address, which is apt to feel like a chore. The supper afterwards is always the best part of the evening. The most ticklish question came last – from a young boy in the school. Who, he asked me, was the most fascinating criminal I had ever met? I played for time. I have not, I said, come here to start you on a life of crime by glorifying criminals. That seemed feeble and pompous. The truthful answer would have been Myra Hindley, but her name, suddenly introduced at the end of the evening, might have left an unhappy taste. Then I had a bright thought. Shane O'Doherty, whom I have already described as the true penitent who desired to apologize to his victims. I was asked at one point what good I thought my visits did to prisoners. I ventured to suggest that I encouraged them to reform their lives and that at the worst persuaded them not to collapse in cynicism and despair. This morning I read some lines in Jean Vanier's *Community and Growth* which put it better than I can: 'People cannot accept their own evil if they do not at the same time feel loved, respected and trusted. They cannot overcome their egoism and fears if they have not been helped to discover that they are lovable.' Without, I hope, undue self-pity I think of myself as someone who needs a full measure of encouragement in just the sense described, whether or not because of experiences in boyhood. My alleged craving for publicity originates, it may be, here. Without Elizabeth, I would never have overcome my temperamental weakness to a point where any kind of achievement was possible.

I found myself involved after the session was over in a brisk argument with the headmaster. We got on to the subject of punishment. He was soon saying that he would expel a boy if he caught him stealing or, for that matter, in possession of drugs. It was not fair on the other parents to retain such a bad influence. I suggested that he should at least get him placed elsewhere. He retorted that if the boy didn't want the privileged education at Latymer he could go into the State system. I suspect that the headmaster is a much kinder man than he presented himself as being. The parents present told me afterwards that he was not accustomed to be argued with on his own premises.

I myself made it a rule when I was chairman of the National Bank that anyone who was dismissed (there were not many during my eight years) had the right of access to me. A young man in one of the Irish branches had got into debt and borrowed £300 which he couldn't repay. He came over to see me in London. I gave him a rosary, which after twenty years he still possesses, before he set off for Alaska. He paid the money back in four months, but later developed mental trouble. We have been in friendly touch ever since and exchange verses, his of slightly higher quality than mine. This was surely a case where my theory that any chairman or headmaster has a responsibility to those who go wrong under his auspices justified itself.

Tuesday, 9 June 1981

Last night Judith and Alec took Elizabeth and me to *Anyone for Denis?* at the Whitehall Theatre. Elizabeth enjoyed it all, suspending her unbelief, however excessive the farce. I enjoyed it nearly all, but couldn't quite swallow a couple of drunken friends of Denis who figured too largely. Angela Thorne, who played the part of Margaret, was by common consent exactly like her, somewhat beautified. Antonia, on an earlier occasion, went round 'behind' and met her. Apparently she had to pad herself quite heavily. Any friend of Margaret, or indeed M. herself, would be delighted with the likely effect on Margaret's image. She had many good lines, but I liked this one particularly: at the end of an address to the public, 'Please remember this. Whatever happens, you are to blame.'

John Wells, Antonia's friend, made himself look exactly like Denis; tall and thin, though I never thought of John as tall and thin, with the narrow, horn-topped glasses. He didn't talk at all like Denis, far too nimminy-pimminy, but as no one knows how Denis talks, and everyone knows how he looks, there was general satisfaction with the likeness.

The star turn in my eyes was Roy Jenkins as the butler, portly, bespectacled, bland. He only let himself go once, when alone on the stage he looked round at the Chequers drawing room and exclaimed in heart-felt terms, 'One day all this will be mine!' The play was peppered with contemporary allusions. 'Tony Wedgwood Benn has just gone into hospital, a psychiatric one of course,' etc., etc. The same actor doubled Roy and Willie Whitelaw, the latter a rather feeble impersonation.

Roy himself was present. I saw him in the foyer and said: 'You were the star turn.' 'I would say caricature rather than satire, wouldn't you?' he replied diffidently. I remember Denis not being amused by the *Private Eye* articles when I had lunch with him, and I myself, 'the most caricatured man' of 1972, felt the same. In the play Roy was addressed at one moment as 'smoothy-chops'. I reminded him, perhaps tactlessly, that when this label was first coined for him in *Private Eye* he remarked to me: 'It's hardly the sobriquet I would have chosen, but it doesn't cut very deep.'

I told Roy that I was sure he was right in standing at Warrington. I was much impressed by his response. 'Of course one can't *win* Warrington.' I recalled, not for the first time, his sense of history, which one could almost compare to Churchill's. He seizes the dramatic moment, but he can put it in perspective. He will make a great song and dance at Warrington and get a great deal of media attention, but he is looking beyond. Without discouraging his supporters he must somehow let it be realized that it will be a positive triumph if he gets any votes at all. My opinion of him rose again, as a statesman I mean. I have always liked him as a person. I am afraid that his claret-loving image has been carried too far and no one could mistake him for a Labour man. But there is a distinction about him which is lacking in our politics today, though you could not call Margaret or Peter Carrington undistinguished.

Six to nine p.m. at 8, Addison Road, HQ of the Richmond Fellowship. First preliminary meeting of our Mental After-Care committee. Present Elly, John Redcliffe-Maud, Professor Wing, Professor Walmsley, the new president of the Royal College of Psychiatry, Peter Thompson, and Brian Rook, chief social worker of the Mental After-Care Association. David Astor attended as a friendly observer. He is enormously interested in the project, but for some reason does not wish to describe himself as a committee member.

The atmosphere could not have been improved on. John and David are experienced and creative committee members. John Wing we deferred to as the super-relevant professional, but if John [Lord] Richardson had been present a different professional seniority might have been established, though Richardson is not a psychiatrist. Everyone seemed conscious of the significance of our venture. All agreed with John Wing in hoping for a hard-hitting report.

The scope of the inquiry led to prolonged though never acrimonious discussion. John Maud, an old Permanent Secretary at the Ministry of Education, easily persuaded us that we must leave out school-children. We agreed to confine ourselves to adults, elastically considered. We all agreed also that the mentally handicapped needed a separate inquiry. John Wing persuaded us that after-care could not be entirely divorced from care in hospitals. I asked what I should say at a press conference if the question arose whether we were going to investigate hospital treatment. It was agreed that this would be outside our project. The terms of reference, though I suppose they could be modified next time, left us to study the community care of the adult mentally ill.

The choice of a name for the community caused unexpected difficulty. Seeing that Elly and the Richmond Fellowship are paying for the whole venture, it seemed right and proper that it should be called The Richmond Fellowship Inquiry, but Peter Thompson objected and the professionals seemed inclined to agree with him. I pointed out that if it did not have the Richmond Fellowship name it would inevitably be called the Longford Inquiry, the last thing I wanted. One Longford Report (on pornography) is enough for a lifetime. The issue was left undecided. I was admittedly a little gratified that the idea of a Longford Report was not unappealing to a professor of psychiatry. But I shall do all I can to make sure that our official name is different, though none of us can dictate to the Press.

We had the usual fun selecting the remaining members of the commission, though I let the discussion become rather ragged. We have already ten members (seven named above, plus Lord Richardson, Lord Winstanley, Baroness Trumpington). We agreed to add one or two members with present or recent experience of this kind of local government administration. Professor Wing, however, and David Astor were determined that in order to carry weight our committee must include two or three names really well known to the public. As always on such occasions, disagreement is total as to who is well-known and who has influence.

My suggestions of Jimmy Savile and Robin Day did not prevail. In the end, we hit on Katharine Whitehorn and Richard Baker, with Margaret Drabble as a possibility. The next day, Lord Richardson told me that what really mattered was that the names should carry weight in professional circles, which is not at all the same as saying that they must be professional. If possible, they should have some previous connection with the subject.

Saturday, 13 June 1981

Yesterday I visited Shane O'Doherty in Gartree Prison. Train to Market Harborough, a few miles to the prison, thoroughly inaccessible to relatives from most parts of England and of course from Shane's home in Derry. An hour with Shane, lunch with the assistant governor in Market Harborough. Three o'clock train to St Pancras, then down to Bernhurst.

Shane, his delicate and attractive face too heavily bearded to suit my fancy, was full of his usual electric energy and almost too articulate. I had to ask more than once to be allowed to get my word in, which he always conceded courteously. He is even more indignant than when I saw him last in Gartree about the failure to transfer him to a prison in Northern Ireland. His sense of grievance is completely justified for reasons that need not be expanded here.

But I came away worried about him. His refusal to see any good in Gartree as compared with the Scrubs is, to say the least, imprudent. He has the utmost goodwill from the Bishop of Derry, Cardinal Hume, his mother in Derry, Phillip Whitehead MP, and myself. What good has all that done him with the authorities? On the face of it no good at all. It has encouraged the strong idealistic strain in his nature which should be of spiritual value in the long run. His mother thinks that when he is eventually released he will become a priest in the Third World.

But has he been at all spoilt by it? Possibly in the short run, but fundamentally he is so virtuous, so natural that I hope and believe that his well-wishers have not done him any lasting damage.

He needs more people to talk to. There were several governors, from the number one downwards, who befriended him actively at the Scrubs. Above all, there was the Catholic chaplain who saw him more or less daily. Here, the Catholic chaplain only comes in once a week, which does not make it easy for a friendship to develop. Shane says that the whole relationship between the governor grades and the prisoners is far less intimate than it was at the Scrubs. I went away promising to put down a parliamentary question about his not being allowed to have a typewriter in his cell (bureaucracy at its worst – no one can think of the reason for the restriction) and to see Phillip Whitehead to discuss the best way to raise once more (a) the transfer to Northern Ireland and (b) his continued retention in Category A. The attitude of the authorities towards Shane I find quite peculiarly depressing. Even the kindest members of the prison service seem unable to deal with an exceptional case like his within the framework of the Home Office Inquiry.

Shane told me interestingly that at Wormwood Scrubs one of the governors had said to him that he and other IRA prisoners were not just in Category A but in 'Special A'. This involved, for example, the presence not only of two officers but of a dog when he moved about the prison. I had always imagined that Ian Brady, for example, was also accompanied by a dog, but he said that this was not so. Today Shane considers that the refusal to transfer him to a prison near his home is a clear example of discriminatory, i.e. political, treatment. He has already applied to the European Commission. Half jokingly, he told me (*re* the H-Block demand) he was going to call for criminal as opposed to political status.

At lunch I passed on the gist of this to the assistant governor. Did he agree, I asked, that the traditions of Gartree, where he had only served six months, were unfavourable to AGs getting to know prisoners well? Not surprisingly, he didn't think so, but also told me that he didn't think it was easy to get to know Shane. He had seen Shane initially and told him that he would be happy to talk to him at any time. Shane had answered coolly that he would take advantage of that offer if any particular matter arose which needed discussion. The AG took this as a brush-off. I accepted the fact that Shane's resentment at being dumped in Gartree might have made him hard to get close to. I accepted also the possibility that the interest of so many well-known friends might have proved unhelpful. On the last point, the assistant governor quickly said that it would be a bad day for the prison service if outside interest in prisons diminished.

I pointed out that the AG had not supervised my talk with Shane that morning. He had left it to a prison officer and missed a good chance of getting to know him better. He took all this in very good part, though mentioning that he had supervised one or two of Shane's visits without obvious benefit. I exercised the privilege of old age and said to the young AG, whose moral earnestness I did not question, 'You have chosen a high-minded vocation, Shane is a thoroughly worthwhile young man and surely it is the difficult cases which provide you with your true challenge.' I assured him that I had lectured Shane that morning, warning him against the sin of arrogance, so that I perceived a mote in both their eyes. It was for them to detect a beam in mine. The AG responded movingly, 'It has been a privilege to meet you, Lord Longford.' That is as may be, but for once I came away with a feeling that I had helped two worthwhile people to get to know each other.

Sunday, 14 June 1981

I have just finished Jean Vanier's *Community and Growth*. It is full of rich emotive and thought-provoking dicta. I quote below the key passage about old age:

> Finally, old people refind the time of confidence which is also wisdom. They cannot be very active, so they have time to observe, to contemplate and to forgive. They have a whole sense of the meaning of human life, of acceptance and of realism. They know that living has not just to do with welcome and loving. They have somehow got past the stage of proving themselves through efficiency.

Obviously, that is an idealized picture, but at seventy-five ought I to be trying to live up to it? For good or ill, my lot is cast in the House of Lords and while my health holds, though my vigour declines slowly but surely, I compete on the subjects that I care about with men and women in their prime. There are in front of my eyes a number of phenomena: Manny Shinwell and Fenner Brockway in their nineties; Barbara Wootton and Douglas Houghton over eighty, active septuagenarians are plentiful. The most popular and effective member of the House is probably Dick Nugent, seventy-plus.

When I look back on the six months since I gave up the chairmanship of S & J, I am not dissatisfied with my attendance and output, though they have been in no way sensational. The time will no doubt come when I must 'make my soul' and concentrate on being a serene old man in the Vanier sense. At the moment I am embarking on the inquiry into mental after-care, which if it succeeds will prove as important as anything in my entire existence. I cannot believe that I am going wrong here. No doubt, as so often, it is all a question of balance. On balance, Vanier has this to say: 'Ask how you can better love your brothers and sisters. You will find rest and that famous balance you are looking for between the exterior and the interior, between prayer and activity, between time for yourself and time for others. Everything will resolve itself through love.' This means surely that in my mental health inquiry I must not only seek to love the mentally ill collectively, whom we are setting out to help, but all those I am thrown into contact with in the inquiry. Most of all my own committee when and if they seem to become tiresome.

The big news yesterday was the firing of six blank shots at the Queen on her way to the Trooping the Colour. I note the matter-of-fact acceptance by everyone of the Queen's coolness during and after the incident. It is assumed by now that this middle-aged woman will always behave calmly and if required heroically, which is no doubt a correct assumption. As a monarchist, I am loyal but not sentimental. Elizabeth is far more easily moved by royal occasions, about which she writes so beautifully. But of the Queen herself I am a passionate admirer.

The Irish election results leave it quite uncertain whether Charlie Haughey or Garret FitzGerald will be the next Taioseach. It is widely said that this is the worst situation. I don't agree. Something like bipartisanship in Irish politics is more likely to emerge this way. The election of two hunger-strikers in the border counties under PR – which could never have happened under the British system – is roughly what I would have expected. The refusal of the party leaders to exploit anti-British feeling does Irish democracy much credit. On Thursday afternoon I came on Humphrey Atkins studying the tape machine in the House of Commons. I said, 'Your shoulders are broad and you will need broad shoulders.' In the same friendly spirit he said to me, 'You are an expert on Southern Irish politics. What would you like to happen?' I said, 'I have known Garret FitzGerald since he was a small child. I have never met Haughey.' There was to say the least an understanding between us that Garret was the finer character, but Humphrey A. said firmly that Haughey was a man he could work with. I was left with the feeling, right or wrong, that he would have liked the Thatcher–Haughey understanding to continue.

Monday, *15 June 1981*

To Windsor for the annual Garter celebration – lunch, procession, service. No new introductions to fill the two vacancies. By now, after ten years, I am quite senior – only a third of the twenty-four (minus two) knights above me. The devotion towards the Queen was warmer than ever, if possible, after Saturday's episode. She was her cool, friendly self as she came round and spoke to the knights and their wives. I am very feeble on these occasions, with a kind of prep-school inhibition against 'sucking up'. The same with most of the others. Talking of prep schools, my old prep-school friend, Bunny Trevelyan, was in a wheelchair. The Queen singled him out for special kindness. I said to him afterwards, 'Humphrey' (which he has been called since he left Furzie Close, though he still has the ears which earned him his nickname), 'next year I'll get into a wheelchair! You can't have the Queen all to yourself.'

Elizabeth said appropriately, 'Congratulations, Ma'am, on your horsemanship.' The Queen brightened at once. Obviously this is the way to speak to her. Indeed she laughed with girlish pleasure and replied, 'It was the Household Cavalry who upset my horse.' Apparently the cavalry officer riding behind her dashed to her assistance when he heard the shots. This caused her horse to buck and rear. But the Queen has a soothing influence on horses and humans.

To my surprise and gratification I was put next to Lady Diana Spencer, the heroine of the hour. When she walked round with Prince Charles, she looked taller than him, with the help of lowish heels (Elizabeth judged they were an inch high). I should guess they are both about five foot ten, he perhaps a little more. I thought that she looked as if she were the heavier – Elizabeth thought the opposite. They are both superlatively fit, with their various sports. I discovered that swimming rates first with her. At school she was captain of that and in addition netball, hockey and tennis. Prince Charles has played little if any tennis, but is beginning to perform under her tuition. We agreed that it was easier than polo, at which he shines. They have skiing in common. I suggested that she would now be taking up horsemanship in one form or another. She said firmly that she probably would, but she wouldn't hurry into it. Her beautiful face, lovely complexion and eyes are set off by a chin which is pronounced in profile. Her striking independence of mind will always remain a keen memory. Curiously enough Elizabeth, who had not met her, finished a recent article by referring to this 'independence'.

In the same spirit Diana told me that Norman Hartnell and the other top dressmakers had implored her to allow them to make her wedding dress, but she had chosen the Emmanuels. She had liked something of theirs that she had seen. I asked whether they were well known. She replied, 'They are now.' Her manners are excellent towards elderly gentlemen and, I should judge, everyone else.

She told me that she first met Prince Charles when she was sixteen. She implied that she fell in love with him at sight, but she 'laid off' because he 'belonged' to her sister. Then, miraculously, the way became clear.

There was a lot to drink at lunch, white wine, red wine, champagne, port, brandy. Not to mention gin and tonic, sherry, whisky and soda previously. Diana never touches alcohol, nor, she told me, do her friends.

She is obviously much attached to her father. She told me of his amazing recovery. We did not speak of her mother nor of her stepmother, whom Elizabeth and I are fond of, and know well. She spoke with patent sincerity of her love for small children. It was clearly a vocation rather than a job, which should equip her perfectly for motherhood.

I said at the end, 'Please let me tell you how absolutely delighted everyone is about your marriage.' Innumerable people must have said this to her already, but she took it with unspoiled good nature. She said, 'I know they are paying fabulous sums to get a view of the procession.' I said I didn't mean that exactly. 'Everyone feels that you are absolutely the right bride.' She said, 'Well, at least I am English.' I looked across the table and said, jokingly, 'Yes, even our beloved Queen Mother hasn't had that advantage.' Diana has all, and more than all, that anyone could expect of a girl of nineteen. But Charles must on no account neglect her education in the widest sense, if she is to be, as she can be, a superlative queen.

Earlier knowledge had brought home to me the disturbed nature of Diana's background. When she was six her mother left the house. There followed public arguments and later the father's second marriage. I find it rather wonderful that she should have survived these experiences and emerge with such a serene and happy nature – so manifestly at peace with herself and the world. Broken homes are traditionally an explanation of delinquency, but occasionally (De

Valera, Bevin, for example) they cause a strong character to become stronger. So I would think it had been in the case of Lady Diana. I wonder, if I meet her again two years from now, whether the royal veil will have fallen. Will she ever be quite so natural again? I hope and believe she will.

Having wished her great future happiness, I felt that I must do the same to Prince Charles. I expressed the hope that he would speak regularly in the Lords. He has twice spoken there and spoken well. He replied, with all his diffident charm, 'The difficulty is to find something to speak about.' But I continued to press him and he showed the way his mind was working. 'I've been thinking of saying something on race relations.' 'Admirable,' I cried, and meant it. I can't imagine a better subject for him.

Is it a coincidence that John Grigg, in an article in *The Observer* on Prince Philip's sixtieth birthday, was advocating race relations as an issue for Philip? But it is a bit late for Prince Philip to discover this as a new passionate interest and just the right moment for Prince Charles. While I am writing this, Lord Scarman is holding a major inquiry into the Brixton riots. Race relations would take Charles far outside this country. He would have a unique role to play in our black, white and brown Commonwealth. In my view the way to begin would be for him to preside over a far-reaching race relations conference.

I look back on today's proceedings through rose-tinted glasses after my meeting with Lady Diana. Prince Charles was very gracious to me and Elizabeth about the books we had sent him, which we ourselves had written. But I cannot quite put out of mind the thought of the fourteen hundred guests on 29 July (including some like Ken Livingstone who have treated the invitation with contempt), among whom we are not included. Relationships with royalty are not, and never have been, quite like those with other people.

Thursday, 18 June 1981

Meeting in John Belstead's room in the House concerning Ian Brady and his demand that he be sent to Broadmoor. I was accompanied by Sir Roger Falk, who has visited him in the Scrubs for the last seven years, also by the well-known criminal lawyer Ben Birnberg, Ian's solicitor.

I opened by stressing the efforts of Reggie Maudling, when Home Secretary, to get Ian sent to Broadmoor in 1971, efforts defeated by

Keith Joseph, the Health Minister, and our strong impression that the Home Office psychiatrist seeing Ian regularly now favours this course. Roger Falk threw in a dramatic warning that if the hospital wing where Ian is housed is closed down there is no saying what steps he would resort to. He was already talking about killing a prison officer or, alternatively, himself. John Belstead had with him one of the top officials and the head of the Prison Medical Service. There was some discussion as to whether a prisoner could be sent to Broadmoor if he was not thought to be treatable, but there appeared to be no doubt that such a transfer could and should take place if two psychiatrists were ready to describe him as mentally ill. We believe that 'mentally ill' is just what Dr Marjot the prison medical officer says he is.

Somewhat to my surprise, it was agreed that if Ian himself had no objection we could see a report which Dr Marjot would be asked to prepare about him. The head of the Prison Medical Service warned us that it might not assist our argument as much as we suppose. I shot him a rather cynical look. We would be enormously unimpressed if Marjot's known opinions were known to have been modified under guidance from his superiors. However, we came away pleased for the time being. At the very least we can demonstrate to Ian that we are fighting his battle energetically. Not that we shall convince him of this at all easily.

Friday, 19 June 1981

Dinner last night at George Weidenfeld's in honour of Elizabeth and her new book on the Queen Mother. Apart from the family the chief guest was the national security adviser in the recent Carter administration. I am inclined to like all Poles, but his self-introduction to Antonia was less than tactful: 'I haven't read any of your books. I haven't read your mother's book. In fact I haven't read a book for five years.' Antonia asked him what he was doing with himself. It appeared that he was writing a book for some vast sum of money. 'Don't you think', she asked him sweetly, 'it would be rather a good thing to read a few books before writing one?' I could not hear his reply.

Later on everyone in his group was asked to name the characteristic feature of various countries. For Britain he supplied the phrase 'cultural hedonism'. It is not known whether he would have revised his opinion after some sharp exchanges with Harold on the subject of Chile. Harold told me afterwards with a gleam in his eye that the National Security Adviser needed to be put through it. Harold is no mean adversary when aroused, particularly if he fancies any implied insult to the Jewish people (which was not the issue here). I had not thought of him as feeling so strongly about politics, but I should have remembered that he refused National Service on grounds of principle.

Edna O'Brien, more dazzling than ever, talking a good deal about loneliness, but I can't think that she is left alone for long, told me later that she had shared a hairdresser for some years with Diana Spencer. But now the future Princess can no longer come to the hairdresser. He has to go to her. I told this to Antonia, who replied that she had shared a hairdresser (next door to the other one) with Mrs Thatcher. But there also the mountain (the hairdresser) had to go to Mahomet (i.e. the heroine). Security considerations were held to make this inevitable but I was left reflecting on the servitude imposed on royalty throughout a lifetime and other great ones when at the peak of their fame. We know they have opportunities and glories denied to the rest of us – but not even to be allowed to go to your hairdresser!

Monday, 22 June 1981

Philip Toynbee died last week. At last I pulled myself together and wrote to Sally:

My dear Sally,

I have been a long time writing. You may have wondered why I did not write sooner. For that I apologize. But the truth is that I cannot begin to tell you even a small part of what I feel about Philip, and what I feel for you now.

There has never been anyone outside my own generation or family for whom I felt anything like as much affection as I did, and always shall, for Philip.

We saw each other so seldom, alas, in all the later years. But for my part, and I hope that it was true of him, my love was as strong and unqualified as ever.

Tributes to him in *The Observer* and elsewhere have all struck an excellent note. I can hardly add to them in general terms. But he was the only undergraduate all the time I was a don who was able to surpass completely the age barrier (more important then than later).

From the moment he approached me after the Mosley meeting, in the Carfax assembly rooms in 1936, we were blood brothers. (We were both at that moment streaming with blood.)

So it went on. As you know I expect I came into some money in 1938 and (full of guilt) bought the Birmingham Labour paper, the *Town Crier*, installing Philip (though still, I suppose, a Communist) as editor. What wonderful high jinks we had together!

At the time of Munich we stood on the steps of the town hall, Edgbaston, and told a hostile mob that we would make it impossible for Neville Chamberlain (then, more than ever, their idol) to show his face again in Birmingham!

Whenever we did come together in later years, as when I paid my short but memorable visit to you, I always felt that the old friendship was as true as ever.

His last book is full of spiritual greatness. No one else could have written it, or lived the life that produced it. But no one but *you* could have cared for him with such infinite love and understanding and quiet strength. I cannot now think of him without thinking equally of you.

Since writing the above I have had a letter from David Astor, always devoted to Philip, who returned the feeling. David says that Philip's life turned out so much better than seemed likely at one time. One must think that Sally saved him from disintegration, drink being the most obvious problem, but by no means the only one. David himself 'discovered' him as an *Observer* writer, though his literary talents were already known, and sustained him through good times and bad (and there were not a few of the latter) with a tenderness peculiarly his own.

When I reached the office I was told that Robert and Cherisse Burdon's trial at the Knightsbridge Crown Court was reaching its climax. Would I come at once to give evidence as to character, as promised, in the event of a conviction? Robert and Cherisse are two young visitors to New Horizon, tormented by a history of drugs but striving gallantly to overcome that dread weakness. They were accused in the Crown Court in Knightsbridge where they were being charged with peddling drugs. I reached the Knightsbridge Crown Court at 11.30. The judge was still drooling on, repeating Robert's evidence at enormous length, and did not conclude his summing-up until one. I returned to the Lords for lunch.

At 4.15 I was summoned back again. The jury were returning. Robert and Cherisse stood in the dock even paler and more drawn than usual. The foreman was asked whether each of them was guilty under four headings.

Robert, it seems, had launched a flat-out attack on the police, whom he accused of extracting a confession by brutally beating him. The judge had said that either Robert or the police were lying. He left no doubt as to whose version he preferred. A verdict of 'guilty' was frankly expected by our able young counsel, who thought that Robert had cooked his goose by his denunciation of the police.

The foreman of the jury mumbled a series of answers to the questions put him, from which it gradually emerged that the jury could not agree on the verdict. They were sent away and told that a majority of ten to two would suffice.

I read *King Lear* for an hour. It is full of so many incomparable phrases that my attempt to write them down soon languished. For me the crucial moment in the play is when Lear for the first time seems to enter into the lives of ordinary suffering humanity.

> Poor naked wretches, whereso'er you are,
> That bide the pelting of this pitiless storm
> How shall your houseless heads and unfed sides,
> Your looped and windowed raggedness, defend you
> From seasons such as these? O, I have ta'en
> Too little care of this!

Robert and Cherisse are poor in the sense of the word used by Father d'Arcy, when he gave me the life's injunction, 'Keep close to the poor.' St Francis de Sales would tell me to love the will of God working itself out through this afflicted couple. I could visualize it more easily through their case than quite a few others.

The jury were summoned back after an hour. More mumbling by the foreman. Still no verdict or apparently any prospect of one. They were duly discharged which means another trial.

The strain on Robert and Cherisse continues. One could only conclude that at least three, maybe more, of the jury agreed with Robert that the police were lying and had in fact extracted a confession by what the judge called 'disgraceful means'. If I had given evidence as to character I would have said that I had known both of them for a number of years at New Horizon, that I had been best man at their wedding and was a godfather of their child. I would have asserted that they were making a gallant, one might almost say an heroic struggle against the curse of drug addiction. Perhaps that will have to be done later.

As I came away I reflected that all human justice is imperfect. I should have hated to have to make my mind up on that jury. But at least they took their duties seriously.

Wednesday, 24 June 1981

Elizabeth and I spent a rather fruitless evening. We had accepted an invitation, paying £12.50 each for the privilege, to what we thought was a party for Prince Charles and his wondrous lady at the Royal Academy. Elizabeth had persuaded herself that the event would be helpful to her book on the Queen. In fact, we hadn't got the picture right at all.

A vast crowd of Friends of the Academy had accepted invitations. Prince Charles and Lady Diana were reported present but even the tallest of us (I myself am still over six feet) could only catch glimpses of the tops of their heads. The sculpture master from Ampleforth showed his formidable sculpture in stone of Joseph, the Virgin Mary and the Baby Jesus – very good in the sight of my untutored eyes. Joseph was the dominating figure. The sculptor told us that Joseph had been too long neglected.

Otherwise it was much like the Buckingham Palace Garden Party where one never meets anyone one knows till one is on the point of leaving. Our most embarrassing afternoon there was when T.S. Eliot greatly honoured Elizabeth, and indirectly me, by asking Elizabeth to 'present' his young wife Valerie. He had been involved in prolonged negotiations with the Lord Chamberlain. I still think that a little extra trouble might have been taken over the most famous writer in the English language at that time. We raced up and down the historic lawn, desperately trying to find a member of the royal family, or, as our standards dropped, an acolyte to whom to introduce the Eliots. But we never came within a mile of meeting the humblest flunkey. A constant menace was the hovering presence of my uncle the 'poet peer' Lord Dunsany, who detested Eliot's poetry and had to be steered away from him. Outside the palace, a photographer came up to us and took a few pictures. But he spoilt the whole effect by asking, 'Names, please.'

The only conversation which sticks in my mind from last night was one with Prue [Lady] Windlesham, fashion editor until recently of *The Times* and a tower of strength as a judge of the Catherine Paken-ham Award. I told Prue that in my opinion normal men didn't dress with a view to appearing attractive. She disagreed totally. She assured me that men dressed either to create an impression of power (e.g. Kissinger, 'Power is the supreme aphrodisiac') or for servitude. I insisted that men of seventy-five and upwards dressed for impotence. I must have been reading too much *King Lear*.

Sunday, 28 June 1981

Elizabeth and I went over to George and Diana Gage at Firle (Thomas was conceived there on our first visit at the end of 1932). George is now father of the House of Lords. Diana has brought him great happiness in old age.

The guest of honour was Harold Macmillan. I used to think that his groping manner was a bit of an affectation, but I was quite wrong. He says that he can't see well enough to read. But as he totters along on his stick he creates an impression of infinite dignity and a sort of mischievous benignity. He greeted Elizabeth with the teasing words, 'You write all these great books about royalty, in spite of Frank's left-wing tendencies!' Elizabeth had been hoping to pick up some useful crumbs for her book on the Queen. They seem to have talked mostly about her security. He considers that world leaders today are threatened from two sources: hired assassins and lunatics – what some of us call 'nutters'. The first category emanated ultimately from the Soviet Union. He did not think that the Soviet Union would have an interest in murdering the Queen. The second group, like the poor, we would always have with us. The royal family, with admirable phlegm, accepted them as an occupational risk. To quote the Queen, 'I've got to be seen to be believed.' Harold M. could only suggest that when royal carriages were used they should go faster than at present; and that royalty should not cluster round like a covey of partidges. For example, there was no need for Prince Charles to be so close to the Queen at the Trooping the Colour.

When my turn came, I rather heavy-handedly asked him what he thought about monetarism. He was at his most bland. 'It is the greatest mistake', he said, 'to lay down a principle. You must have principles, of course. But to proclaim them is a sure means of producing an ugly confrontation.' And it left one very little room for manoeuvre.

He never forgets, I am sure, and he frequently reminds us, that he is a crofter's grandson and a successful bourgeois publisher. When we went in to lunch, I naturally stood back for the former prime minister. He would not allow it. With absolute firmness he insisted on giving way to what he called 'the nobility'. Of course he could have had all sorts of titles and honours, including the Garter. But he has preferred to remain just Mr Harold Macmillan.

The only time I ever stayed in a house with him was when Elizabeth and I stayed with Eddie, Duke of Devonshire, whose sister Lady Dorothy was Harold's wife. We played four rounds of golf during the weekend and talked far into the night. No one in our time, I should imagine, ever sat longer over his port than Eddie 'Hartington'. He had been close beside my father when he fell at Gallipoli. As the night wore on, he told me my father's last words to him in three different forms. In the first version he addressed him as 'Lord Hartington'; in the second 'Hartington'; in the third 'Harty boy'.

Macmillan in those days was a slightly subdued figure. This was 1938. He was at loggerheads with his party over appeasement and unemployment. He was forty-four and had held no office. He toyed with the idea, no doubt not quite seriously, of joining the Labour Party. (Other accounts confirm my recollection here.) But he finished by dismissing the idea with the words, 'But when it comes to throwing in my lot with your wild men of the left, I must remember that I am a very rich man.' To be fair he did not mean that he was not prepared for financial sacrifices, but that his background would make mutual confidence impossible.

As we came away on Sunday I felt that we had been moving in elevated company, both in the worldly and the unworldly senses of the word.

Wednesday, 1 July 1981

Oliver Plunkett Day. In 1681 the saint was hanged, drawn and quartered at Tyburn. I missed the big Mass in the afternoon through attendance at the House, but joined the relatively small crowd in the morning while Cardinal O'Fiaich placed a wreath on the place of execution close to Marble Arch. The noise of the traffic made it difficult to hear anything but in a muted way it was historical and moving. A television interviewer took me unawares. In reply to him I was not very convincing. I found myself saying that the ceremony was a symbol of reconciliation, but was hard put to it to explain my meaning.

The Cardinal preached in English in the afternoon, stressing the perfidy of the Catholics who gave evidence against St Oliver and his good relations with Protestants. Sound ecumenical stuff. Elizabeth took to the Cardinal hugely at a big party later in the day. She likes all dynamic people, male or female. The Cardinal is nothing if not dynamic and very jolly with it. Elizabeth was aware of his academic eminence as a Maynooth professor and of his admiration for Thomas's book *The Year of Liberty, 1798*. She pleased him by re-calling her own research work at Maynooth when writing her book on Wellington.

I had not seen him since Thomas motored me over to lunch with him at Armagh in 1978. Since then he has not had at all a good press in England; he is looked on as an Irish Nationalist, which of course he is, if by Nationalist is meant a patriot who longs to see a united Ireland. All too many English people, Catholics and non-Catholics, yearn for the excommunication of the IRA, whose violence has been denounced repeatedly by the Cardinal and the other bishops.

I can't help recalling my last meeting with Dev shortly before he died. He kept insisting that he had not been excommunicated fifty years earlier during the civil war 1922-3, although the Irish bishops had condemned the Republicans whom he was nominally leading. Some years later the Pope of the day had agreed with him that he had not in fact been excommunicated. But supposing, I persisted, the Pope had disagreed with you and said you *had* been excommunicated? Dev replied with that deadpan humour that I had come to know so well, 'I should have considered that His Holiness was misinformed.' Personally, I was glad that the Cardinal should have made a brief but quite spectacular appearance in England. It was high time that his bogey-man image here was superseded.

Malcolm rang up this evening in a state of unusual excitement. A mysterious lady was coming to stay with him and Kitty for a week, participating in a television programme. He was very anxious that we should come to dinner on Saturday week when the programme would be finished. He was not going to tell us who the lady was. Elizabeth and I spent some time guessing and rang up to suggest some likely names – Mother Theresa, Jackie Kennedy, Rosalind Carter, Margaret Trudeau. He relented and told us that it was Svetlana, Stalin's daughter, a strong Christian these days who I know has been in correspondence with Malcolm. Of course, we shall be fascinated to meet her and to find out if we can what she really thought and felt about the old tyrant.

Thursday, 2 July 1981

Rather an amusing flare-up at our S & J management committee today. William told us that Billie Jean King was short of funds because her sponsors had dropped out after the revelations of her lesbian affair. Her memoirs, to be suitably ghosted, were on offer. There was an immediate outcry among the five women present about the atrocious behaviour of the sponsors and general sympathy for Billie Jean. I disingenuously asked whether Sir Charles Forte was likely to approve of a book in which Billie Jean 'told all'. William held his peace but our zestful young feminists literally shrieked when I suggested that there ought to be more sympathy for her discarded girl-friend, now in a wheelchair, than for her. They accused this unfortunate girl-friend of blackmailing their heroine. Spirited young women seem to feel challenged when any man makes the mildest comment on the private life of any member of their sex. I might have defended myself on the ground that I was probably one of the few men in London who had addressed three different groups of lesbians, but I felt that I had caused enough annoyance for one morning.

I went along in the late afternoon to hear the Northern Ireland debate in the House of Commons. I was in time for the end of Jim Callaghan's surprising emergence as a champion of an independent Ulster. In a thin house he sat down in more or less total silence. Later it emerged that Michael Foot had tried to dissuade him from speaking. Personally I have always recognized the theoretical argument, put to me some years ago by Bill Craig, that allegiance to Ulster is the only allegiance in the near future which could unite Protestants and Catholics in the Province. At the moment, everyone is asserting loudly that it is 'simply not on'. But I am sure that something of this kind will prove to be a necessary transitional form on the way to a united Ireland.

Wednesday, 8 July 1981

I travelled to Warrington on Monday to report on the run-up to the Warrington by-election for *The Universe*, returning very early Tuesday morning. I gave dinner to Judith, our family poet, on Tuesday evening and, as so often in her company, felt impelled to break into verse. The following lines emerged:

After Warrington

Warrington died.
Perhaps it never lived,
Except in minds attuned to that conception.
Warrington died.

Statistics cannot make or mar a soul.
The unemployment figures may be twice the 1980 level.
'Do not fear,' they say.
'This town is not like Toxteth.'
All the while the blaze of looted buildings brings the word
Across the narrowing skies.

No one that I met in Warrington doubts that the Labour candidate, Doug Hoyle, an effective electioneer with a strong local connection, will hold the seat for Labour. But the relative success or failure of Roy Jenkins in his exciting intervention is of vast importance for the future of the SDP and of British politics.

I attended a question time organized by the churches at which all the main candidates performed (three were invited, a fourth, the ecologist, made his way in). Roy cut an impressive figure. His election literature reminds one that he was the son of a miner – which, listening to his old-fashioned, aristocratic accent, comes as something of a surprise. But he was every inch the former Chancellor, Home Secretary and President of the European Commission. He was at his most statesmanlike when the question of abortion came up. Few people are aware of the crucial role Roy played as Home Secretary in promoting the 1967 Abortion Reform Act.

He is also on record as saying that the permissive society is the civilized society. No one was crude enough to ask him whether he was proud of his part in putting through the 1967 Act. He said he did not favour any changes at present, but would always consider arguments put to him in the future. Difficult to know how to interpret that – Catholics would obviously like to take it to mean that he would narrow rather than widen the Act.

I was fortunate to have a private conversation with Doug Hoyle, the Labour candidate, who showed a compassion and care for the outcast and disadvantaged – in which we should include the millions of unemployed – that convinced me that it is still Labour who have a deeper understanding of the human background and of our obligation to transform it.

Uncle Arthur always used to say that the working class in Hackney Wick would vote Labour because of the 'class thing'. It may sound a bit like Karl Marx, but Uncle Arthur was an Old Etonian merchant banker, as well as long-term resident in the East End. I should say that Doug would know more about winning elections than Roy Jenkins. Receiving the baton on the last stage of the relay, he is not likely to let it drop or be overtaken. From the considerable experience of constituencies in the north-west of England, he knows all about the significance of parish priests. He was very warm in his approach to me, recalling the help that Elizabeth and I had given in past elections. There is no doubt that I am easily appealed to by any left-wing figure of working-class background who treats me as a comrade. Good luck to you, Doug!

Friday, 10 July 1981

Long debate in the House of Lords yesterday on Northern Ireland. Among those who spoke were Jack Donaldson, at one time a junior minister in the Northern Ireland Office, Lord Moyola, a former PM of the Province, Lord Brookeborough, a live wire in his own right but best known in this connection as the son of the Northern Ireland Prime Minister (a disastrous one in my eyes) from 1943 to 1963. I expressed the fervent hope that the Labour Party would come out with a declaration of support for the principle of a united Ireland. A federal style would leave a Belfast government the power to make its own rules regarding divorce, etc. I submitted the thesis that the Ulstermen, when they saw the shape of the future, would enter the negotiating process.

After we had 'done our stuff' we fraternized happily in the 'Bishop's Bar'. Ivone Kirkpatrick once remarked of Quintin Hailsham after Quintin had denounced Bobbity Salisbury at somewhat inordinate length, 'He looked as if he had had a good day's shooting.' So with us in the Bishop's Bar. Moyola raised the question at one point, 'Do you think that anything we said, or anyone else has said, has made the slightest difference?' We agreed that the question was quite out of order and if persisted in would remove the pleasures of parliamentary debating. But in answer to Moyola I would say, marginally, Yes. A score of well-meaning peers should not be disappointed with that assessment.

Two-thirty to three o'clock: radio interview on LBC with some phone-ins about the state of the country. In practice this meant the riots which have during the last week been unprecedented in my lifetime. If I were writing about even the most abbreviated history of this period I would have mentioned last week Ted Heath's two public warnings that Thatcherite economics would produce race riots and widespread violence of all kinds. No statesman was ever proved right so quickly, in spite of all the insinuations that he was speaking entirely to spite Margaret Thatcher.

I said that in the short term everything must be done to assist the police. In the short and medium term we need a completely new economic policy which would avert the existence of whole communities of unemployed young people. All concerned, governments, churches, all the rest of us, must work together to persuade parents to show an altogether different degree of responsibility for the conduct of their children, but it might take a long time to bring about a change. I was asked whether I believed that it was likely that there was a conspiracy at work. I said that there appeared to be no doubt that various organizations were doing all in their power to stir up trouble. I gave the same kind of answer which I had heard Roy Hattersley, the Labour home affairs spokesman, giving on the radio. I added a special tribute to Willie Whitelaw's personality. Judging by television, he is well-suited to coping with this crisis.

Saturday, 11 July 1981

Have now nearly completed Cardinal Hume's *Searching for God*. A great book by any contemporary standard. I know of no piece of work by any British writer during my lifetime which should be of such direct spiritual assistance. Father d'Arcy? C. S. Lewis? William Temple? Much that they wrote was of permanent value, but they have left nothing so systematically instructive. I can only compare *Searching for God* with St Francis de Sales's *Introduction to the Devout Life*, and that was published in 1616.

It is all the more remarkable that the book consists of edited addresses given over a decade to Ampleforth monks with no thought of publication. If I had to single out Cardinal Hume's distinctive combination of qualities I should mention his closeness to God and his ability to express this in terms of practical conduct. It makes me all the sadder that though he has been Archbishop of Westminster now for over five years, I am not on the periphery of his circle. [Later note – I feel closer now.]

Cardinal Hume was talking exclusively to monks. How far can we transfer the message to the rest of us? At one point he writes: 'There are five things to which we must be faithful – prayer, obedience, hard work, community life, poverty.' On the face of it, prayer and hard work are imperative duties for all of us. Not so obedience, community life and poverty. But one can't leave it there. Community life? Obviously a family man living in the world can never live a community life resembling that of a religious. Moreover most men when they retire lose a good deal of the community life of their profession which will not often be fully compensated for by, shall we say, voluntary work in their neighbourhood. Since giving up the chairmanship of S & J, I am spending a good deal more time in the Lords than for many years past. Long ago, before I became leader, some peers said of me, 'He talks a lot about equality, but he doesn't treat us as equals.' Perhaps, as time goes on, with Cardinal Wolsey I will learn what it is to be 'little'. Not masochistically but 'in community'.

What does he tell us that can be applied to our lives without adaptation? I take a passage which gives the flavour of his insights and is simpler than some others. 'At the root of most people's problems is insecurity and with this goes fear. Insecurity needs to be healed with compassion and concern so that love may cast it out.' The text from St John's Epistle, 'Perfect love casteth out fear', has long been one of my favourites, but I have always thought of it in terms of my own love casting ·out *my own* fear. The whole new vista opens up when one realizes that one's love can cast out the fear of others and make the whole difference to the happiness and goodness of their lives.

After reading this and other passages several times, I still find it hard to understand what is meant by loving others 'in God'. It is well over fifty years since my dear lamented friend Evan Durbin, a Baptist lay preacher, told me that all pleasures (including drinking cider, the utmost indulgence he allowed himself) should be pleasures in God. To be honest, I am still very much in the dark. Does it mean that I love Elizabeth as God or Christ loves me in the spirit in which Christ laid down the Commandment, 'Love one another as I have loved you', or does it mean that when I am properly filled with the Divine Spirit the love of God acts through me in my love of others? Or something much more profound, or much more simple? I must keep on trying to obtain a glimpse of the necessary light. One day I may even venture to ask Cardinal Hume himself, but I think I will wait until (if it ever happens again) I find myself sitting next to him at a dinner. And even then I might conclude that it was hardly the right moment.

Sunday, 12 July 1981

To dinner last night with Kitty and Malcolm for the eagerly-awaited meeting with Svetlana. On the way over I forecast to Elizabeth that she would be short and sturdy like her father. Elizabeth had the opposite picture. I was more or less right, but Svetlana was even broader in shoulder and beam than I had expected. Plump with it and very cosy. Her eyes are blue and her hair, though she is in her middle fifties, still fair. One felt at home with her from the first moment. She had herself become part of the Muggeridge family after her *Week in the Country* – the name of the forthcoming BBC programme. The latter was, incidentally, Malcolm's own idea, which shows that his initiative in this area is in no way diminished by his much-publicized dislike of the medium.

Naturally, we began by talking about the making of the programme, the enthusiasm of the BBC team, etc. Svetlana herself, under the highly expert tuition of Malcolm, seemed to have found no difficulty in 'going public' after ten years in retirement. She said that she expected a spate of letters (and more appearances?) when the programme is shown. After that, a return to a happy obscurity in Maryland with her ten-year-old daughter by her second marriage (which ended in divorce).

Svetlana was uninhibited in talking about Stalin, though we did not attempt to probe very deeply. She gave an amazing account of the twelve hours that passed after his stroke before permission could be obtained from the Politburo to call a doctor. I suggested from a rather hazy recollection of the first of her two books that she had 'remained fond of him'. She demurred. I made a mental note to re-read her book and study the circumstances of her mother's suicide. I suggested that as Stalin did not leave the seminary where he was training for the priesthood until he was twenty-one, religion must have meant a lot to him in his formative years. She smiled rather sceptically.

I told her that I knew Irish rebels whose strong Catholicism had been destroyed or weakened in revolutionary movements. She replied rather cryptically that her father's rejection of religion was not in favour of a national, Georgian revolution, which she seemed to think more respectable, but of social democracy, which to her seemed to derive from atheistic Marxism. I found myself telling her what Ernie Bevin had said after his first meeting with her father: 'He's just a working chap, like you and me, trying to make his way in the world.' Another inscrutable smile. I was left doubtful whether she had heard of Bevin.

We talked about Marxism. I told her that I used to lecture on it at Oxford. She said that she and her friends had had Marxism 'stuffed down their throats' at university until they became utterly bored with it. She said the same was true of the present generation.

Where did her Christianity originate? She told us that deep down the Russian people had always remained religious, mostly Christian, though there were now thirty million Muslims. She didn't have to go outside Russia for her Christianity; it was 'all around' her in her grandmother and other relatives. Yet she told us that it is to this day illegal to possess a Bible, though Bibles are widely passed from hand to hand.

In America, like Malcolm she refuses to belong to any one church. It is the 'message' not the institution which counts with her. But she significantly does *not* visit Russian Orthodox churches. They would link her too much with Russia, which she would seem to have repudiated as decisively as Brendan Bracken repudiated Ireland. 'I am an American,' she stated, with obvious satisfaction. Her American citizenship was obtained with the utmost difficulty. She told us with immense vividness of her escape to India and eventually, via Switzerland, to America. She was held up for three days in Rome while the American Government made desperate efforts to avoid receiving such a controversial guest. Russian leaders visiting the USA tried to have her treated as a nut-case. It took years before her American citizenship was granted. She is not allowed to communicate with her two older children, from whom she has not heard for five years. We did not ask her to measure the price that she had paid for her liberation.

Elizabeth invited her to tell us what she thought of England. She had never been here before and had had a rather narrow introduction this time. A reception by the BBC, a whisk round London, then the warmth of Malcolm and Kitty's home and the peaceful security of Robertsbridge. Her reply could be summed up in the final word she used, 'gentle'.

What then, she was asked inevitably, about the riots? She replied without hesitation, 'They only concern one per cent of the people.' At that point we all became vociferous. Malcolm confessed to an uneasy feeling about the situation. It was curious that the riots only seemed to occur where there were large immigrant communities. Malcolm has a penchant for Enoch which always rather nettles me. I can't think why. I hasten to point out that the facts acknowledged by the Home Secretary were quite contrary to the Powell hypothesis. Malcolm, the courteous host, withdrew the suggestion, whatever may have been his inner feelings. Malcolm is so habitually opposed to stock progressive reactions that the idea that unemployment was at the bottom of the trouble was not likely to appeal to him, although in my eyes, it is the largest cause. We could agree that the permissive society in some sense had much to answer for, and pinpoint parental neglect as the most obvious of all the scapegoats. Svetlana smiled serenely throughout.

At one moment Nixon's name came up. Svetlana and Malcolm showed themselves well disposed towards him. I said that I had met Nixon twice since his downfall and felt sure that he had gained by suffering. Kitty said, 'Don't we all.' I compromised: 'Some of us do, some of us don't.'

I said to Svetlana, 'You have suffered far more than most people.' Nixon at the time of his fall had made a vow, which it seemed to me he had kept, to eschew bitterness. Had she been able to eschew it? She said that she felt no bitterness to individuals, but, if I understood her correctly, was not ashamed to feel bitter and indignant towards institutions and ideologies.

Kitty quoted de Caussade to the effect that God will make sure that in the end His will prevails. She agreed with me that de Caussade had at one moment been suspected of quietism, of leaving it all to God and doing nothing ourselves. All present joined in a vote of no confidence in quietism.

At a moment when Malcolm was talking to Elizabeth I said to Svetlana that he was a super-pessimist in worldly matters – an optimist ultimately through his belief in God's infinite mercy. She said that she by no means always agreed with him, but admired him immensely, above all because of 'his courage'. After studying his work from afar she had taken the bold step of entering into correspondence with him. I should say that they have a great deal in common quite apart from Malcolm's lifelong interest in Russia from his Moscow days onwards and his devotion to Tolstoy and Dostoevsky. Both of them are patently conscious of the other world, though Svetlana through her extraordinary family background and Malcolm through his exceptional talent are deeply versed in this one.

Parting question to myself: Is there any necessary conflict in being religious in Malcolm's and Kitty's sense, totally confident that is in the ultimate working of God's providence, and being 'an agent of change' as I am now officially catalogued? And Svetlana, where does she stand? On Malcolm's side of the division, no doubt, but with differences which we shall know more about when we see the programme.

Tuesday, 14 July 1981

Last night we had the first fully-organized meeting of our Mental After-Care Inquiry. After a good deal of discussion an official name was agreed on: The Richmond Fellowship Inquiry into Community Care. It is not so convenient, I feel, or readily understood as the Inquiry into Mental After-Care which I have been telling people about, but it leaves us free, among other advantages, to consider those who have not been to mental homes, but who would benefit by the sort of community care we are planning.

Those present last night under Elly's hospitable roof, in addition to Elly and myself, were Lords Richardson, Redcliffe-Maud and Winstanley, the first and third being doctors, though not psychiatrists; Professor Wing of the Institute of Psychiatry, Ken Coleman of the Westminister Borough Mental Health Department, and Peter Thompson. Professor Wing suggested that we should all call each other by our Christian names, even where we were strangers. Good psychiatry!

I was inwardly nervous about the meeting, in spite of the expertness and great goodwill of all concerned. Where were we to go from here? How were we, so to speak, to get under way? John Maud asked me what I had in mind when I started the Inquiry. I could only mutter something about my passion for a neglected cause. I could fairly point out that the Government had expressed goodwill towards our effort, as indeed had the members of the committee by their presence.

John Richardson moved the whole operation forward. He pointed out that the minister in the Lords had expressed goodwill. He suggested that on behalf of the committee I should write to the top minister concerned, asking for an interview and at the same time setting out the kind of information which we feel his department might be able to supply to us. This led on to a plan for an expert drafting group to prepare the letter to the minister: Elly, John Wing, Michael Winstanley and Ken Coleman.

Before the end of the meeting, a small working group was taking shape, which I had always hoped for. John Richardson said to me afterwards, speaking from a vast experience of mingled politics, medicine and administration, 'Rather a good meeting, I thought.' I thought so too.

Buckingham Palace Garden Party this afternoon. Elizabeth has described our experiences so dextrously that I reproduce her account below:

B.P. Garden Party. On the way there, Frank said he would try to avoid talking to any of the peers whom he sees every day. It did not quite work out like this. As we walked up from Grosvenor Gate, we saw a dazzling mass of flamingoes – more than last year – but for at least ten minutes no one else of any interest whatever. I said, 'Perhaps this is going to be the time when we know *no one*', and Frank said, 'It's a lesson to people who think it's a small world and they know everyone in it.' At that moment I caught sight of Norah Phillips, but did not make for her, on Frank's principle of not seeing peers. Next moment Anne Wall and her husband said hallo! This encounter illustrated another principle of B.P. parties, namely that one either sees no one or else one's nearest neighbour in Sussex. Anne belonged to the second group, as she is lunching with us at the House of Lords – tomorrow! She looked lovely dressed in blue. (She is the Queen's Assistant Press Secretary.) In the middle of the lawn in front of the steps we met a priest from Corby and his friend, a retired headmaster from Darlington. I asked the latter if they were having riots. He said no, though things were very bad. I asked why not. He thought a bit and then said, 'I believe it's the very tight family discipline you find in these mining families. When I began teaching, I could not get the children to answer back, ask questions or respond at all.' 'They did not dare challenge Dad?' 'No.' 'That's rather different from what we hear in the South where children are all supposed to begin arguments with their parents with the words, 'Teacher says . . ."' '

Then Denis Thatcher came up, very jovial. He said they had got up at 5 a.m. to visit Toxteth riot area yesterday. I asked if he had enjoyed *Anyone for Denis?* He said, 'No, I can't say I enjoyed it, but I did enjoy raising £20,000 for our charities. [The tickets were £50 each.] I told the manager, etc., "I'll come any Sunday you name if I can get £20,000 again."' Margaret Thatcher came up, dressed in white and wearing a little white hat. Her cheeks were very pale too and she looked drawn and much smaller (stooping?) than I had remembered. Nevertheless she still looked game and immaculate, so I congratulated her on having emerged from her 5 a.m. start so well. She asked me what I was writing, and I told her about my *Queen as Monarch* and how the reign was one whole generation. She said, 'What a pity it rained for her Coronation.' We talked of 'changes' and I quickly asked if I could talk to her about them 'when you are not so busy'. She said, 'in the recess'. I found myself feeling much older and more confident than her and *almost* protective! (She seemed shorter than me, say 5ft 4, and I only had low heels.) Denis looked taller and older than I remembered him, and Frank as always thought he was wonderful!

After that we met Lord [Martin] Ingleby in his wheelchair with his family. He told us that the other day Mrs Thatcher had seen him in the corridor and said, 'Hallo, Lord Ingleby', though she did not know him. Frank said, 'I suppose she's got your vote now?' He said, 'No, I shall stick to the cross-benches.'

The only peer Frank had said beforehand he would consent to talk to was Gladwyn [Jebb], and sure enough we met him and Cynthia; she looking charming in a pink and green print dress with a green-frilled parasol. She begged us to join *her* party, the SDP. She was annoyed at Hugh Thomas getting so right-wing. He is now an outstanding Tory peer. 'He once said he would follow Roy Jenkins but he had no party. And now,' added Cynthia melodramatically, 'Roy *has* a party, but it's too late!' 'But he could change sides again,' I said. 'No one would blame him, and after all Churchill said, "One can't re-rat" – and did!' Cynthia then explained that Hugh had begun as a Conservative, so that would mean three changes and he couldn't re-re-rat!

I only add a footnote. Denis is just about the most friendly man I have ever met, not with the vague benevolence of the professional politician, but with a personal warmth that leaves no doubt that he is really pleased to see someone whom he regards as a friend. Two years ago we were trying in S & J to get a book out of him. He gave me lunch at the Savoy Grill. Some years earlier, he and Margaret, before she became leader of the Opposition, had come over for dinner with us at Bernhurst. Denis and I are equally passionate about rugger. He was for many years a leading referee and described to me his finest hour. He had had to warn a player guilty of misbehaviour. The captain of the team had come up and made a protest. Denis said to him, 'If he does that again, he'll go off, and within ten seconds you'll go off after him.' After the game in the bar the captain had said to him, 'Would you really have sent me off?' Denis replied, 'Of course.' 'Thank you very much, sir,' said the captain. 'Quite right!' Denis avoids talking politics, but he left me no doubt that this was a little parable about the need for discipline.

Thursday, 16 July 1981

Lunch for Greg Noel, deputy director of the Melting Pot. He had come hotfoot from the scene of the latest riots and of the appalling destruction during the police raids two days earlier. Greg said that at least eleven houses were wrecked by the police. Lord Scarman, who came with his wife to tea at the Melting Pot (a gesture much appreciated), had just visited the scene of the police damage and was, it seemed, much shocked. Greg has high hopes, I hope not too high, of the Scarman Report. He says that the effect of community unemployment cannot be exaggerated, especially on the school leavers, who have never had the chance of working and are assuming that unemployment is the natural order. *Hope* must be given them at all costs. He kept coming back to 'hope'.

Greg's immediate remedy is a major extension of training schemes for the young. They keep the young people off the streets, they put some earned money into their pockets which reduces the urge to steal, and they give the youths *some* skill at least, so that they have *some* hope of a job afterwards. He was even more indignant about the police behaviour than when I visited the Melting Pot after the first riots. He kept repeating requests to meet someone with a real 'power of decision'. When the Conservatives were in opposition, Whitelaw had visited the Melting Pot and shown much sympathy. Since he became Home Secretary, it had been impossible to make contact with him. I agreed to consult Scarman, who had spoken nicely to Greg about me, and ask him how best to bring some pressure.

Later I spent some time in the Press Gallery of the Commons. When I arrived, Margaret Thatcher was answering questions. Listening to the noisy Labour back-benchers, I felt, like Elizabeth at the Garden Party, quite sorry for her. I said as much to Hugh Thomas sitting next to me. Hugh replied, 'There is no need to pity her. She is much more serene inside than you suppose. She is answering these questions deliberately in a low key. On radio, she will come out much better than her opponents!' I am sure that what Hugh says is true, also that Margaret T. enjoys a battle. Nevertheless, like Cardinal Hume, she looks tired. Most of us would have been worn out in her position long ago. But her passion for activity must add to her troubles. Still, the blessed recess is at hand.

In the evening dinner with Mary [Duchess of] Roxburghe for Bron Astor's dance for her two entrancing daughters, one at Oxford after Charterhouse, the other at Downside. One is sorry to hear that Downside are terminating their experiment with girls before Ampleforth have started. At dinner I sat next to Mary, full of political and social antennae and a lady little over forty and looking less, who for twenty years has 'planned parties'. She had worked for two years with Bron on this one. On her left was a gentleman from *The Tatler*, whose immediate claim to fame was his possession of a semi-official list of suitable young men for dances. When my four sisters went to dances, half a century ago, there was a list of this kind. I was amused to find that it still persisted and was in the control of this pleasant journalist.

I can't remember when I last went to a debutante dance. Forty years ago? Elizabeth and I have been to a certain number of 'dances' since we married, but not deb dances for many years. Bron and the girls, seventeen and sixteen years old, made a lovely picture as they received us. There was a huge marquee in the garden. The vast majority of those present were young and therefore unknown to us, but we had some happy conversations with David and Brigid Astor and a charming daughter of theirs. Also with the Catholic Archbishop of Southwark, who as Bishop of Arundel played a large part when I received the Grand Cross of St Gregory; and with Norman [St John-Stevas], whose imitation of Mrs Thatcher sacking him is apparently a star turn in society.

Elizabeth and I returned to Chelsea and heard the Warrington result, with the heavy poll for Roy Jenkins. Short of a victory for the SDP, it could hardly have been more surprising.

Friday, 17 July 1981

To the Lords for one more of these Friday sessions, very unlike the old days. Entering the guest room, I was greeted by a cheery group of Fred Peart, Bob Boothby and others. What did I think of Warrington? I replied (some subconscious loyalty at work, perhaps), 'A flash in the pan.' This was greeted with general derision. I tried again, but I was then called away to meet a guest. A little later I ran into Cledwyn Hughes. He had no doubt about the right comment: the best thing that could happen to the party. I felt at once that he was right. Dora Gaitskell, when I told her, was not sure at first, but then gave a ruling in her best Queen Victoria vein: 'Most salutary.' Then I met Bertie Denham, Government Chief Whip. I told him that 'it would be very good for our party', to which he quickly responded, 'and for ours'. A perceptive man. What could I have meant by my comment, but what could he have meant by his?

Diana Mosley and Margaret from S & J came down to spend a night with us. Diana, who has a natural flare for picking up gossip even when living abroad, had heard that there was at last a real movement to displace Margaret Thatcher. The Conservative peers are led by three heavyweight Cabinet Ministers with whom Bertie must be in close touch: Lords Soames, Hailsham and Carrington. Are they up to anything just now, or nothing? Or was Bertie referring to a possible U-turn?

Diana and Margaret reached Bernhurst at 7.15. We had a long peaceful evening. We still hope that Diana will write a life of the Kaiser. I feel that she *will* write it, given sustained encouragement. It is a pleasure to see her happy relationship with Margaret. Margaret is wonderful with all authors, but best of all with Diana.

Saturday, 18 July 1981

A further long gossip this morning. I do hope that one day (and the days for all concerned are shortening) Diana will write a book about the stupendous personalities she has known, and known *well*. Churchill, Hitler, Goebbels, Lytton Strachey, the Duke of Windsor and, of course, Tom. She knew Hitler even better than I realized. Nothing will ever make her say or think that she wasn't immensely fond of him. When he was in Berlin he was often lonely at night (Eva Braun and Unity were in Munich). Diana would sit and talk to him long into the night. At this time, as always throughout the long years of marriage, she was passionately in love with Tom Mosley. We can rule out, therefore, impropriety of any sort.

She still thinks of Hitler as very amusing with a varied though patchy knowledge of history and philosophy, and a really good knowledge of music. Alan Bullock had said of him in his biography that he never got beyond Wagner and Beethoven. Diana, reviewing it, had asked whether Professor Bullock had progressed far beyond Beethoven. Hitler never said a word in her presence which indicated that he might possess a cruel side to his nature. He was her friend, not Tom Mosley's, who never cared for him. I remember his telling me once that Mussolini was more manly. It is difficult today (and she is all too well aware of this) to believe that a highly intelligent woman like Diana could be unaware of what Hitler was already doing to the Jews, or not have any inkling of what he might be capable of later. I fall back on the thought that she was in her early twenties and the excitement of it all swept her off her balance. Now a kind of dogged loyalty prevents her admitting the enormity of her error, though speaking generally about those days she did once say, 'I was wrong.'

Now, many years later, after much suffering of her own in addition to witnessing so much suffering inflicted by the Nazis, I would describe her as a very balanced woman, very brave too, and still beautiful. She vividly described her two hours' interrogation by the Birkett Committee when she appealed against her internment. Tom's interrogation went on for five days. The grounds for the internment have never been made plain, nor has the transcript been made available, though this doesn't surprise me. Public feeling was no doubt the actual reason for the incarceration. The public probably shared my own impression that Tom Mosley and Hitler were much closer than they were. It remains a shoddy tale. One is glad but not surprised to hear that Tom's old friend Bob Boothby, and Dick Stokes, an untiring champion of neglected causes, visited him in prison and did what they could to help him.

After the war, Tom Mosley was often pressed to raise the question of his wartime treatment but, says Diana, he was always interested in the future, not the past. 'That was part of his greatness.' I noticed this trait when Elizabeth and I had dinner with them in 1962, but in the last year of his life I found him returning often to the question of whether he had not committed a tragic mistake in leaving the Labour

Party. Could he conceivably, by following another course, have helped to avert a war? He reminded me of Dev going over and over the question of whether he should have led the Irish delegates to London in autumn 1921. But neither showed any trace of bitterness, and the same would be true of Richard Nixon. It would be difficult to imagine, however, three men more unlike each other.

Thursday, 23 July 1981

I talked rather more than usual (in these latter days) at our S & J meeting. Incidentally, William is looking altogether happier than last year. I *don't* think that this is due to his being in undisputed command, though as I have probably noted before it was high time I gave up the chairmanship. We have had a better year than we expected and better I fancy than most publishers of our size. Trust House Forte are providing one of their accountants to supervise the working of our accounts department. This takes a weight off William's mind. Accounting details have taken up far too much of his time and energy.

He is always hoping, understandably, to repeat the colossal success of the *Third World War*, a work of semi-fiction invented by him, though brilliantly executed by Sean Hackett and others. He would like to think that our best-selling author, Ted Heath, could fill the bill. I urged that Ted, though he could write a fine book about the future, has not the kind of imagination required for semi-fiction. We toy with the idea of Denis Healey if available. At the end of the morning, I suddenly think of William Clark, recently retired from a high position on the World Bank. He has the highly relevant qualification of having written an excellent novel about Number 10 Downing Street.

A pleasant end-of-term meeting of the Labour peers. A general recognition that by the time we meet again after the Labour Party Conference an unpleasant party situation will confront us. Agreed to hold a special meeting on the state of the party on 7 October. Individually, Labour peers express their opinions boldly, but collectively we are terrified of calling undue attention to ourselves. Things, however, would seem to be at last coming to a head. The National Executive has now come out unequivocally (1) for a united Ireland in principle. Excellent. (2) For unilateral disarmament, quite awful though expected. Denis Healey's position, win or lose the deputy leadership, becomes ever more impossible. The same might be said of Michael Foot's. But (1) he is a known unilateralist; (2) he can fairly say that the parliamentary party forced him to take the job.

Some talk with Chris Mayhew, a newly-arrived Liberal peer, forty years ago my pupil and Labour president of the Oxford Union, for whom I forecast a premiership one day. His only regret is that he did not leave the Labour party much earlier, once things had 'become hopeless'. He told me what I did not know before that in 1969 he and others had made a plan to topple Harold, then PM. But it involved 'Roy and Jim'. Jim wrecked it by wooing the trade unions and in pursuit of that aim coming out against Babara Castle's *In Place of Strife*. I have no doubt that Chris will prove himself one of the best speakers in the Lords.

Half an hour with Miles Norfolk just back from the Maze Prison. The invitations to the peers, including one to myself, were absurdly late. So Miles went along with Rodney Elton the under minister. Probably it was the best outcome. It was certainly a revelation to Miles, who had never been to Northern Ireland and only twice to the South. I had felt hitherto that his Irish sympathies were under-developed, but there is no one better at taking human beings as he finds them.

The visit had appalled and startled Miles. He talked to more than one of the hunger strikers, including a prisoner called Quinn, who made a deep impression on him. He had no idea that IRA hunger strikers were like that. My reaction, with less excuse, was similar when I first met some IRA prisoners several years ago. Miles said to Quinn, 'We admire your courage very much and we pray for you, but please believe that you cannot help your cause this way.' Quinn, in an exhausted condition, could only murmur, 'We won't give in, we won't give in.' I said to Miles, a former Guards officer and general, 'They regard themselves as soldiers going to their deaths if ordered to do so.' (I did not make a comparision with my own father at Gallipoli, leading his own brigade to certain death when it was perfectly clear that the whole exercise was a nonsense.) Miles understood all this better than I did.

What a splendid man he is! If occasionally the Conservative Whips get at him he is quick to see the joke afterwards. He is going to think matters over. He will probably ask Atkins to see him and myself, but if we are to do anything real we probably ought to ask to see Mrs Thatcher. There is nothing much that can be altered at the moment except 'the tone', but in the long run 'the tone' could be of far-reaching importance.

Wednesday, 29 July 1981

Prince Charles's Wedding. A day which has brought much happiness and I feel sure lasting benefit to the nation in a renewed sense of unity. Having prowled about among the crowds early on, I watched the wedding itself on television with Elizabeth; then went to lunch with Kevin and Ruth. Three of their most attractive friends were present. Janet Hobhouse, half American, beautiful but rather sad highbrow writer; Sophie Baker, also beautiful but by no means sad, photographer, long-time friend of all the children; a broad-shouldered, dynamic architect, recent escort of Princess Margaret, though some years younger. We watched the second part of the programme covering the royal appearances on the balcony and an earlier interview with Charles and Diana. Janet summed up our sophisticated feelings: 'The country is in good hands.'

Subjectively, my emotions as I watched were ambivalent. I was admittedly disappointed at not being asked – a disappointment not quite simple or genuine. Even when I have attended royal functions of this order I have never entered thoroughly into the spirit of the occasion. I am not really a ceremonial man. After I finished my book on St Francis 'dying naked on the naked earth', I visited Assisi and was jarred by the sight of the huge church which was raised immediately after his death. I repeat that my feelings on such an occasion are mixed. When I attended the re-opening of Cologne Cathedral in 1948, having just ceased to be Minister for Germany, I was shown the floodlit cathedral in the evening by Dr Adenauer, raised to an unusual pitch of enthusiasm by the enormous attendance. I said, rather sententiously, 'We come to Germany to teach you many things, democracy for example, but this is something that we can learn from you.'

I felt still more vividly the overwhelming force of religion joined to national feeling when I stood among the huge crowds at Phoenix Park, Dublin, and Knock in the west of Ireland to applaud the Pope in 1979. I wrote in the *Catholic Herald* at that time that in England only a royal occasion could make any comparable impact. At the time of the Queen's Coronation I wrote an article for the *Guardian* called 'Thoughts in the Abbey'. I concluded that religion would be the guiding star of her reign. How right I have proved, though I did not foresee how powerfully the family would also figure.

Prince Charles and his bride do not give me today a clear indication of how their life will be directed, but we can be sure that under all circumstances they will exhibit decency and courage. At this moment who can ask for more? When I saw this beautiful girl standing there before the altar with millions focused on her, I had the horrid fear that, like Iphigenia in Greek legend, she was becoming a kind of human sacrifice. At the time of the funeral of George VI, dear old Pethwick Lawrence said to Elizabeth about the present Queen, 'Poor little creature. Pray Heaven that they don't work her to death.' There seems to be an awareness of this danger in the case of the new Princess of Wales. The children will no doubt be her salvation.

Saturday, 1 August 1981

Dinner last night with Malcolm and Kitty. We took with us our enterprising and appealing grandson Benjie Fraser, aged twenty-two, and his enchanting girl-friend, still at St Paul's. She is the daughter of Caroline [née Blackwood] by her second husband, a Polish musician. Caroline was married earlier to Lucian Freud and by her third marriage to the illustrious American poet, the late Robert Frost. She has herself won an enviable literary reputation. I was best man to her grandfather Basil, Marquess of Dufferin and Ava, when he married Maureen Guinness at St Margaret's Westminster in 1931. Basil was killed in Burma in 1946. He had suffered ill health, not unconnected with his way of life, but he had made a noble recovery. On his death I was able to write in *The Times*, 'Before he left for the East, he was already a conqueror.' John Betjeman loved him dearly and wrote an obituary poem which ended with the words, 'By a soldier's body in Burma'. Maureen, in her seventies now but still glamorous to me, is having a ghastly time at the moment. She got rid of her butler for what sounded like excellent reasons, but she is undergoing a prolonged and humiliating experience before an appeals tribunal. I offered to attend the tribunal to show solidarity. But she decided on reflection that the publicity was quite bad enough without that!

Malcolm was at his most exhilarating. Attractive young people bring out in him what alcohol, which he has not touched for twenty years, achieves in others. He rang me this morning to describe Benjie as his favourite of all the Fraser children. I am not sure how far he knows the others. His final judgement on the world was delivered with devastating good humour: 'A disintegrating civilization invariably expresses itself in an access of total gibberish.' All the same, he was ready to agree that the Royal Wedding would do more good than harm. He makes a great boast of having pulled up his television aerials, but if he wishes to see a programme he has no difficulty in finding a helpful neighbour.

His main assault last night was on the slavery of the consensus under which we all live in these days. Like Marxists, and it may be said, Catholics, and indeed all system-mongers, he has no difficulty in fitting everything in to his simplified picture; the wedding, the anti-weddingites, Mrs Thatcher, Michael Foot, even the rioters and of course the media are portrayed as usual as the heart of the evil. I asked him, 'How do you, the most successful broadcaster of today, define your own role within the consensus?' He replied with a parable from, I think, Kipling. 'In an Indian village there was an image of Kali, worshipped by all the villagers, except a few Christians. One of the latter persisted in throwing stones at the idol. For a long time he was gravely maltreated but after a while the village got tired of beating him up. He became tolerated and then a valued institution. When he died the village approached the Christian group and asked them to appoint a substitute.'

Malcolm considers that in the instinctive calculations of the forces of the consensus he himself plays a similar part. On the way home, Benjie and Evgenia confessed themselves captivated by his wit and wisdom. Wit, certainly, wisdom possibly in the sense that G.K. Chesterton distilled it through his wealth of paradoxes. Malcolm would not make the same impact without his electric blue eyes, gleaming white hair and vitality, which seems to increase as he approaches the eighties. But there is also his profound conviction that there is a different and better world than this one, though it is about the only idea that he can't quite put into words.

An unexpected and most impressive letter in *The Times* this morning from Kevin [Pakenham]. 'Monetarism', he writes, 'may not yet be buried but it is in an advanced state of decomposition.... Could we not go back to a policy of credit guidance to the clearing banks both in aggregate and sectorally?' He takes the fifties and sixties as relatively successful periods when this method was followed. I rang Denis Healey this morning to ask him to come early to dinner tomorrow to have a talk with Kevin whom he has always appreciated. He said that he would and added, 'That's a first-class letter of his in *The Times*. It's what I have been saying myself.' I told this to Kevin and added, 'Denis's comment is typical of a politician, but now I come to think of it it is what I have been saying myself.' Kevin, always tactful, agreed I had been.

In six of the eight years I was chairman of the National Bank (under six Conservative chancellors) bank lending was restricted by special request of the authorities. Left to themselves the bank chairmen would have followed their competitive instincts. I was always struck by the difference between their point of view and the public interest stand-point of the Bank of England. Since then the banks have been given their heads with unsatisfactory results. But if Kevin had his way would it really be the end of monetarism, or rather a method of making monetarism more effective? It would certainly be a sharper inter-ference with the market economy.

Monday, 3 August 1981

Bernhurst. A big party by our standards last night. Denis Healey, the star guest. Others present: Jack and Frankie Donaldson, Benjie and Evgenia, Kevin, and Judith.

Denis was in uproarious form. He arrived at 6.45 and didn't leave until 11.15, having talked for at least four out of the four and a half hours of the intervening time, which is just what we wanted. The young people, Benjie and Evgenia, were entranced. Judith, who has not been too well lately, visibly cheered up as Denis bellowed on.

His culture is wonderfully wide – no politician of his generation or mine equals it. He is admittedly no Lytton Strachey in appearance: he has been compared before now to an Irish navvy. His grandfather came from Ireland; I don't know what the family were doing pre-viously. Denis by now is very rubicund and weighs perhaps sixteen stone, yet he seems in the best possible health. When he heard that Evgenia's father was Polish he informed us that he knows two sen-tences in every language (he is in fact a good linguist). One is – 'I welcome you on behalf of the Labour Party with every hope of a successful congress'; the other is 'I love you'. Embarrassment follows if one gets the two mixed up, using the first one in bed (a joke). He produced the two sentences in what he assured us was good Polish.

Naturally we pressed him about his prospects for the deputy leader-ship. For our benefit at least he maintained an air of confidence ('He would, wouldn't he?', to quote Mandy Rice-Davies). The TGWU will vote for Silkin initially. When he is eliminated, Denis hopes that they will at the worst abstain. If they go against him, i.e. vote for Benn, and the miners do the same, it will be 'very close'. I tackled him on the awkwardness of his position *if he is elected*. How can he support unilateralism, etc.? He said in effect, though not in these words, that there would be two Labour foreign policies, one parliamentary, the other executive, supported by the Conference. He intoned optimistically about likely developments which would break the control of the Left over the Executive and enable decisions to be reversed next year. I felt that the hope was father to the expectation.

Benjie told me afterwards that he was struck by the contempt shown by Denis whenever the SDP were mentioned. He was asked about Roy Jenkins and dismissed him cheerfully. Six of us heard his remark, but none of us could agree on it afterwards. After he left, Jack, who is very fond of Denis, said that he was more than ever glad that he had joined the SDP. Denis missed his chance last year, now he is fighting hard but belatedly.

The morning papers had been full of the rebellious utterances of Pym and Thorneycroft. Denis felt sure that Margaret Thatcher would not be overthrown. He thinks that when really up against it she will make the necessary adjustments. As the election draws near both parties will 'move towards the centre'. The SDP will be well and truly scuppered.

Many people in the political world would say that at the moment Denis, in spite of his outstanding gifts and experience, occupies a most unenviable position. No one would have guessed it yesterday evening. I am left asking myself, 'Why is Denis not more popular?' He delighted everyone last night, but of course we all gave him his head and played up to him, even those of us like Jack and Frankie who have defected from the Labour Party. Evgenia said delightedly, 'He made himself so vulnerable', which appeared to be a high compliment. But I remember an American journalist saying after Denis's defeat by Michael Foot for the leadership, 'He has kicked too many shins for his own good.' The word 'bully' is used about him every now and then as it was about Dick Crossman and Hugh Dalton. It seems to be applied most often to large men with loud voices. My provocative but valued friend Randolph Churchill once said to me that he had an overwhelming desire to express himself. The same attribute may be a partial explanation why Denis raises so many hackles. An alpha man.

Tuesday, 4 August 1981

Lunch yesterday with the editor of *The Universe*, a striking young woman who says that she is of Lithuanian origin, though you would never think it. I have been doing a certain amount for the *Universe* lately. She wants me to write for them regularly, on Catholic affairs and on some other matters. *The Universe*, sold widely at church doors, cannot afford to offend the bishops, though I am sure that the young editress will be otherwise daring. I did not feel, nor did she, that I would be the right person to do any kind of gossip column. It was agreed that I should do a monthly interview, starting with Cardinal O'Fiaich, whom I am hoping to see this Sunday. I am very happy at the thought of making a small contribution to the Church in this fashion.

Have more or less finished Thucydides' *The Peloponnesian War*, skipping, I am afraid, rather shamefully. How badly the Athenians come out of the whole story! What made war inevitable, says Thucydides, was the growth of Athenian power and the fear which this caused in Sparta. Remembered that my revered H.A.L. Fisher began his *History of Europe* with the sentence, 'We Europeans are the children of Hellas'. I took down his three-volume work and turned to the chapter 'Athens in Sparta'. 'The Athenian empire, the brilliant growth of two generations, shared the fate of every polity which rises by the repression of local liberties. From within it was exposed to the discontents of unwilling subjects, from without to the enmity of jealous rivals.' Yet we who did the Classics at school were brought up to admire Athens without much stress being laid on the evils so well brought out by Thucydides and the Warden. One always hears that Harold Macmillan spends much time reading Thucydides. He will probably himself go down to history as associated with 'the wind of change in Africa' more than any other great act of policy. Is it possible that it was Thucydides who warned him against the perils of holding down subject peoples indefinitely?

Wednesday, 5 August 1981

Elizabeth went off this morning to stay with Harold and Antonia in Ischia. I must somehow survive in her absence. Harold Nicolson and his wife operated what was ultimately a beautiful marriage based quite largely on letter writing. It seemed natural to him to spend Monday to Friday away from his wife. Personally if I am away from Elizabeth for a short while I feel diminished and I have never understood the philosophy of taking a holiday.

Friday, 7 August 1981

I had an hour with Myra this morning. To my selfish relief, she was looking remarkably well. She had heard that the two Price sisters, for whom I think her living tomb was originally constructed, had both been released because of anorexia. She had also heard that they were now studying for degrees. 'Why can't I get anorexia?' she quipped. When I reported the comment to the wing governor and the Governor of the prison, they understood the point perfectly. I had expected this to be rather a marking-time visit while we wait for the Home Office decision in December as to whether she can be considered for parole. But in fact we had the beginnings of a good discussion about remorse, repentance and resentment. She says that she will write to me about resentment and the spiritual problem it presents for her. She was well aware that the world was full of suffering far more intense than her own. We agreed, however, that one's own suffering meant something different from the sufferings, however widespread and appalling, of others. This brought us back inevitably to the question of how a loving God could permit so much agony along with so much love and happiness. I came away feeling better. I hope she did likewise.

Monday, 10 August 1981

Returned from a dash round a large part of Ireland over the weekend. Saturday, lunch in Dublin with Dr Moira Woods, mother of eight, friend of the official IRA, whose detestation for the Provos is unlimited, *femme fatale* of every British–Irish conference. Then down to Tullynally. Sunday, 4 p.m. open-air Mass at Cooloure, the incredibly romantic house by the lake, which Thomas has placed at the disposal of a Catholic youth movement. It brings down children in large numbers from Dublin slums. Two ministers addressed us. One, a young school teacher in her twenties, recently elected to the Dail and at once made an under-secretary, possibly a Shirley Williams of the future. The other, a local member of parliament, chief whip of the Fine Gael Party. He explained the intricacies of the Irish constitution, highly relevant when Fine Gael had such a razor-thin majority.

Next morning Thomas motored me seventy-five miles to lunch with Cardinal O'Fiaich. The Cardinal was as dynamic and jovial as ever; with his powerful head and square body, he reminded me irresistably of Maurice Bowra, though a larger man. I thought I detected some shadows round his eyes which were not there when Thomas and I went and saw him in 1978. It is difficult to say which of us did most of the talking.

We soon got down to the hunger strike. He had no doubt that the day of peaceful settlement has been postponed for the moment. The position of any government in Dublin has been rendered extremely difficult through no possible fault of their own. The 'destabilizing effect' of the hunger strike and the resulting deaths is an unpleasant but incontrovertible fact. In the North the polarization has been palpably augmented. I had not myself realized how hard the Cardinal has been working to bring the Catholics and Protestants together. He has been organizing social gatherings of a mixed character which will for the moment have to be suspended.

During a handsome lunch the Cardinal gave us an entertaining account of his private meeting with Mrs Thatcher at the beginning of July. He had never met anyone so reluctant to concede a point, even for the sake of the argument. He took with him one of his bishops as an ally. For the purposes of the record, his secretary later rang up to discover exactly who was present. He was told the Prime Minister, Mr Atkins, the Cardinal and the Cardinal's 'hatchet man'. We agreed that that particular press secretary might find himself posted far away. I told him that I had forecast when she came to into power that she would not last two years. Her cabinet colleagues would not stand her dictatorial methods for much longer. Wrong!

I had three hours with Cardinal O'Fiaich altogether. His attitude to Thomas as a fellow Irish historian was delightful. Situated in Armagh, like the Protestant Primate, he takes an all-Irish point of view more easily than the politicians in either North or South. I ended up my article for *The Universe:* 'I came away happy to see him in such good health and heart, carrying his heavy burdens so buoyantly. But I would not like to guess at his inner sorrow.'

Tuesday, 11 August 1981

Spent part of the day writing my interview article about the Cardinal for *The Universe*. When I took it round the editor began suggesting subjects for future interviews. It will be amusing to see if any of them materialize: Archbishop Warlock (in connection with the Liverpool riots); Cardinal Hume; Margaret Thatcher; Shirley Williams; Mother Theresa (when in England). Growing more excited, we agreed that I ought to see Reagan and, of course, the Pope. As in our management committees, the longer the discussion continues the more ambitious the targets.

In the evening I gave dinner to Judith at the Garrick, before taking her to the one-man show about Evelyn Waugh at the Arts Theatre. She was in sparkling form at dinner, but quit the one-man show at the interval. If I had not a long-sustained interest in Evelyn, as Bron's godfather and so on, I dare say I should have done likewise. It made him out totally repulsive, which is very untrue to history, though he had an offensive side. The only redeeming feature of his character in the one-man show was his affection for Nancy Mitford, which was certainly true to life, and the self-disgust which is presented quite poignantly. Evelyn in fact had many friends who were devoted to him, though we sometimes encouraged his enormities. All that was missing from the sketch.

Wednesday, 12 August 1981

Was taken round two Richmond Fellowship homes this morning in the preliminary stage of our Mental After-Care Inquiry. The special feature of these homes is the community approach to the therapy. I have no doubt that many people are benefiting while they are in the homes. The problem of their mental health when they leave is one with which the staff are fully familiar.

Went down to Bernhurst to await Elizabeth's arrival in the middle of the night. During my alleged holiday I have enjoyed myself a lot in reading Cicero's *Selected Works*, particularly a practical code of behaviour on duties, and an essay on old age. Cicero's code of moral and political conduct is one which will always command the respect of those interested in public affairs. He makes the assumption that what is beneficial to the community is in accordance with Nature and that it is our obligation to pursue it before all else accordingly. There is no difficulty in relating it to a Christian social philosophy, although it would need much adaptation. He wrote his essay on old age when he was sixty-two (in fact my age when I resigned from the Cabinet and first lectured on the essay). But Cato, the hero of the essay on old age, is presented as a man of eighty-four, so that at seventy-five I come somewhere between the author and his subject.

Perhaps this sentence is the one which I absorb with most alacrity: 'Old age far from being sluggish and feeble is really very lively and perpetually active and still busy with the pursuits of earlier years.' If one reads the essay carefully, one could apply this to one's own condition with suitable qualifications. Some people, according to Cato, never stop learning, however old they are. 'In my later years,' said Cato, 'I have learned to read Greek.' This autumn I mean to learn to appreciate music through GLC courses or otherwise. I am sure that Cato and Cicero would have approved.

Two a.m.: Elizabeth arrives, very belatedly via Naples and Gatwick. I am there to greet her on the doorstep. All human life returns.

Thursday, 20 August 1981

Visited Broadmoor yesterday starting from and returning to Bernhurst, my base for August and September. Was taken down from Waterloo by Willem van der Eyken, the secretary of our Inquiry and the key figure in the Richmond Fellowship. We arrived at Broadmoor at 12.45. I recall a rather plentiful buffet on the last occasion. This time we were asked to content ourselves with a temperance cafeteria. Either the staff are exceptionally abstemious or they make up for their lunchtime restraint in the evening. Dr Udwin, the senior psychiatrist and acting superintendent, and I have by now established a rather peculiar basis of friendship, after one or two stormy passages. He, if anyone, is entitled to say, 'Thank God I've got a sense of humour.' He is viciously attacked by the Press whenever a prisoner escapes, which is seldom, or, what is slightly more common, a prisoner released from Broadmoor commits a serious crime.

Like my son Kevin and my late Uncle Arthur he can always be relied upon to put a heterodox viewpoint. I started on the conventional assumption that many more patients could be released from the mental hospitals, including Broadmoor, if only better facilities were provided for them in the community. Dr Udwin will have none of that. He is amused that the Press regard him as much too eager to release patients. In fact by current standards he is a retentionist. Three-quarters of the patients at Broadmoor are schizophrenics, including the two whom I was seeing later. Dr Udwin views it as positively harmful to suggest they ought to be released more rapidly than at present. For many of them a hospital is the only tolerable answer. He applied his remarks, which were supported by several colleagues present, not just to special hospitals but to mental hospitals generally. I reminded him that in the last twenty-five years the numbers of the mentally ill in hospitals had been more than halved. Did he regard this as a mistake? He said, 'Yes, as regards two-thirds of them.' He was in fact extremely sceptical about the whole idea of community care, however much effort was put into it. All this is good provocative stuff for John Wing and the other members of our committee.

I visited two patients, Ron Kray and John Neish. I had played some small part in bringing Ron and Reg Kray together in Parkhurst, but Ron seems to be better where he is. He told me that since a boy he had suffered from mental trouble. What tragedies might have been averted if he had been treated earlier? He is now much more preoccupied with Reg's situation than his own. Reg in Long Lartin Prison is still in Category A after fourteen years. Ron's concern for his brother is edifying and I am sure that Reg would show a similar attitude.

A pleasant talk with John Neish, who seemed in quite good health this time but even so brought home to me the sheer unpleasantness of schizophrenia. It comes over you like a horrible cloud. John is a gifted poet. I wrote the preface to the last volume of his poems. More significantly, Southern Television recently employed two actors to read his poems for half an hour, paying £300 for the privilege. John is using the money to assist the publication of his next volume. He hopes to move into an ordinary mental hospital in the New Year, with the possibility of release a year or two later. But what kind of life will be open to him then? Richmond Fellowship, please step forward.

Friday, 21 August 1981

Went up to London for the day. Ran into Frank Field, dark-eyed, handsome, clerical-looking – my idea of a model Socialist MP. For years he made the Child Poverty Action Group the most effective of all reforming lobbies. He has written several books on poverty and equality and has always been ready to help me.

He is, to my mild regret, a member of the Tribune group and would describe himself, I suppose, as moderate Left. I fear that he favours unilateral disarmament, like many Labour MPs whom I would sympathize with on social issues. He tells me that at the moment

Benn is likely to be elected deputy leader, though nothing is certain. Frank himself intends to vote for John Silkin; if and when John is eliminated, Frank will abstain. I reproached him mildly for the first course, and more strenuously for his proposed abstentionism – the sin against the Holy Ghost. He agreed that it was an unheroic course, but Denis Healey had 'not been a good deputy leader'. He seemed to take it for granted that Benn would be as bad or worse. Assuming that John *is* eliminated, everything will depend on the way that the TGWU allocate their votes. If they abstain Denis will just about 'make it' – if they vote for Benn, Benn would win. I suspect from my talk with Denis at Bernhurst recently that this is not far from his own analysis. Frank and others are working hard to persuade the TGWU to abstain on the second round. In other words, he would prefer a Healey to a Benn victory if only because Michael Foot would still remain as leader.

He had begun by remarking, 'I have read of the great parties, Liberals for example, tearing themselves to pieces. I never thought till now that it would happen to us.' But whatever the thunder and lightning around him, Frank will go on working to end poverty and promote a more equal society.

Saturday, 22 August 1981

Am pursuing, diffidently, my plan of learning something about music. The purpose is in no way academic, but as the more strenuous physical pursuits become too much for me I feel, increasingly, the need for a new aesthetic enjoyment which will last me as long as I am spared. I hope to take a course this winter in the history of the appreciation of music and to listen regularly to Radio Three. In the meanwhile I have completed *The Language of Music* by Deryck Cooke, and H. C. Colles's *The Growth of Music*. There is much in both books which I am incapable of understanding. I jot down, however, one or two points which are plain enough. Deryck Cooke seems to feel that he is saying something highly controversial in writing: 'The appeal of music is directly to the emotions and should be responded to in this way. The widespread view of music as *purely* music limits the listener's understanding of the great masterpieces to their purely aural beauty – i.e. to their surface attraction – and to their purely technical construction.' Something that Colles says about Schubert gives me my marching orders for the moment. 'It is not necessary for us to submit his flood of beautiful things to close analysis but it is very necessary to take every opportunity of hearing them and knowing them practically.' I can hardly wait.

Monday, 24 August 1981

Visited Glyndebourne this morning with Elizabeth for the Southern Television recording of *A Midsummer Night's Dream*. Martin Jackson, now a big shot in Southern Television, kindly sent us tickets. He did not warn us explicitly, though it was on the back of the programme, that we ought to wear evening dress. We were somewhat conspicuous in our day clothes. This evening dress idea in the morning would have appealed to John Christie, founder of Glyndebourne, most Etonian of eccentrics and most eccentric of Etonians. When he was a master at Eton it was known to the boys that he would only inherit a fortune at the age of thirty if he earned his living first. We realized that he could not be expected to take his teaching duties very seriously. For the first and last time in my life I was top of the class in science, because I was top in school order at the beginning of the Half. He left us at the end of the Half in our initial positions at the beginning of it. Later and perhaps then he had only one eye. He sometimes failed to insert the false one. He was a great friend and cricketing admirer of my housemaster, C.M. Wells. When I looked round at Glyndebourne yesterday, I recognized old John Christie as one of the most creative figures of my lifetime.

With my new-found passion for self-education in music, I was determined to enjoy the opera. Though not a visual person, I could share Elizabeth's enthusiasm for the setting. I took more trouble than ever before to master the intricacies of the plot with the help of the programme, so I did not suffer from that 'lost' feeling which has often afflicted me in opera. And of course the fact that it was Benjamin Britten and thoroughly English made it all a good deal easier. But I can't pretend that I am yet 'into opera'.

Felix Barker, one of the leading dramatic critics of our time, and his most companionable wife Anthea joined us for wine and food by the waterside, in lovely sunshine. Naturally I attempted to pick Felix's brains. He disclaims any right to pronounce on opera, lacking the necessary ear. He has of course seen *Midsummer Night's Dream* many times. (Elizabeth has seen it more than once.) He could not help recognizing that the operatic effects slowed up the action. I suppose you cannot enjoy opera fully unless you love music, and if you do love music the drama and decor will add to the exhilaration. As far as I am concerned, all that still lies in the future.

We discussed at some length the question of whether opera can ever be amusing. The scene where Bottom, wearing an ass's head, seduces Titania got a few laughs. In other circumstances it might have been voted pornographic, but it was all so frivolous that the word would hardly apply. Elizabeth enjoyed the whole experience. I was very glad to have been present.

Wednesday, 26 August 1981

Dinner last night at the Garrick, where William Armstrong and I were hosts to William Clark, who we hope will write a well-documented fantasy about the coming confrontation between North and South. It looks as if a memorable book will eventuate. William Clark in a Theophrastus series would be 'the knowledgeable man'. The Brandt Report was mentioned. It at once emerged that William had initiated the Brandt Committee when deputy chairman of the World Bank. Also that he had persuaded Brandt and colleagues with some difficulty to accept Ted Heath as a member. To start with he did not hit it off with them at all well. But later Brandt fell ill and Ted was invited to become joint acting chairman. His achievement in that role was notable. William has been chosen by *The Observer*'s journalists as one of their two representatives on the new Anderson Rowland Board. He will look after their interests with extreme astuteness and be very amusing about it at the same time.

This morning Willem called for me at 8.30 to take me to the Maudsley, where we were shown the rehabilitation section of the hospital. I must revise my assumption that you can draw a sharp line between the care of the mentally ill in institutions and their after-care in the community. The Maudsley have made a lot of progress in providing what can only be called after-care themselves. One more topic to be sorted out in committee.

Later today came a sudden exciting development in my affairs. Elizabeth had been asked on behalf of the Catholic Church in England to write a popular book about the Pope in time for his visit next year. The publishers would be a combination of Michael Joseph and Rainbird. Elizabeth felt eventually that she was too tied up with her book on the Queen. She suggested that I should propose myself. This I timidly did and was accepted with alacrity. So I have now to write 50,000 words in little more than two months. Rainbird promise assistance with the research, but it is a tall order however looked at.

Friday, 28 August 1981

Lunch, Gay Hussar, for Mary Warnock, a member of our Mental After-Care Committee. Mary is as striking a figure as any woman of her generation. Married to Geoffrey Warnock, the principal of Hertford College, Oxford, he a philosopher – and she a philosopher. Headmistress for some years of the Oxford High School for Girls, a leading member of the Independent Broadcasting Authority. A mass of dark hair, vivacious, good figure, large, heavy, horn-rimmed glasses which suit her well. Her special value to us is her recent chairmanship of a weighty government committee on education of the handicapped, physical and mental. She and John Redcliffe-Maud, chairman of a royal commission on local government, should know all there is to know about the right approach to the local authorities. She is clearly prepared to join in taking evidence, including that from the mentally afflicted.

Three p.m.: visit to the top people at Rainbird's *re* the book on the Pope. Much impressed with their dynamism. Agreed that we must meet Monseigneur Brown, Administrator of Westminster Cathedral, as soon as possible to work out plans. Rainbird's have promised assistance with research, but where is this help going to come from in practice? We agree that an interview with the Pope as soon as possible can be reasonably requested.

Four forty-five p.m.: made a dash down to the Oval to catch sight of the second day of the last Test. Memories, memories. They begin with England's recovery of the Ashes in 1926. But the Oval compared with Lords is to me Cambridge compared with Oxford. Not second-rate but not quite first-rate either. This time the turnstiles were closed and I was treated with scant deference. Then a friend of William Armstrong came out and offered me his ticket. The tone of the local Cerberus changed instantly, 'This way if you please, sir.' But the cricket was unbelievably boring. Tavare recently made the slowest fifty in Test history. But Boycott seemed anxious to outdo him. While I watched, neither made a semblance of a stroke. I left the ground to catch an earlier train than I had intended.

In the ticket office at the Oval Tube Station a burly middle-aged man, perhaps a bricklayer, accosted me. 'How is Myra Hindley?' This question has been put to me with many different shades of meaning. I said she ought to have been set free years ago. He continued rather sadly, 'Will they ever let her out?' I said she has been there sixteen years. He said, 'It's a hell of a long time. Good luck to you in all you are doing.' I wish that Myra could have heard his kindly tone of voice.

Monday, 31 August 1981

Elizabeth's birthday weekend. She was seventy-five yesterday. Her figure is unchanged during the last fifty years. She has only once been plump, when we lived in Stoke-on-Trent and taught for the WEA, stuffing ourselves with huge sandwiches in the intervals. Yesterday she completed, as frequently, forty-eight lengths of our pool. She does it all with the minimum of effort and I with the maximum, which at least gives me additional exercise.

At lunch on Saturday, the guests included Professor Pat Grosskurth, looking about thirty, though she has a daughter of that age, who is writing about Melanie Klein and her bitter struggles with the other school of Freudian psychoanalysis. We agreed that most people, including Pat and myself, benefit from psychiatric treatment at least once in their life. Most, but not all. I can't imagine Elizabeth requiring or accepting it. Also present was Pat's good-looking boy-friend, Bob, and Harford and Robbie Montgomery Hyde. Robbie is as happy as any wife ever was, no psychoanalysis for her. Harford was a Conservative MP from 1950 to 1959, by which date his Ulster constituency found him about as palatable as Bournemouth found Nigel Nicolson. They both were ultra-liberal on hanging and homosexuality. Harford is just about the greatest living expert on Oscar Wilde, whose rooms he inhabited at Magdalen. He and I talked a good deal about Eden, about whom a very disparaging book has appeared in the last few days, amidst a good deal of general acclamation.

My mind goes back to a summer's day at Warwick Castle in 1950 when I, Minister of Civil Aviation, and Anthony Eden, deputy leader of the Opposition, were speaking to a vast Bank Holiday crowd on behalf of the United Nations. We all drank a lot of champagne at lunch, at least I did. I don't know about Anthony Eden. We then repaired to the garden and sat bare-headed under the blazing sun. By the time Anthony Eden came to speak, he was visibly affected. He began, 'I never can forget what I said to the people of Sydney during my tour of Australia', but at that point he collapsed in a faint beside me. He rose indomitably and began again where he left off. 'I never can forget ...' but again he fainted. This time in my arms. But he wasn't done with yet. He rose for the third time, murmuring to me, with the same graceful courtesy, 'Sorry to be such a bore, Frank', and for the third time was beginning to say, 'I never can forget ...' when our host Lord Warwick, Anthony's kinsman, intervened and prevented him from continuing. I shall never forget (my words this time, not his) the sheer guts with which he was determined that the show should go on.

Six years later, when he collapsed at the time of Suez, I was aware that this was a man who would push himself to the point of self-destruction. Incidentally, that same day at Warwick Castle he went off after tea to make a speech elsewhere, was in excellent form at dinner, and left early on Sunday morning to fulfil other speaking engagements. I am sure that vanity was a weakness, accentuated by his phenomenal success as a good-looking young man. But taking his whole life, including the First World War, I am sure that courage was his outstanding attribute.

On Elizabeth's birthday her dear friend Elma Dangerfield, the life and soul of the Byron Society, of which Elizabeth is a kind of mother-heroine, arrived with her lodger. The other guests were equally dear friends, Graham and Dorothy Watson. We were particularly happy also to have Elizabeth's sister Kitty with us, who bears up so bravely under the loss of Donald. He was a very capable editor of the *Sunday Telegraph* and would have made a great headmaster of Winchester, where he taught with much success for some years. Elma almost convinced me that Bacon did write Shakespeare, though she conceded that Shakespeare might have had a hand in the plays. By the end of lunch I was taking almost anything from her as gospel truth, including the statement that Leicester was secretly married to Elizabeth I and that Essex was her son by him. Also that Bacon was Elizabeth's son. But I must really, having sobered down, now go into all this more carefully.

We had asked Graham to lunch with no *arrière pensée*. Margaret however was very anxious that I should discover whether Mary Soames's daughter Emma was right in saying that Mary would like to do a book about her grandmother, but that Graham was not permitting it at the moment. Without creating any vestige of bad blood, I was able to clear up the issue. It seems that Mary was going to be busy for at least a year, but Graham, who retires for the last time, said that there was no reason whatever why we should not try to persuade her to do a book on her grandmother after that.

I also inevitably took advantage of the presence of Graham to tell him of my agreement to write a book about the Pope in a great hurry. I asked him whether I ought to pay his firm the agent's fee, seeing that I have negotiated the offer myself. He was completely dispassionate. He gave the ruling that there would be no need to pay the usual 10 per cent unless I was expecting Curtis Brown to negotiate additional rights.

I remember some years ago being taken to task by one of the most respected members of the Garrick for asking a literary agent to lunch there. 'Surely', I said, 'you would ask Graham Watson?' 'Oh, I would make an exception for Graham', he replied. Nothing of that sort could happen today. The status of literary agents has been much improved. But Graham Watson is still a man apart.

Saturday, 5 September 1981

Joy, joy, joy! Michael telephoned from America to say that the beautiful Mimi has had a daughter. Michael is in ecstasies which he transmitted to us. This makes twenty-two grandchildren in all.

Saturday, 12 September 1981

Returned last night from a flying visit to the TUC Conference at Blackpool. Was and still am considerably depressed, partly due to my having felt 'out of it'. I met no one I knew well and not many I had met previously. The Labour Party Conference in comparison is a gathering of old friends and friendly acquaintances, like the Eton and Harrow match in ancient days. The only member of the House of Lords I encountered was the kindly Hughie Scanlon, former President of the AEU – friend of Antonia's on *Any Questions* and today one of the two or three best speakers in the House of Lords. Talking to this mellow, elderly gentleman, gold-rimmed like myself, with his charming Catholic wife beside him, it is difficult to recall that he was once the dangerous Leftist to whom Harold Wilson, when Prime Minister, had to issue the request, 'Take your tanks off my lawn, Hughie.'

September 1981

Admittedly I found plenty of people to talk to in one way or another. I was by no means left to my own devices. One ex-miner, now a local hotel proprietor, who had evidently dined well, came across the hotel lounge after dinner to salute me. 'I have always admired you for sticking up for yourself under attack. You remind me of Arthur Scargill.' Obviously a high compliment from him. But the fact that I was an outsider may have helped me to form a more dispassionate view than I tend to at Labour Conferences where jolly fraternization produces a somewhat rosy sentiment.

Michael Foot is making a desperate, very belated effort to stop Benn. But what an unattractive battle cry! Terry Lancaster in the *Daily Mirror* points out this week that there is no difference between Foot and Benn on the main policy issues, e.g. unilateralism, withdrawal from the EEC and abolition of the House of Lords, etc. Foot sees himself as fighting heroically for the rights of MPs. But I can imagine no audience becoming emotional on that topic. So a united momentum of argument against Tony Benn is barely feasible. Of course everyone excoriates Thatcherism. Everyone also agrees that anti-Thatcherism is not sufficient.

The event that led to my visit as the correspondent of *The Universe* was the much-heralded debate between Healey, Benn and Silkin, the three candidates for the deputy leadership. It fully came up to expectations. I had a little trouble at the beginning. A steward on duty refused to accept my Transport House Press card as entitling me to sit in the seats reserved for the Press. I subsided into the front row of the ordinary stalls. The same steward continued to guard the Press preserve as though his life depended on it until the burly Eric Heffer, accompanied by his pretty and petite wife, brushed him aside and plonked himself and his wife in the forbidden area. Frank Johnson in *The Times* described the incident vividly. The steward in his account finished by announcing, 'There are two concepts of liberty involved.' As Johnson remarks, he was rather a theoretical steward, and may I add a very happy one next morning to find himself the hero of so much comment.

The meeting was held up for ten minutes by some extraordinary whirring noises variously attributed to the television cameras and the microphones. Everyone was enormously good-tempered demanding to know where all the electricians had got to, but eventually they grew restive and the meeting proceeded, whirring or no whirring. Who won the debate? In decibels Tony Benn hands down. But the audience was

173

so overwhelmingly on his side from the start that it was never a fair contest. John Silkin spoke rather better than I expected, though making some rather blatant claims about his personal merits. I was inclined to regard his intrusion as somewhat irrelevant. But next day two journalists told me on the way back to London that they did not rule out the chance of his being not just deputy leader but leader of the party some day. I don't believe that myself. It gives him some justification, however, for his persistent candidatures.

The audience, or quite a section of it, mostly young, were quite unpleasant to Denis Healey. Robert Carvel, doyen of political commentators, found their attitude the most unattractive feature of the conference. Considering all the denunciations of Benn by Healey, Foot, Shore, Hattersley, etc., at other fringe meetings, it was surprising there was no back-lash from Healey's supporters in reply to the Bennite heckling.

Benn put on a superlative performance. He sedulously refrained from anything that could be called 'personalities'. He remained cold, calm and collected throughout whilst stirring up fire and turmoil. Every answer he gave was perfectly adjusted to the requirements of the majority of the audience.

One recalls that Prince Bülow once said, 'Real politicians are animated by two motives only – love of country and love of power.' I do not doubt that Tony Benn is powerfully stirred by a desire to promote the public good. But I have always (ever since his ultimately successful bid to renounce his peerage) regarded him as quite abnormally ambitious. Admittedly strong ambition is a necessary condition of reaching the top in politics, especially in our democratic age. (Wilson, Callaghan, Heath, Thatcher would never have got to Downing Street without it.) Is this equally true of all professions? I would think that politics being the most competitive demands ambition in its most extreme form. But most politicians of quality and others who succeed in the world are more capable of laughing at themselves than Tony appears to be. Of course he may have a thorough laugh against himself at home but I rather doubt it.

As I return to Bernhurst and try to sort all this out with Elizabeth, I am bound to ask whether our decision to remain in the Labour Party has been in any way shaken. At this moment I would not assert, nor I think would Elizabeth, that we could not conceive of leaving the Labour Party under any circumstances. But I feel, as I think she does, that it would be inglorious, indeed dishonourable to do so after forty-five years in the party and nine years as a minister, without making at least one far more strenuous effort than hitherto within the party for truth and justice. Certainly I have no excuse for not trying persistently to 'get in' at the coming Brighton Conference whatever the humiliation and mortification involved. I do not flatter myself that that in itself will amount to anything, but when the Lords reassemble I must seek out like-minded spirits – who have not yet defected!

Having scribbled the above notes I am conscious that there is one thing lacking. The Labour MP who expresses most adequately my own convictions about equality and poverty (Frank Field) and the undisputed leader in the battle for penal reform (Robert Kilroy-Silk) are both left-wing Tribunites. Speaking generally, the trouble about Healeyites is that a desire for redistribution of wealth in favour of the poor is not conspicuous among them. If the moderates are ever to achieve any momentum of argument, men like Roy Hattersley and Peter Shore must be called upon to provide a radical inspiration sadly lacking at present.

Tuesday, 15 September 1981

Elizabeth and I listened last night to the news of the Cabinet reshuffle – the sacking of three 'wets', the down-grading of Prior, the end for Thorneycroft as chairman of the Tory Party. Is it *Schadenfreude* that makes us enjoy the toppling of prominent persons from their pedestal? In the train from Etchingham this morning there was general amused satisfaction. 'It makes us feel they're no better than we are.' I bought all the morning papers for once. They were fairly predictable. The *Express*, *Mail* and *Sun* delighted, the leftish papers, *Guardian* and *Mirror*, very critical, the *Telegraph* favourable, but not as favourable as I had expected. *The Times* even less enthusiastic.

Poor Jim Prior made an ass of himself, or allowed an ass to be made of him. It may well be that he took the right course in accepting Northern Ireland. But the announcements made on his behalf during the weekend that he would never consent made him appear weak and, as a railway porter said to me, 'He wasn't likely to give up his wage packet.' I am sure that that is an untrue way of looking at it, but he will take a long time to recover his position in the country. I should like to think that he would have a real success in Northern Ireland. But how can one make such a prophecy?

Wednesday, 16 September 1981

Yesterday at 11 a.m. attended the press conference organized by the new Prison Reform Trust, inspired and partly paid for, like many other idealistic projects, by David Astor. David gives me credit for the original suggestion that somehow public opinion towards penal matters must be radically improved. Though invited to the press conference and made welcome, I have definitely not been invited to be a trustee or an executive member of the new body. The idea is that fresh faces and fresh voices should be introduced into the penal scene. The trouble about that is that these novices, however distinguished elsewhere, may take years to learn about prisons and the Trust initially intends to operate for only three years.

The chairman, Sir Monty Finniston, an industrialist of the highest repute, was very much an innocent abroad yesterday. The director, Dr Stephen Shaw, is highly qualified in penal matters; much will obviously depend on him. The star at yesterday's conference was Peter Timms, now a Methodist minister after many years as a prison governor. I have often visited him at Maidstone. He is also a moving spirit in the Christian Prison Fellowship.

I suggested that the churches, collectively speaking, had up till now brought little influence to bear on penal matters, although individual clergy, including bishops and Cardinal Hume, had acted fully in accordance with the words of the gospel, 'I was in prison and you came to me.' The new Trust is bound to do *some* good; whether it can do *much* good remains to be seen. It is at the worst a gallant adventure.

Spent the evening with Ashton Gibson, founder of the Melting Pot. Ashton has started a separate enterprise in quite a different part of London – Hackney – and without any support at all initially has built up quite an impressive affair. He tells me that their annual budget is now £250,000, £160,000 coming from Hackney borough council.

Ashton married a white woman in his youth and has had eight children, those that I have met most charming. He tells me, however, that his marriage broke up some years ago and he now intends to marry a lady in Barbados whom he has known for many years. He asked Elizabeth and me to come to Barbados for the wedding, offering to put us up. I expressed a deep sense of appreciation, but regretted that we could not afford the journey.

I took him to dinner at the Garrick. As we left, we encountered Sir Michael Havers, Attorney-General. I said jokily, 'I'm glad you survived the Government reshuffle.' He said, referring to a recent incident, 'I would rather be employed by Lew Grade than Margaret. You get the sack; you get £500,000 with it.' In a flash Ashton was involved in a discussion with the good-tempered Sir Michael, seeking to obtain legal advice that might be worth thousands of pounds.

Ashton has under his wing a number of young blacks who are being charged with rioting offences. He has found black lawyers reluctant to do more on such occasions, when the young men have been caught red-handed, than put in a plea of guilty and then argue for extenuating circumstances. Ashton is convinced that when the circumstances are extenuating enough, such as unemployment, social deprivation, police harassment, it ought to be possible to present them as 'not guilty'. Havers apparently agreed that Ashton should write to him. I can't believe that Ashton's argument will succeed with him or the courts, and yet there was something noble, to which Havers responded, in the way he leapt into the breach on behalf of his youngsters.

Thursday, 17 September 1981

Very helpful working lunch with my new friends at Rainbird. Elizabeth Blair gave me the sort of editorial guidance that I needed most. Luckily I had drawn up some chapter headings and a rough synopsis. She improved both and gave me some firm guide-lines. The photographer turned out to have taken an art degree in Rome and to be extremely well informed in a rather anarchistic Irish fashion. He described the Pope as a disaster and in another moment as touched by God. I am very lucky to find a photographer so unusually equipped and a shorthand-typist, Carey, who is a university graduate and longing to do research rather than shorthand-typing.

This evening a jolly little meeting to initiate a branch of the WEA in Hurst Green – a far cry from Stoke-on-Trent in 1929–31, when I got engaged to Elizabeth in the station waiting-room, while we were both WEA lecturers. The general desire was to have a class in international relations. I said that this was the only subject which I would not join in – I had too much of it in my ordinary existence. Why could we not have musical appreciation or archaeology, or indeed anything cultural? All very good-tempered, of course. I am very much in favour of this new initiative.

Friday, 18 September 1981

Ten thirty a.m.: received H-Block delegation at the Irish Club. My visitors consisted of five wives or mothers of H-Block protesters, none of them on hunger strike at the moment though any of them might be called on to 'volunteer' at any time. Also one apparently hard-line Republican, possibly ex-H-Block, who had 'buried' one brother-in-law hunger striker, plus two young men – Englishmen as far as I could make out – who were in some way responsible for organizing the visit. Owen Carron, the newly-elected representative for Fermanagh and Tyrone and formerly election agent of Bobby Sands, had come to London with a party of about a hundred relatives including our little party. Altogether I was with them rather more than an hour and have little idea what impression I made on them. I had warned one of the organizers the night before that they would probably be wasting their time in coming to see me. I took the same line as Cardinal O'Fiaich, who had denounced violence repeatedly and kept on calling on the hunger strikers to abandon their task. Nevertheless I was told they wanted to see me and in the end the party was larger than I expected.

On reflection I was a bit too anxious to warn them that they would 'get nothing out of me' even before they had developed their case. The exchanges between myself and the hard-line Republican were quite tense, but my abiding memory is of the sadness and sincerity of the women. I have no doubt that if it were left to them they would wish their relatives to give up their fast, but they are certainly not going to let them down by admitting that to me or anyone else. I was able to point to what I had said in the House of Lords, that there are 'elements of nobility' in anyone who is prepared to die for a cause, even a bad cause. I think that emotionally speaking that provided a link between me and the visitors, but a lot of the time was spent in their denunciation of the British authorities and the treatment of the prisoners in the Maze. I assured them that I was a political opponent of Mrs Thatcher. In my experience after many years of visiting prisons prisoners were never treated as well as they should be in England or in any other country.

The Republican hard-liner was well equipped for a certain line of argument. He pressed me to say whether, if I were Mrs Thatcher, I would agree to the five demands. I told him that I was anxious to say nothing which could possibly encourage the hunger strikers to continue. In other words I avoided the question but finally I dictated an answer which I hope they will repeat faithfully. I was ready for any prison reforms in the North of Ireland, including the abolition of prison clothing which could reasonably be demanded by penal reformers in England. I think that that is another way of saying that I would be ready for some concessions but not necessarily the ones they are asking for. Of course I would be entirely in favour of abolishing prison clothing everywhere else. It has not existed in England for many years in the case of women.

After some heated but still quite amicable exchanges I said to the hard-liner, 'I am just as good an Irishman as you are. I have written two books, or to be accurate one and a half books, which I believe have been of real service to Ireland. What have you done compared with that?' He was not at all impressed by my having written a joint life of De Valera, who he said was an American anyway. In that case, I said, I suppose you would call Patrick Pearse (Commander-in-Chief in the 1916 Rising) an Englishman. He was quite prepared for that also. I said that he counted nobody an Irishman who didn't agree with him. He said, 'Would you kill a British soldier?' I said, 'Of course not. It's lucky I don't know your name or else I might have to ring up Scotland Yard.' He said, 'If there were a war between England and Ireland, which side would you fight on?' By this time most people were laughing. Nevertheless I came away with an enhanced recognition of what Yeats would call their 'terrible sincerity'. Perhaps I should just add that the hard-liner kept repeating that he had buried one brother-in-law and couldn't be expected to weaken or persuade others to weaken. I said, 'Surely if you have buried one brother-in-law that's a good reason for not wanting to bury another?' But that argument fell on stony ground.

Tuesday, 22 September 1981

Visited Derek Worlock at Archbishop's House, Liverpool, for *The Universe* and the book about the Pope. Archbishop Worlock loves Liverpool and Liverpool, or a large part of it, loves him. He and his great friend and ally, the Anglican Bishop Shepherd, are full of sorrow not only about the recent riots, but about the underlying causes immediate and long-term. Certainly there is no city in Britain where the Christian bishops and other religious notables are looked to so eagerly for leadership.

The Archbishop paid earnest tribute to 'the loyalty and faith' of

Christians in Liverpool. But he stressed that they faced 'a great challenge'. There is a great danger that 'what we do and say in church will seem less and less relevant to their actual lives'. It is essential to demonstrate the social message of the gospel 'not just in words but by example in action'.

The unemployment situation has of course become worse and worse and is now abominable. But the social deprivation and, what the Archbishop refers to with considerable passion, the 'alienation' have been long-standing evils. The churches in Liverpool and other agencies are promoting projects of various kinds helpful to employment. But something more profound is needed.

The message that the Archbishop does not tire of proclaiming is the need for reconciliation not retribution. But the alienation existing most obviously among the young blacks goes very deep. The black community have been in Liverpool for two or three generations. They dislike being called an ethnic minority. Yet there are still no black councillors and only a handful of black policemen. When I asked why they have made so little effort to get their own people in, I was told that they shrug their shoulders. 'They don't think it does any good.'

One man could hardly have done more than Archbishop Worlock to promote peace during the riots. Accompanied by his faithful secretary he has been out night after night in the danger zones. He has been criticized outside rather than inside Liverpool for showing undue tenderness to the 'defence committee'. Certainly he has shown practical sympathy towards their humanitarian purposes. But in no way to their hostility towards the police, although he understands all too well the long-standing nature of that hostility.

Thursday, 24 September 1981

To S & J in the morning for the management committee meeting. Then back to Bernhurst for Elizabeth's apotheosis – a whole day with Southern Television who were doing a profile of her. Nine years ago, during my pornography notoriety, the BBC did a programme about me for *Panorama*. A crew of five descended on us. This time there were twenty of them. Over-manning could hardly be carried further.

The charming interviewer with the dark good looks of her Roumanian background told me that Elizabeth was every woman graduate's ideal person. Elizabeth had 'wowed' them for several hours by the time I arrived. Unaccountably I became rather skittish. Television tends to have this effect on me. Elizabeth appeared to have told them that she was a rebel. I thought that 'radical' was a better word. I think that she is too naturally happy a person to have the disgruntlement, the chip on the shoulder, which is almost always discoverable in rebels. Radical she certainly is. She would be on the progressive or humanitarian side in all situations, even when completing a biography of Queen Victoria, the Queen Mother or the Queen.

Friday, 25 September 1981

To London for the day, pushing ahead very hard with the book on the Pope. Down to Maidstone for the evening – two hours with a discussion group in the Rule 43 wing – the prisoners being those who had asked for segregation to avoid maltreatment. Only one of our group of a dozen described his own offences. He had been in prison sixteen times for improper advances to young boys; he admitted a certain immaturity in his personality, but felt that he was growing up. He was now drawn towards boys of sixteen rather than twelve. I felt desperately sorry for him. He was by now over sixty and had convinced himself that he didn't do anybody any harm. I told him that I had once had improper advances made to me, in a non-corridor train in Ireland, and had been scared of such trains for years. I fear that that did not make any impression. He will come out soon. I can only hope that this cursed temptation will gradually evaporate. An enlightened and enlightening evening, though, as always on these occasions, those who probably needed help most were inarticulate.

Tuesday, 29 September 1981

Elizabeth and I spent yesterday at the Labour Party Conference at Brighton. The bashing of Mrs Thatcher and her policies was predictable and understandable, if rather monotonous.

Roy Hattersley won general approval with a speech on race. His strong championship of Denis Healey seemed for the moment forgiven by the Bennites, among whom forgiveness is not a prevailing virtue. Healey himself, opening the economic debate, was treated with reasonable cordiality. Benn, winding up, reminded me more and more of Stafford Cripps (without the glasses). Ice-cold manner, infallible capacity for striking the emotive notes, perfect control of himself and of the effect to be produced. A standing ovation for him was attempted at the end but did not quite come off – too many of us remained seated.

Benn carries the young with him because, apart from his great skill as a rhetorician, he alone seems to hold out *hope*. He entertains a socialist vision (sincerely, I personally feel sure) of the kind that the constituency activists want to believe in. He tells them in effect that given the faith and the will-power it will all be quite easy. (In his speech on Monday he warned them that it would not be so easy after all, but no one took the disclaimer seriously.) Those who have served with him in two governments know all too well that things are not remotely like that. They cannot believe that he is unaware of his own gross over-simplifications. Hence the antagonism among the MPs is directed not only against the policies but against the man.

Lunch with Jon Snow, just back from Angola. He gave me some vivid impressions of his first meeting with the Pope on the way to Mexico – useful for my book. He has always believed that Benn held out the prospect of the kind of socialism that mattered to him. But he confessed himself shocked, since his arrival at Brighton, by the antics and bullying methods of his supporters.

Saturday, 3 October 1981

An unsatisfactory week. From the personal standpoint, certainly; from the public angle probably. Though the outcome is not yet clarified. I tried in vain on Wednesday at the Labour Party Conference to get myself called. But the time devoted to floor speakers was not much more than three-quarters of an hour, and there were champions of multilateralism who had stronger claims than I had (the Labour Party spokesman in the House of Commons, Manny Shinwell, former Defence Minister, Michael Stewart, former Foreign Secretary) and none of us were called. So my personal grievance must be seen in perspective. I came away with the sad feeling that speeches in the House of Lords, however statesmanlike, were not going to have much influence at a Labour Party Conference, with the chairman usually reflecting the emotions of the audience. I say to myself, 'If I am really serious about influencing the Labour Party I must realize that letters to *The Times*, the *Guardian* or left-wing journals are going to have much more effect than speechifying.' There was a certain optimism at the end of the week because the moderates won five seats on the Executive.

Against that all the left-wing resolutions were carried overwhelmingly. It remains to be seen whether these right-wing gains will have brought about any substantial changes by next October. If not, the position of Denis Healey and lesser persons on the right of the party will be horrifyingly endangered.

Denis scraped in as deputy leader this time, which gives him a chance, but a slender one, of reversing the votes at next year's conference.

Next Wednesday I shall set off for Rome. Agnellus Andrew has arranged interviews for me, not, alas, with the Pope; but I shall be meeting Archbishop Deskur, his chief in the communications office at the Vatican. Archbishop Deskur is possibly the Pope's oldest and best friend, but has had an appalling stroke which confines him to a wheelchair.

Wednesday, 7 October 1981

Afternoon aeroplane to Rome.

Dinner with Agnellus Andrew, a spell-binder publicly and privately. When I was writing my book on St Francis, he insisted that I should have a chapter called 'St Francis and contemporary lepers'. I changed it to 'outcasts', but the idea was the same, and it was certainly the best chapter.

Thursday, 8 October 1981

Called on my sister Pansy at her flat a few minutes from the English College. Delighted to find her such a happy woman. She has 'come home'. She told me that she felt Rome to be the centre of the world and, though she didn't say this, I am sure that she finds herself closer to God in Rome than anywhere else. She took me round to St Peter's Square and showed me where she stood the previous day when the Pope gave the first of his renewed weekly audiences, before perhaps 50,000 people. She also showed me the spot from which he was shot. I asked her whether it was true that she had come to live in Rome, and indeed been received into the Catholic Church, out of 'love of the Pope'. She said that that was an exaggerated way of putting it. But it was certainly the election of this particular pope, whom she had never heard of before, who gave her the necessary inspiration. She was amazed at his gift for languages. Pansy, Mary, Violet: the three sisters, each so distinctive and each in my eyes still so young. Julia, if she had lived, would have been one such.

Ten-thirty to eleven-thirty a.m.: interview with Archbishop Deskur at the Vatican. Amusing to note that Peter Hebblethwaite, reviewing a book by Dr Huntston Williams, writes: 'It is astonishing to read that Archbishop Deskur "reigns over 300 journalists" in the Vatican Press Office. He has not been seen in Rome since the pontificate began. He is convalescing in Switzerland.' Archbishop Deskur, as already mentioned, had a very bad stroke at almost the same moment that the Pope was elected. Immediately on election, the Pope called on him in the hospital, which scandalized his advisers. 'You're a Pope now, and you can't do that sort of thing!' The Pope replied, 'If I can't do it as Pope, I'll do it as Karol Wojtyla in a black cassock.' So they had to give way. The Archbishop is head of the communications office. Agnellus Andrew, who made my appointment, is his number two. He began by making two apologies: (1) for his English, which is in fact excellent, though he speaks slowly perhaps because of his stroke; (2) for his memory which is nothing like it was. This is accepted generally. But for my purposes he was able to answer the questions I put to him better perhaps than anyone else alive.

He first met the Pope in 1943 when they came together in the secret seminary in Bishop Sapieha's palace. They had become more and more intimate. In later years the Pope stayed with him many times in Rome. I jotted down fourteen answers to questions I put to him. In almost every case he threw new light on the Pope's life or character. I will record here a few points which struck me most forcibly.

Archbishop Deskur repeated again and again the Pope's detestation of Marxism. Not just atheism, but Marxism. The Pope, ever since he has known him, has been emotionally involved with the workers following his life in the quarry and the factory. But in the Pope's eyes Marxism is the worst enemy of the workers. It would destroy their freedom utterly. The Archbishop stressed the Pope's contribution to the crucial Council documents: *Lumen Gentium* and *Gaudium et Spes*. The Archbishop had been his theological adviser for five years at the Council.

How come, I asked, that Karol Wojtyla, who was still only an auxiliary bishop, should be given the opportunity to play such a decisive part? He told me that the answer to that was simple. The present Pope was Paul VI's 'great discovery'.

In this connection he emphasized the significance of Paul VI's inviting him to give the Lenten addresses which later became *The Sign of Contradiction*. He wanted not to test him out, but to exhibit his prowess before some of the cardinals, who would fairly soon be called to choose Paul's successor.

I asked him what influence the Pope had had in producing the present situation in Poland. Enormous influence, replied the Archbishop. Everyone had told me already that the uprising of the Polish workers could not have taken place without the Pope's visit, and the boost to morale that he gave them. The Archbishop added that his speeches, carefully studied, laid down the course of action that Solidarity had followed. Solidarity have now written to the Pope to ask his permission to incorporate his latest encyclical in their programme.

I asked him whether he could put into words the Polishness of the Pope. He said that Poles were natural poets and certainly the Pope must have written far more poetry than any previous pope. But he added that what he called the 'cordiality to individuals' is extremely Polish. The Pope always tried to persuade anyone who came to see him to stop to lunch or supper. Last year the Pope decided that in the Year of the Disabled he must do his bit, so he asked his disabled friend Deskur to lunch every Sunday. I agreed with the Archbishop that that seemed very Polish. A Pole, so he said, would never welcome anyone without giving him something. He produced coffee for me and Polish cakes. At 11.30 in the morning I had no appetite for them but chose the smallest. He offered me a present which I felt was too large to take away. Looking back it would have been more gracious to accept it.

He had much to say along well-known lines about the Pope's attitude to women, artificial birth control and other matters of public controversy. I will only add here that in reply to my question, Is the Pope a mystic? he stated confidently, Yes indeed. He was aware that in England the Pope was regarded as a conservative theologian. He asked me to make the point that St John of the Cross on whom the Pope wrote his first thesis, and also St Theresa of Avila to whom he was devoted, were *liberal* mystics and on that account in conflict with the official teachings of the time. I have never learnt more from anyone in a single hour about a subject I was deeply involved in.

Saturday, 10 October 1981

A hard morning, translating the Rome adventure into the book on the Pope. The speed at which that operation has to be conducted wakes me up a bit early in the morning, but does not appear to be doing any permanent damage.

I spent the evening and night with our own bishop, Cormac Murphy O'Connor, who was head of the English College for six years in Rome. Talking to him and Agnellus had helped me a lot in getting the right atmosphere, though neither gave me the inside stuff that could only come from somebody like Deskur who had known the Pope from the beginning.

Cormac is going to look into the question of an interview with the Pope. If it had not been for the 'incident' (the attempted assassination) there would have been no great difficulty.

Tuesday, 13 October 1981

Spent two hours with Elizabeth watching the first instalment of *Brideshead* on television. General applause in the Press this morning, well deserved, though I wouldn't wish to spend two hours watching anything on television many nights in the year. Evelyn Waugh had a marvellous grasp of stylized dialogue, here exemplified in the army and the Oxford aesthetes. He was less happy here and in his novels in portraying society dialogue. It has always been so unstylized that no one can hit it off perfectly.

The film has already produced an argument as to whether the relationship between the hero and Sebastian was homosexual. The homosexual implications are certainly much more obvious in the film than they were in the book, but no one will ever be able to put this correctly. In the Oxford of that period there was a lot of actual homosexualism and a lot of pretended homosexualism, as in the OUDS 'Smokers' (smoking concerts) for example.

> I'm just a jumper-boy
> A high-necked jumper-boy
> My mother's only joy.
> I swear it's true and
> When I do my tricks,
> With Joy or Helen Trix,
> I'm in an awful fix,
> Because I only know the way
> To jump a boy.

I will strenuously deny that in his maturity Evelyn had any homosexual leanings. It has been stated, more or less authoritatively, that he had a homosexual period at Oxford before I knew him. He brought a friend to stay at Tullynally, when I was engaged, who may have been the original of Sebastian. Later Evelyn had seven children. But I know that this is not a complete defence. When I, with others, started the New Bridge for ex-prisoners it was said that the Home Office treated us as a gang of homosexuals out to help fellow-homosexuals. When I pointed out in reply that I had eight children I was told that the answer was, 'Oh! that's just cover!'

That apart, I hope that Evelyn would have liked the film. It's obviously going to be an enormous success.

Wednesday, 14 October 1981

Impossible not to refer, however briefly, to the extraordinary political situation. Even the *Telegraph* admits that the shadow of Heath hangs over the Conservative Conference. If Ted has been watching the Churchill programme (*The Wilderness Years*), he must detect resemblances between his position and that of Winston.

However, when I said to William Rees-Mogg at the Garrick yesterday, 'Are you going to the Conservative Conference at Blackpool?' he replied, 'Too much organized hypocrisy and disloyalty for me.' I said, 'You will at least agree that Ted ought to be given a fair hearing?' He said, 'I like Ted'; but went on to imply that he allowed his personal feelings to become too evident. I said, 'That's what people said about Churchill before the war.' William said, 'Ted isn't Churchill.' I commented, 'He's not likely to get the same opportunity.' William finished the conversation by remarking blandly, 'No, and he's not so bright.'

I look forward with unusual eagerness to Ted's speech at the Conference today. He is a big man with a petty side. He will have prepared his four-minute speech meticulously. A real test of nerve and temper.

Thursday, 15 October 1981

I broke off yesterday eagerly awaiting Ted Heath's intervention. I can't see how he could have done any better. Elizabeth always says that he is better as a comic than statesmanlike speaker. His initial joke was excellent, when he said, 'I hope that no one will applaud – it might irritate his neighbour.' I watched Margaret Thatcher carefully.

She obviously thought this was her idea of Conservative wit, and applauded genuinely. He is said to have been out-voted by the Conference, but that of course is as absurd as saying that Brynmor John would have been out-voted at the Labour Conference on multilateral disarmament, if he had been allowed to speak. Ted did well, but as at the Labour Conference everyone thought that they had come out on top.

Friday, 16 October 1981

Lunched in the City, taking the chair for the National Bank Pensioners, including my dear friend Peggy Fitzgerald and many other old comrades. It is undeniable that I am always happy in resuming contact with the National Bank staff; possibly this is a form of senile vanity, but there was undeniably in those days an extraordinary spirit of devotion to our common purpose and therefore of friendship, which has been well maintained in the years between.

Went with Elizabeth to the first afternoon of *The French Lieutenant's Woman*, the novel by John Fowles, the screenplay by Harold. I had been fascinated by the novel and, with one qualification, felt that Harold dramatized it superbly. I had been irritated when reading the book by the author's tiresome commentary. Harold had tried to overcome this difficulty by introducing a sub-plot. But I could not feel that this expedient worked out well and the critics have not been kind to it. Fowles, however, who ought to know, has written a glowing tribute to Harold's adaptation of his story, one true artist saluting another.

Thursday, 22 October 1981

Attended large meeting of peers and MPs to hear American Defence Secretary Caspar Weinberger on nuclear defence. He looked like a rather smaller, thinner, somewhat more worried version of Reagan. In round terms he indicated that at this moment the Soviet forces and those of the West were roughly in balance, but that the Russians had taken decisions in the last few years which would make them much stronger than the West, unless we accelerated, which indeed was what we were doing. He made one rather successful joke. He said he understood that there would be 250,000 people protesting in Hyde Park on Sunday. By a curious chance after every CND meeting throughout the world it was always announced that 250,000 people had been present. He supposed they were the same 250,000, moving round quite rapidly.

Friday, 23 October 1981

A frantic rush to get 'The Pope' ready – Liz and Carey pulling me along, delightfully but remorselessly. Quite late in the day I was asked to obtain a number of opinions from prominent Catholics; I shan't receive Shirley Williams's contribution for a week or so. Elizabeth has turned in a thousand words, instead of the three to four hundred suggested, on the historical aspects of the Pope's visit. We are all thrilled with them. Condensed beauty, as Uncle Eddie used to say. She can indeed claim St Thomas More, the subject of her piece, as her favourite saint. Margaret Thatcher says the same of St Francis of Assisi. I won't press the comparison further. Miles Norfolk has written about the corruptness of the Catholic Church before the Reformation. It comes well from him as head of the Catholic laity, but perhaps from him only.

The Croydon by-election result was almost exactly what Elizabeth forecast yesterday, victory for the Alliance. Therefore I have no startling reaction this morning. There is a consensus, a bit overdone in my eyes, that this is not such a bad result for the Tories, but a profound humiliation for the Labour Party. I admit to Elizabeth privately that if anything could warn the Labour Party of the perils that attend their headlong movement towards the Left, this might be it. But we read today that a Labour MP is not to be re-selected. His place is taken by a leading member of the Militant Tendency, so that there are no signs that the warning is sinking in. Of course we pin a few hopes to the improvement in the Executive, but if I were a Labour MP I would be full of alarm and despondency.

Monday, 26 October 1981

William had asked me to join him in giving lunch to Ardiles, the famous Argentinian World Cup footballer, now playing for Spurs, described on occasion as the best footballer in this country. I keep an eye on soccer, but read the news rather more carefully this time. William's hero is Liam Brady of Arsenal, who is also a great midfield player but is now playing in Italy. I was anxious to discover from Ardiles how he felt his game compared with Brady's and how much defence figured in the make-up of the perfect mid-field player. However, Ardiles could not arrive in time, so the lunch was cancelled.

I repaired to the Garrick, seated myself at the top table and soon found myself engaged in further discussions about nuclear disarmament with Gladwyn Jebb and Charles Wintour, editor for many years of the *Evening Standard*. I found them both surprisingly soft. I may have misunderstood them, but Gladwyn seemed to be saying that we should never use nuclear weapons first, that it would be better to be overrun by the Russians. There is no doubt that Reagan has given nuclear disarmers plenty of ammunition and that there is a lot of so-called concern, though much of it is no doubt manufactured. I still think that the young men whom I taught at Oxford in the thirties were facing a much more dangerous future than the present generation. But I am bound to ask myself whether I am becoming a little too provocative on this subject. The Pope, I learn, holds his positions with absolute firmness, but is a great practitioner of dialogue. This presumably means not only listening to what other people say but appearing to take them seriously. I must try to learn from the Pope. If Weinberger is right, as I believe he is, we should be in a pitiful position a few years from now, unless Western armaments were rapidly increased. There is going to be 'the hell of an argument'.

Wednesday, 28 October 1981

Television performance with Anne McHardy about our book *Ulster* which was published last Thursday. Anne is full of charm in what I call a Welsh way. She is very reluctant, however, to appear on television or even be photographed. On this occasion she spoke out well and confidently and was considered most photogenic. Val [Pakenham] had done a lot of research for my part of the book. She will write a fine book herself when she is convinced that she can.

Handed in my 50,000 words to Rainbird three days before schedule, though there was a little cleaning up to be done on the last chapter. The whole thing would have been quite impossible without the superlative assistance of Elizabeth [Blair] and Carey [Smith]. Of the contributions I received a young woman training to be a teacher at Strawberry Hill made the most arresting comment. She praised the Pope highly as might be expected and added, 'Even when I disagree with him, as over contraception, I feel that he is prepared to dialogue with me.'

Thursday, 29 October 1981

S & J sales conference. A general spirit of optimism. Our 'reps' take round the books of Virago, the feminist publishers. Two striking female personalities, Carmen Callil and Ursula Owen, represented them at lunch. I seem unable to avoid involving myself in arguments about unilateral disarmament. Sure enough, I was soon at it hammer and tongs with them. But I found myself utterly enjoying their company and they didn't seem to object to mine.

I was visited later at the Lords by Ruth Dudley Edwards, author of a superlative life of Patrick Pearse. She is now deep into a biography of Victor Gollancz. When she read his books she thought he was a saint. When she read his correspondence she thought the opposite. Now she has settled down into a middle position, recognizing that there were plenty of warts on him, but much to admire and love. She knew from my book *Five Lives* that I considered that he had had a far-reaching influence on me, particularly in connection with Germany during the great hunger. We agreed that he had an extraordinary power of making one feel an unprofitable servant and pushing one on towards ever higher ideals. For many years my own private motto has been, 'Hate the sin and love the sinner.' Victor at his best gave you a unique expression to those words in action. But sometimes he went a bit too far, even for me, when for example he announced during the war, 'I adore Hitler.' Those who knew him best knew best how to take that sort of extravagance.

We were joined over drinks by Elizabeth and Alec Home. She had been interviewing him for her book on the Queen. Unlike other recent prime ministers, he was a long-time friend of the royal family and probably understood the Queen better therefore than the others, though they have vied with one another in praising her qualities. Alec told Elizabeth one thing that did surprise me. He said that no future prime minister should be expected to go through what he went through when he took over. The Whips had played a crucial part in his selection but were afterwards accused very unfairly of misrepresenting the views of the MPs whom they had consulted. Alec Home was sure that the Queen had played no part whatever in the choice of himself. When Elizabeth sees Rab Butler she may discover whether Rab still cherishes the belief attributed to him that influences near the throne played some part in securing the appointment of a friend of their family. Be that as it may, there is no denying that Macmillan did what he could to keep Rab out. At least everyone makes that assumption.

Then on to an S & J party for Elizabeth and me in honour of our golden wedding. We were presented with 150 daffodil bulbs which showed a touching appreciation of Elizabeth's life as a gardener. William, Margaret and Vikki have seen the gardens she created at Bernhurst from the post-war mess of concrete and barbed wire. We were both touched by the manifest feeling of affection shown us by the young people who had subscribed to the present. But it was the incomparable Gwen who alone could recite Wordsworth's poem about the daffodils, which she did quite beautifully to the admiration of all. In my few remarks I said that in a fairly varied existence I had never met such a happy atmosphere.

Saturday, 31 October 1981

To Durham yesterday morning. I spent the last half of the journey in animated talk with two young women; one working on contracts in Penguins, the other till recently a key person in *Time Out*, now working for the breakaway *City Limits*. They were not dissimilar, though younger, to the Virago leaders that I had met on Wednesday. We discussed them cordially. The *City Limits* young woman gave me an absorbing account of the struggle in *Time Out* that led to a sit-in by the staff and their eventual secession. She assured me that the idea of all being paid the same had really worked in *Time Out* and was now being applied successfully in the new paper. I told her that I had tried it when we began New Horizon but found human nature too strong for us. Bernard Shaw was the only socialist who had seriously advocated complete equality of income, and he certainly hadn't practised it himself. I admired their dream. She knew Ken Livingstone quite well and said that his integrity was recognized by all who had much to do with him. She herself was a convinced Marxist though she had no use for the Militants. Contrary to what I have heard, she told me that Ken was not interested in Marx.

Both ladies talked admiringly of E.P. Thompson of anti-nuclear fame. I told her that my Virago friends also admired him strongly and looked down on me for not having read his history of the British working classes. My companions admitted, however, that he had a flaw. What could this be? It was explained to me that his book, *The Poverty of Theory*, had thrown him into conflict with a number of Marxist theoreticians and he had not appeared to advantage in the resulting controversy.

They were going for the day to Durham for the wedding of the brother of the journalist on *City Limits*. He had been living with a lady for ten years, whom he was now marrying. He was an engineer, but unemployed without hope of work in Newcastle. For some reason which I did not quite understand, it was more profitable to marry. The picture of the employment situation in Newcastle that they gave me was quite appalling. Of course, the new Minister for Employment might urge him to 'get on his bike', but to someone who had always lived in that part of the world that would seem a rather grim jest.

The 'official' purpose of my visit was to act as chairman of the judges in the University Debating Championship (Northern Region, including Scotland). But first a look round Durham Prison and an hour with Myra. In Durham Prison (all men except for the ineffable women's block) working hours average sixteen a week and there is no 'association' at all. I was told that this is typical of local prisons. The work situation is not likely to improve and may even get worse while we have three million unemployed. The lack of association is attributed to staff shortage, though Durham is hardly, if at all, over-crowded and has its full complement of staff. By this time I would have hoped to have initiated a sharp debate about prisons in the Lords if it had not been for 'The Pope'. I really must get on with it now.

Myra looked well, as she did last time. I told her so, but she repeated that she 'can't help it'. If only she could get anorexia! She is doubly keyed up. She is waiting anxiously for the December decision on whether she can be at last considered for parole, and an exam on Monday which should complete the first part of her honours course. Her essays for the latter purpose which count towards the degree have been so highly marked that though a natural pessimist she is optimistic about the result on Monday. All the same, she is working late at night until she falls asleep over her books. I gave her Elizabeth's *Nine Victorian Women*, very much her kind of book, I feel sure. I wonder which of the nine she identifies with. The whole lot perhaps. I identify her more easily with *The French Lieutenant's Woman*. She gave me an entertaining account of the visit of John Harris, the chairman of the Parole Board, and half a dozen of his colleagues. They saw a number of the women prisoners in a group for about three-quarters of an hour. They are apparently aware that they are criticized for not meeting prisoners. They are much mistaken if they think that this kind of hasty exercise will lessen the criticism.

Myra, 'remembering to smile' she assured me, had asked John Harris whether parole was refused to so-called notorious prisoners if it was thought that public opinion would be adverse to granting it. Harris was cagey. I can just see him, making those nervous gestures, so reminiscent of Roy Jenkins with his clever brain working overtime. He replied, 'Some account would have to be taken of public feeling.' 'Why?' asked Myra. 'Because,' he said, 'nothing must be done to discredit the Parole Board.' 'Ah,' said Myra, 'I see, jobs are at stake. But would you not call that a political decison?' He hummed and hawed and admitted that such a case might have to go the Cabinet. 'Would that not involve a political decision?' she pressed him. 'You might call it that,' he conceded. 'Jobs at stake,' she repeated. One can only hope that these tart comments have not retarded her parole, but after sixteen years in prison, when at last someone deciding her destiny appeared on the scene, one can understand the release of her pent-up feelings. I was glad to hear that the reports being put in about her were more favourable than ever. Now it is up to Willie Whitelaw. He is a decent man and I rely on him to do the decent thing.

A discussion with Myra about prison life led me to discover for the first time that it is a prison offence which can be punished quite severely for women prisoners to kiss or embrace one another. I am much shocked and will in due course explore this additional inhumanity. I can't believe that the women's organizations would regard this as acceptable. Since then I have asked a priest whether nuns were allowed to kiss each other, bearing in mind warnings against particular friendships. He said smilingly, 'Perhaps in public, not in private.' Perhaps the whole area is one which no one in authority likes to discuss.

Dinner at Durham University with the students was as enjoyable as always and the debating level well up to standard. I was presented with life membership of the Durham Union. I accepted gratefully, but warned them that they might have me on their hands for longer than they supposed. The House of Lords was a great preservative. Philip Noel-Baker, ninety-two, Fenner Brockway, ninety-three, and Shinwell, ninety-seven, were all going strong. They seemed prepared to take the risk.

The best of the twelve finalists was a young woman who comes from a Glasgow family of nine, but was representing Edinburgh. She was far more successful than the others in relating her speech to what had gone before and involving the audience in the argument. She made a mild joke at my expense. When I came to sum up I picked her out for special praise and said that in time I felt that she would become another Margaret Thatcher. I could see that she didn't like the remark and went up to apologize to her afterwards.

She replied, 'I had a crack at you, you got your own back. Fair enough.' I told her that she had a real talent for debating and hoped she would go one day into Parliament. She replied that the Westminster Parliament was far too much a branch of the public school establishment for her to want to join it. Small, quick and resolute, I am sure that she will go far, but hope that her life will not work out quite as she plans it at the moment.

Monday, 2 November 1981

A varied day, starting up from Bernhurst. Called in at the office to meet a young woman whose fiancé is being prosecuted, with two other men, for robbing and killing a jeweller. A horrible crime, whoever committed it. She swears, with obvious sincerity, that he was with her at the time. No one could be more convinced than she is about anyone's innocence. I could do little to help her, but possibly talking to me made her feel somewhat better.

Twelve o'clock: funeral of Richard Llewelyn-Davies at Golders Green crematorium. *The Times* paid ample tribute to his achievement as architect and professor of architecture. It did not mention his boyhood in Dublin, where I used to stay with his mother. When I was writing my book on the 1922 Treaty she, who had known Michael Collins so intimately, gave me much help. But she later wished to withdraw some of the things that he had said to her, magnificent sayings like, 'There will be no more unattended funerals'; 'No more lonely scaffolds for our men'. Luckily, the book had already gone to press. Elizabeth and I were tremendously fond of her. She was equally intimate with Irish Nationalists of one kind or another and the world of Cambridge 'Apostles', Bloomsbury, etc., through her husband. Richard, though privately educated, was soon elected an Apostle when he went to Cambridge, and in politics was far to the Left in those days, like so many of his most brilliant contemporaries.

Richard and Pat have always, I suppose, been humanists. In the circumstances, the service was a moving blend. Donald Soper was at his most ingenious, though altogether genuine, in discovering a likeness between Richard as Professor of Urban Planning and St Augustine, author of *The City of God*. Tessa Rothschild followed with three poems, ending with Heraclitus and then saying, 'Goodbye, dear, dear Richard' in the direction of the coffin, which seemed completely appropriate. We then had some classical music and sang Blake's 'Jerusalem'. Pat said to me afterwards, 'I hope you didn't find the whole thing too unorthodox.' All things considered, it could not have been improved on.

Pat's wonderful buoyancy prevented the company being too downcast. I may be wrong, but I detected a kind of wistful hopefulness in the non-Christian audience.

Two-thirty: visit to Ian Brady. A few days ago I received the report of his psychiatrist, for which I had pressed so hard. It is a very well-considered document based on two years' interviewing of Ian and showing itself favourable to his going to a special hospital, presumably Broadmoor. This, of course, is what the Home Office favoured ten years ago but were tripped up by Keith Joseph, then Minister of Health. But this time I have a document in my hands, as has Ian's solicitor, which gives us much better ammunition. Ian showed no special excitement over the news. But that is his way. He leaves me in no doubt that he does like me to visit him, which is all the encouragement I need.

Wednesday, 4 November 1981

Yesterday was our day of golden wedding celebrations. Five p.m. photograph at Patrick Lichfield's studio; six o'clock cocktail party at Antonia's; 8.30 dinner at Rachel's. The first was attended by forty of us: Elizabeth and myself, fourteen children or spouses, twenty-two grandchildren, Flora's husband, Robert, and Mimi's daughter, Lindsay. The second by the same group plus another fifty guests. The third by Elizabeth and myself and the fourteen children or spouses.

The Lichfield photograph was reprinted in *The Times* with an accompanying commentary by Philip Howard. Philip writes frequently about the proper use of words and is well qualified for that purpose. '. . . In the middle sits Elizabeth, the calm centre of the family hubbub, and the sweetest singer in that nest of singing birds. Behind her stands Frank: brilliant and perverse, brave and foolish, crusader and polemicist, as usual agreeably shaggy, as always lovable, improbable patriarch of a dynasty of eagles. He needs an *apologia pro vita sua* less than most of our generation, though he will keep on writing them. His monuments stand and sit all round him.' Coming from Philip those words are very gratifying. But what I really feel about the whole event was said to Elizabeth as we drove home. She said, 'This is the happiest day of my life since our wedding. Don't you feel the same?' I said, 'This is *your* achievement but what makes you proud and happy makes me proud and happy too.'

Lichfield was far removed from the old-fashioned idea of a male photographer. No cissy he. He had noticeably broad shoulders and wove his way towards us like a boxer protecting his chin. Antonia told me that to avoid being bullied in the Navy he took up the noble art and won at least one championship. His shock of hair and lined face completed an impressive image. He got on with the job at an admirable pace. It was all done in twenty minutes. I asked him whether this was the largest group he had photographed. He said, 'No, there were fifty-seven in the Royal Wedding picture.' I said, 'I suppose it was easier not having to cope with so many small children.' (One of our little ones punched baby Alexandra in the face and made her cry.) He said it was harder dealing with royal persons. One could not order them about so readily.

Antonia's party would have been joyous without the bountiful champagne. Michael and Mimi had come over especially from America partly for the occasion, partly to parade Alexandra with infinite pride – justified. Alexandra was to be christened the next day. They gave us a reproduction of *The Times* report of our wedding (3 November 1931) with a list of those present on that occasion. Elizabeth's brothers John and Michael and her sister Kitty, my sisters Mary and Violet (Pansy being in Rome) were with us again this time. There were only three other survivors. Maureen Dufferin, bloody but unbowed and still full of fun after her ghastly court struggle with her butler, David Astor and Esmond Warner. I made a short speech which, to drop into publishers' jargon, was widely acclaimed. In the circumstances it would have been difficult not to be applauded, but I suppose I make this kind of speech better than any other kind, after early training at Lord Birkenhead's knee at Charlton.

I can't resist putting down on paper one or two successful remarks. 'A famous prime minister once said, at any rate Harold Wilson once said, "A week is a long time in politics." Fifty years has seemed a long time in marriage to me. It must have seemed an eternity to Elizabeth. ... Not long ago I went to a wedding in Yorkshire where the best man addressed the host in this way: "Eric, you are going in to bat on a sticky wicket, don't try to score all the runs on the first night. Remember you've got a partner who is a better stroke player than you are. Think of yourself as Boycott and her as Botham."' I added that I had always followed that advice. Finally I recalled the occasion when President Kennedy went to see his father, terribly afflicted with a stroke, confined to a wheelchair and unable to speak. Jack Kennedy, as he went away, remarked to his companion, 'He has made all this – the presidency, everything – possible, and look at him now.' I asked them to apply those words to Elizabeth who was looking radiant: 'She has made all this possible, and look at her now.'

Alan Taylor was there with his wife. She urged me to invite Alan to speak. After all, he was my oldest friend. I said that Esmond Warner had been in my house at Eton which was hardly true of Alan. Well then, she said, your second oldest friend. Not true, as it happens, but I was much flattered that she and Alan would like to think it was. So Alan spoke and Harold [Pinter] replied, both appropriately. Alan boasted that he and I had both 'made it' – 'it' being fifty years of marriage. He admitted that in his case there had been marriage, divorce, re-marriage, divorce, re-marriage – the rest of the recital was drowned in laughter.

Elizabeth cut the cake and reserved her speech for dinner, where she proved herself, in Philip Howard's words, 'the sweetest singer'. I went to sleep in a haze of gratitude – to God, to the family generally, and, above all, Elizabeth.

Tuesday, 10 November 1981

At 6 p.m. I presented myself at the Speaker's House for a party connected with the disabled. George Thomas, the Speaker, is by common consent the most popular Speaker of all time. He is the first Speaker whose musical Welsh voice has been heard day after day on the radio. 'Order! Order!' will always be associated with George. I reminded him of his treatment of Jack Profumo. Jack, after many years working for Toynbee Hall, still did not feel himself worthy to re-enter the Palace of Westminster. On one occasion it was unavoidable, because of a meeting suddenly arranged there. Jack rang George Thomas's office to ask if the Speaker had any objection to his making this one visit. George not only had no objection, but when Jack arrived was there to welcome him with open arms which, in his case, would mean an embrace. George was obviously not displeased by my recital. But just as obviously he regarded the step he had taken as so natural as to be hardly worth mentioning.

Michael Foot arrived. He is attracting a lot of flak just now. But where the disabled are concerned he is beyond criticism. He has been much abused because of his dishevelled appearance at the Cenotaph on Sunday. I have run into the same sort of comments myself and I said to Michael, 'I am proud to belong to a party whose leader is as badly dressed as I am.' After his usual slight hesitation, his humour took over and he replied, 'That's the most severe criticism I have had yet.' Snowdon, who has done as much for the disabled as anyone known to me, was naturally present. I said to him: 'Your rival Lichfield photographed forty of us last week and told me that he had photographed fifty-seven members of the Royal Family at the time of the Prince of Wales's wedding.' Did Snowdon take any panoramic photographs of this kind? He said definitely, 'No!' He liked to do one or at the most two people. Not long ago he took a photograph of Antonia and a writer friend of hers, whose name had escaped his memory. They were seated in a restaurant, each of them at a different table, each waiting, it would seem, for a companion, not associated with each other. It sounded quite weird to me. But I don't doubt that it aroused much interest and speculation. I told him that Lichfield looked like a boxer. Tony, as I more or less call him, said in a dead-pan voice, 'Yes, I believe he boxed at Harrow.' Old Etonians like Tony and, I suppose, myself, have a special way of pronouncing the name of that school.

The leader of the official Ulster Unionists, Jim Molyneux, was there. I said that I hoped he didn't mind shaking hands with me. He was very civil, as he always is in that super-quiet Northern Ireland way (emotion comes out at other moments). Gerry Fitt hove to and soon the two Northern Irishmen of contradictory parties were absorbed in local gossip. There was a lot of talk about Frank Maguire, till his death the independent MP for Fermanagh–Tyrone, who hardly ever came to Westminster. On one occasion, however, Fitt, Molyneux, Paisley and Maguire were all going back to Northern Ireland together. Paisley was drinking orange juice. Maguire said to Paisley, 'Be a man,

Paisley. Have a drink.' Paisley said, 'Yes, I'll have a drink; I'll have a bitter lemon.' Maguire wasn't satisfied. 'I don't call that being a man, Paisley. You're supposed to be such a tough guy. Don't be afraid to mix your drinks.'

Wednesday, 11 November 1981

A mixed bag of news about 'The Pope'. Liz Blair rang up to say that Michael Joseph were not at all satisfied with the present form of the Epilogue. I had collected nine contributions from English Catholics thinking that was what they wanted. But no. They needed a potted history of English Catholics since the Reformation. And quickly! Luckily Elizabeth's piece on Thomas More is much admired. Miles Norfolk's is also just right. But what on earth am I to say to the other seven contributors who so nobly responded to my last-minute request?

However, the news from Rome is encouraging. Bishop Agnellus has only seen the last chapter, the summation not the Epilogue, but likes it very much. So does Archbishop Deskur. Monseigneur Brown is flying out to Rome with the complete text. It is hoped that the Pope will read it, provide some introductory words, and receive me in the immediate future. Liz also tells me that we have received an official Imprimatur from the Westminster Diocese.

I attended a Foyle's lunch in honour of 'Young Winston', who has just published a book about the peril of the West. He spoke so well and vigorously in an old-fashioned, rhetorical style that I an surprised he has not got further already. Perhaps even for a Churchill he is a little too sharp in his criticism of Thatcherite policies. He told us bitterly that the proportion of our national income spent on defence was less under Margaret Thatcher than under Harold Wilson. I suppose in his place, with the television serial about the pre-war Churchill so fresh in our minds, it would be difficult not to identify with the Winston of the thirties. The man we would not listen to until it was almost too late.

My agreeable neighbours were Max Beloff, not for the first time at one of these lunches, and an engaging lady – a former model, it proved – who was not on the list of guests and was seated between me and Harry Pincher. With my usual desire to bring people together I began, 'I wonder if you know Harry Pincher.' She replied, 'I ought to. It's true he is my third husband, but I have been married to him for quite some time.' She told me that since the present spy mania started the media have never left them alone for a moment.

Friday, 13 November 1981

Two p.m.: attended, by urgent request, Knightsbridge Crown Court. I had come to support our young friends Robert and Cherisse Burdon who were being charged with selling drugs. I had attended the same court on an earlier occasion when the jury disagreed. I could only be useful, I understood, by giving evidence to character in the event of a conviction. It soon became evident that there would not be a decision today. The solicitor, however, begged me to remain visible for a reasonable period. My name had been mentioned more than once in the case. Judges and juries were inclined to be sceptical when defendants introduced the names of well-known people. I spent, therefore, an hour in court. I was struck by the nervous tension which appeared to prevail among the jury. All anxious to perform their task correctly. When they first came in there was some youthful jocularity, but when the judge entered and the case began, a preternatural solemnity descended upon them. I understand that Cherisse made an excellent impression but Robert had overdone his attack on the police.

Tuesday, 17 November 1981

Ian Paisley's extraordinary performance in the House of Commons yesterday fills the headlines. The assassination of Robert Bradford was bound to stir terrifying emotion. He was, after Paisley, the most hard-line of the Ulster MPs, but he seems to have been popular in a personal sense, and to have been deeply loved by his wife.

Not long ago I heard him speak in the House of Commons. He followed immediately after Jim Callaghan, who had advocated, amid general surprise, an independent Ulster. Bradford spoke attractively and well. He argued interestingly that an independent Ulster would be at the mercy of world forces, the United States, Europe, etc., coercing her into union with the South. This sense of being alone in a hostile world is, I suppose, held in common with South Africa. It goes hand in hand, no doubt, with the belief that though they do not care all that much for the British, without British protection they would be helpless.

Another, even more obvious, comparison for Paisley is with Carson.

On Thursday, 19 March 1914, Carson launched a terrific attack on Churchill in the House of Commons and then left dramatically for Belfast. Some people, as Anne and I record in our book, 'thought he was going to proclaim the provisional government of Ulster'. If ever I performed an act of sabotage in Northern Ireland, it would be to blow up that appalling statue of Carson outside Stormont. But I must not entertain dangerous thoughts.

The reception of *Ulster* has been a little disappointing. Reviewers have commented on its 'usefulness' but have rightly also noted its lack of conclusiveness. Bernard Crick wrote in the *Guardian* that each of us might have written a better book on our own. Without living in that tortured province, I could never have done a worth-while book by myself. The same is not true of Anne, though perhaps the best book she could have written would have been limited to the years of her direct experience. But I am glad all the same that we did the book, and Anne, with her beguiling charm, has been a pleasure to work with.

Saturday, 21 November 1981

Returned to Bernhurst after speaking at the Cambridge Union. The motion, 'That politics is an honourable profession', was proposed by me (plus undergraduates) and opposed by John Stonehouse (plus undergraduates). A floor debate intervened between the four undergraduates on the paper and the visitors. Not the Oxford tradition, but it at least made sure that John and I remained till all the undergraduates had spoken.

John looked very much 'better' in all senses than when we spoke together at the Union just after he came out of prison. He has always been handsome, but the strained and indeed tragic look had disappeared. Sheila, his most gallant companion for so long and through so much, has now taken to large horn-rimmed glasses and made a very piquant figure – attracting much attention during the evening. She must have been through as much as John – possibly more. John, after a year's social work, has started to write the best-sellers which he told me was his intention when I visited him in Norwich Prison. The first one had been accepted with enthusiasm by Jonathan Cape and will be appearing shortly. The next one is well on the way. Sheila told me that writing is a lonely life, which most authors discover. I should describe them without hesitation as a very happy pair.

The debate had a curious ending. The president put the motion to a vote of the House and it was easily carried. But when everyone had recorded their votes by walking through the doors we were well beaten. I myself spoke quite creditably and held the attention with ministerial reminiscences. But I showed a bit too obviously that I didn't care a damn which way the result went (always fatal if you want to win). I don't know what John thought about the actual motion, but he made a most powerful appeal for a better world and imposed *his* motion on the majority of the audience. He was careful to avoid attacking individuals. He was wonderfully generous about me, though he recalled the curious fact that when I went to Germany as minister I had an Irish passport (how on earth did he know that?). Apart from myself he singled out as honest politicians Enoch Powell and Tony Benn. Malcolm [Muggeridge], hearing this tonight, suggested that they had all got eccentricity in common, though he did not use the word eccentricity. Perhaps I come into the same category. What I do think all those three have in common is an obsessional temperament. A former pupil of mine now a judge knew Tony B. and John S. extremely well just after the war. John S. was his best man. It was he rather than Tony who he thought would have the great future.

Undergraduates, and I don't say this only to excuse my defeat, have an ambivalent attitude to politics and politicians. The political career starting at the Union attracts them and yet they have an oddly cynical view of political behaviour. When I was explaining why I did not resign over Germany in 1947, a bright young woman asked me repeatedly, 'So you put your career before your honour?' I kept trying to explain that I was trying to do what was best for the cause of justice for Germany. But she couldn't see it even when I mentioned my later resignation from the Wilson Cabinet.

Tuesday, 24 November 1981

Mary Craig gave me lunch yesterday, as full of life and sparkle as ever. She is producimg at least three books in connection with the Pope's visit. She feels, as I do, considerable frustration at not having met the Pope, an omission which each of us seeks to rectify. I tell her that I expect to see him next week and will do everything to assist her purpose, except agree to her accompanying me into his presence – she would steal the act far too completely.

We talked quite a lot about Richard Ingrams. In a recent article some alleged friend of mine was quoted as saying that I am a 'peculiar' person, and the same word 'peculiar' is used about my 'causes' in William Hickey this morning. Mary and I agree that Richard, whom she is devoted to, and I find full of charm, is very peculiar. When Mary interviewed him on television she insisted on knowing how someone so genuinely religious and so pleasant and modest to meet could have indulged for many years in widespread character assassination through *Private Eye*. Mary's own impression was that Richard was not only embarrassed but hurt. For quite a while afterwards she felt that he and his wife, whom she is also very fond of, were hostile. However, she has now been asked to lunch by them, so she assumes that all is forgiven. Richard really does seem, more than most of us, to be two people. I must be careful not to be too subjective here. He is always so charming to me when we meet, but in the past (though not recently) has written such acid things. He and Malcolm are devoted to each other.

Some years ago I might have levelled against Malcolm the same dual personality charge, but not in these latter, gentle, mellow days. Mary thinks that Richard might become a Catholic. His wife is RC. *Private Eye* has been an enormous, unpredictable success in a worldly sense. But I am under the impression that Richard would like to find a nobler vocation. I say to Mary that his rise and rise and rise raises the whole question of humour in society. *Private Eye* amuses us all, and to provide amusement is, other things being equal, a sign of grace. But where do morals come in? Not prominently in the world of *Private Eye*. Yet deep down Richard Ingrams, I am sure, is a moralist. An intriguing figure indeed.

Saturday, 28 November 1981

At Bernhurst. A hectic week, personally and nationally. In the big world, the publication of the Scarman Report on the Brixton riots may have enormous consequences or hardly any. Everyone approves of it except extreme Lefties. Greg Noel of the Melting Pot considers the report 'fairly good', though he doubts whether the proposals for independent complaints machinery against the police are firm enough. Meanwhile, Ashton Gibson, the founder of the Melting Pot but now head of Caribbean House, has hit the headlines with a scheme for voluntary repatriation of West Indians. I have tried to avoid commenting favourably or unfavourably, though asserting my pride in being a patron of Caribbean House. The *News of the World* has produced a poll to support the argument that Powell was right. They claim that their poll demonstrates that most West Indians want to return home. I can't criticize Ashton in what he is seeking to achieve, but I expect that most black leaders will say – indeed they are saying – that he is playing into the racialists' hands.

Shirley Williams's victory by 5,000 votes at the Crosby by-election was no great surprise. Earlier this year when the Alliance started William Rees-Mogg bet Robin Day in the Garrick a magnum of champagne that the Alliance would win more seats than any other party at the next general election. I thought he was off his rocker and bet another bottle with him, as did one or two other members. I certainly would not make the bet now, although if I had to guess I should expect to see all three 'groups' come out about equal. The comments since Shirley's victory have been predictable. Licking of wounds by the two main parties ('main' for how much longer?) and ecstasy among the winners.

Will it help the Labour Party to 'pull itself together'? And what can pulling itself together mean when the fissures are so deep? So long as Michael Foot is at the top the leadership will be enigmatic, but if he departed, willingly or otherwise, who could hold the party together at all? Peter Shore is the only name mentioned in this connection, though Dennis Healey and Roy Hattersley are better known to me personally and, like Peter Shore, highly reputable figures.

On Tuesday I became involved in a major dispute in the Lords with Quintin [Hailsham], who was infuriated by my contention that the judges were thwarting the will of the people by refusing shortened sentences in spite of the request of the Home Secretary. Quintin, head of the judiciary, felt their honour and his to be impugned. He interrupted me no less than four times. He accused me of not accepting his word. I pointed out that a moment earlier he had done the same to me, and added, in a neater phrase than usually occurs to me, 'What is sauce for the goose is sauce for the exalted gander.'

All week since then I have been congratulated. Hugh Jenkins, my new left-wing friend in the Lords, said that I had 'justified a patrician element in the Labour Party'. I have also received letters of commendation from those who heard our interchange on the radio. None of the speeches that I have made over the years about penal reform has ever aroused so much public attention. But the mood of triumphalism has slipped away. I sent Quintin a note saying that I was very sorry if 'any words of mine had caused him pain or indignation. That is the last thing I would wish, especially after your recent kindness to Elizabeth.' He had given her most valuable help over her book on the Queen. He replied generously, though conceding nothing, 'I remain your friend.' I am proud to be treated as such.

Yesterday was the day of the British–Irish Conference at Lambeth Palace. Archbishop Runcie greeted us warmly. There were four sessions of the conference, plus a dinner in the evening at which Garret FitzGerald spoke felicitously, his good nature shining through as always, his determination to liberalize the Irish constitution undoubted.

After eight hours or so of discussions (apart from the dinner) my head was buzzing. The speech which made the biggest impact, though not a pleasant one, was that of Harold McCusker, the official Unionist MP. He spoke with a harsh sincerity, stressing more than once his anger and resentment at British policy. Obviously he felt betrayed, though unlike Paisley I don't think he called anyone a traitor. Some allowance was made for his distress over the assassination of his friend and colleague Robert Bradford. Even so, the audience generally were taken aback by his extreme bitterness, though one or two Protestant colleagues from Northern Ireland presumably shared it.

McCusker said that the question was now being widely asked among Unionists, 'Are we paying too high a price for staying in the United Kingdom?' and the answer 'Yes' was being increasingly given. He referred more than once to a 'momentum' that was sweeping through the Province in favour of extreme courses such as those of Paisley. He had no use for Paisley's policies, but 'He's got more leadership in him than all the rest of us put together.'

I was sitting next to McCusker. When he sat down I asked him, 'Are you saying that in the last resort you would now go for an independent Ulster?' He said, 'Yes, that is so.' I am still not quite sure what he and others like him mean by British betrayal. In the short run they want tougher security measures without making it in the least plain what they have in mind, but in the long run they are convinced that all British governments, openly or secretly, would like to achieve a united Ireland. This I hope is true. The Labour spokesman, Don Concannon, said so officially.

A great deal of the morning was spent on the question of extradition. Among northern Unionists there is a loud demand that the Dublin Government should agree to extradite political offenders, i.e. members of the IRA who take refuge in the South. The Irish Attorney-General explained concisely the constitutional difficulties on the Irish side, but informed the conference that he and the British Attorney-General were trying to find a way round some of them. There was a crushing intervention by the Chief Constable for Northern Ireland, denounced repeatedly by Paisley. A big man in all senses, calm and cogent. He explained that what really mattered was not extradition but close co-operation between the police forces of Northern and Southern Ireland. This was excellent already and was being further improved. I asked him afterwards whether extradition from the South for political offenders would make the slightest difference. He said, 'No difference whatever.'

The Conference was one more triumph for Marigold Johnson. Everything she organizes is as potent as anything written by Paul.

Tuesday, 1 December 1981

Setting off this afternoon for Rome where I have been assured that this time I shall meet the Pope. At the very least I shall be seated in the front row of a large gathering and he will speak to me and others at the end of the meeting. But Agnellus, who has worked hard to make this possible, assures me that there is every prospect of a private audience in a separate apartment.

Wednesday, 2 December 1981

Returned tonight from Rome where the private audience with the Pope came about as hoped for. I remember asking myself when I formed part of the vast audiences at Phoenix Park and Knock what England could offer in any way comparable to these papal occasions. It could only, I felt sure, be royal. Drawing closer to the Pope and encountering the Vatican entourage, the similarities and dissimilarities with Buckingham Palace kept occuring to me. In each case criticism, at any rate on the surface, is stilled. Total devotion takes over. In each case the visitor is thoroughly indoctrinated before he enters the presence. (Compare my strong gin and tonics before lunching alone with the Queen.) The Queen has to take relatively few executive decisions except on the advice of her ministers. The Pope has enormous responsibilities for moral leadership which include many executive decisions particularly in regard to the clergy. But as people I can see one profound likeness. There is, in each case, total commitment to duty.

At 11 a.m. yesterday the vast audience, close on 10,000 including delegations from many countries, waited tensely. Then at the back of the hall there was a sudden flurry. Among the throng a bulky figure in white could be seen making his way slowly forward. He moved up the aisle speaking to many and being spoken to by still more, some of them evidently feeling that to touch him was sufficient. Half-way up the aisle he paused and moved back again to speak, it seemed, to young people whom he felt he might have neglected. Eventually he reached the platform. Messages of welcome were recited from many delegations. He replied in half a dozen languages. Each group applauded fervently when they were mentioned.

The theological meat was yet to be offered. This winter he has been delivering a series of addresses on the Resurrection. Yesterday he dealt with marriage in the after-life. An argument too intricate to be spelt out here. One or two points were made plain to all. There would be a resurrection of the body. We should still be men and women but there would be no more procreation. We would have achieved a higher state of being.

To the surprise of visitors from overseas, a circus party then put on a dazzling display of acrobatics. Each performer as he finished his or her act came forward and received the Pope's benediction. His thoughts throughout were inscrutable.

By now I was growing anxious. My private audience was programmed for 12.30 and it was at least an hour later than that. I could not be sure that anyone was aware of my presence. In those infinitely august surroundings I felt, in Donne's words, 'like an ant on the great ant heap of the world'. Then all cares were dispelled. I was led into an interview chamber and carefully stationed on a particular spot for the purposes of the photograph which was taken later. The Holy Father entered quietly, moving without haste but covering the ground with speed, his physical power even more pronounced than I expected, his slight stoop also observable.

I had been advised that he might resist any attempt to kiss his ring but, whether or not out of courtesy, he seemed to welcome the gesture. I ventured to say that it was very good of him to see me. He replied, 'It is very good of *you* to come to see *me*.' Conventional words but carrying complete conviction. He really felt that it was good of someone to come all this way from England to see him.

I had brought an illuminated letter from our parish priest and the other members of the parish. The Pope asked me to convey his best wishes to 'all members of your parish and particularly your parish priest'. He dwelt on the words parish priest with evident pleasure. He told me, 'I give my blessing to your book.' He added, with a touch of possibly Polish humour, 'It must have been a difficult job.' The last word pronounced in the American fashion.

The overwhelming memory is of his gentleness. In my time I have called on many prominent persons. Courtesy has been invariable, kindness has been common and an instinctive assertion of personality commoner still. There was nothing whatever of the attempt to impress in Pope John Paul II. He had spent the previous two and a half hours giving and receiving love. He was still living in a haze of universal benevolence. For the time being he focused on me alone.

Thursday, 3 December 1981

I have just presided over the twelfth meeting for the award of the Catherine Pakenham Memorial Prize. Elizabeth was, for the first time, absent through slight indisposition. Antonia telephoned her to tell her that the tone and style of the gathering were more confident than ever. There is a consciousness that the Prize is now well-established. Certainly the entries were more numerous and I gather of higher average quality than ever before. Rachel has taken over from Elizabeth as chairman of the judges and delivered the judges' report with fine aplomb. I was told more than once that she was 'just like Elizabeth' in the way she did it.

Valerie Grove, Marina Warner and Suzy Menkes have brought a fine new 'zip' to the judges' bench. Valerie describes the whole adventure in today's *Standard* with a generous professionalism that these still younger journalists would do well to copy.

I, as usual, embarked on a short speech welcoming and thanking everyone. I told the audience that at that hour yesterday (this was roughly true) I was being received in private audience by the Pope. I could only hope that some of his sanctity had rubbed off on me. If so I gladly passed it on to them. A moment's incredulity, and then happy laughter.

Friday, 4 December 1981

To Dublin last night for a debate at Trinity College on pornography.
It is not my favourite subject these days. I have exhausted all I have
to say of value about it. But I feel I must support the good old cause
when called upon.

Trinity was forbidden (theoretically) to Catholics for many years,
but now 70 per cent of the students are Catholic. With its historic
buildings in the heart of Dublin it is a worthy expression of the culture
of the whole island. My host was in fact a Presbyterian from the North.
He would make an excellent Cabinet Minister in a united Ireland.
Mary Kenny was one of the speakers. She was educated in Dublin,
though not at Trinity, and played on the audience as on an old fiddle,
to quote what was said of Robert Peel in the House of Commons. She
was the most liberated woman at one time in the whole of Ireland but
now, as engaging a figure as ever, she is an uncompromising champion
of family values.

My mind inevitably went back to the time a few years ago when
she and I spoke together at Queen's University, Belfast. I travelled
over with a party from England who were attending the funeral of an
Irish friend who had been kidnapped, tortured and murdered. I was
disconcerted at the dinner before the debate to be told by the president
that this being Rag Week it was quite likely that I would be kidnapped. Later, during the debate, the attempt was made. I hung on
to my chair as, very belatedly and half-heartedly, the stewards came
to my assistance. Mary Kenny threw herself nobly into the fray. What
was extraordinary was that no one alluded to the incident afterwards.
For the only time in my life I locked the door of my hotel bedroom.

I should mention that at dinner, when the president told me about
the kidnapping prospect, I had asked him how I would know whether
it was or was not serious. Referring to the methods in use at the time
he replied, 'When you've got the hood over your head and the elec-
tronic noises in your ears you'll know whether it is serious.' The
students could never understand why being kidnapped at that time in
Northern Ireland was not a laughing matter for the kidnappee.

Returning from Dublin, I made my way this afternoon to Brixton
Prison to see Tony O'Callaghan. I used to visit Tony in Maidstone.
He had been 'out' for three years, and in a good job where he is a shop
steward. His wife Karen and he have two small children. They are a
happy and attractive pair. Suddenly he was accused of a share in an

armed robbery. I cannot believe that he is guilty. Even if he were I should, of course, stand by him.

After a quarter of an hour I was told that 'time was up'. I stood on my rights, became distinctly pompous and insisted on seeing the Governor. I told him that I had been visiting prisons for over forty years, including Brixton many times, and had never been restricted to less than half an hour. My visits were usually much longer. I realized that some misunderstanding had occurred, but a point of principle was here involved affecting all MPs and peers. As always I should obey the orders of the Governor within his own prison, but if cut down to fifteen minutes in this way I would take the matter up afterwards with the Home Secretary. In the end I got my way, but this role of an angry old man does not suit me.

Sunday, 13 December 1981

Jon Snow has just rung up from Rome. He has been sent there by ITN to cope with the Polish crisis. Shocking that I hadn't realized how grave the situation has become. The papers didn't say much about it this morning. Jon was going to give me lunch tomorrow having just got back from El Salvador. I hope that he will be back by Wednesday evening when the Order of Christian Unity are presenting him with their annual 'Valiant for Truth' award, by no means the first television award to come his way. Elizabeth and I are much honoured to be two of his four allotted guests. Funnily enough, when he was co-ordinator of New Horizon I never credited him, in spite of all his nervous energy, with this extraordinary physical stamina, which he has shown in every continent. How wrong I was.

I asked him whether the Pope was playing an active role in the crisis. He said that the Pope was understood to be much distressed. Jon doubted if he knew much more of what was happening 'than we do', meaning ITN. But can this be so, when the Pope is so closely in touch with the Primate, for instance? Yet Jon has a very shrewd instinct in such matters.

It is a long time since we were forced, by the terrible snow in this case, to spend the weekend in London. Elizabeth and I agree that for once Bernhurst would have been unbearable. Yesterday afternoon we went to the film *Gallipoli*, said to be the most successful money-spinner in the history of the Australian film industry. I suppose that I was biased against it. The Australians were represented as conducting suicidal assaults on entrenched Turkish positions, to provide safe landings for the British at Suvla Bay, which was where my father was later killed. The Australian scenes were wonderfully vivid, but I personally thought the slaughter of the gallant Australians a little too horrifying. What do we mean when we say that violence ought to be limited in films and television? Taken literally, that would exclude most war films. Some people will defend them on the grounds that they generate a horror of war. Others that they stir heroic feeling. At any rate, Elizabeth, Kevin and I all disliked the film for one reason or another.

Today I visited the Zoo – the first time for half a century. It was already arctic before a blizzard started – after that sheer torture. Very few visitors had braved the elements. I spent a long time, as did others, looking for the lions, to discover in the end that they were not on view. The moat was frozen over, so that they would have been able to escape and maybe pounce on us. I saw pandas, vermin of all kinds, an elephant, rhinoceros, lots of fish and birds. The snakes were the most disturbing phenomenon, with a great deal of emphasis on their poisonous qualities. Do we really feel that there is a sacred duty to preserve every species of viper? If so, for what reason?

I have now read the revised draft of the proposed evidence of our committee to the DHSS on community care. We shall be considering it on Tuesday. I like our document very much, as an interim comment. I was very pleased yesterday to find that John Maud and Michael Winstanley are also favourable. Naturally it owes most of its merit to John Wing. When I last saw Elly she seemed somewhat apprehensive that John Wing's hospital emphasis would come out too strongly. I must assume that she and he will both be happy with the present draft. It certainly puts the DHSS right on a vital issue – the possibility that community care can be rendered most effectively in many cases by the hospitals themselves. We seek to refute the sharp dichotomy between institutional and community care, between medical and social treatment.

Wednesday, 16 December 1981

Marina Warner's wedding this morning at a church in Kentish Town to John Dewe Mathews, one of seven tall, nice-looking brothers who were all at Ampleforth. Marina was, like Antonia, educated at St Mary's, Ascot, and Oxford. She is sometimes referred to, not absurdly, as a younger Antonia (she is thirty-four, Antonia forty-nine). They possess the same passionate scholarship. Antonia used this actual phrase in reviewing Marina's learned book on Joan of Arc. It applies to both equally, though Antonia is perhaps more conscious of her readers. Both are as attractive on paper as in the flesh, a rare phenomenon. But physically they belong to very different types. Marina, slim and dark, reflects the Italian beauty of her mother Ilia. Esmond, her father and my oldest friend, encounters surprise, that he should be so closely connected with such beautiful women, as I do in my case. Marina's sister Laura is also a scholar beauty.

As Marina's godfather I was of course delighted that the wedding was taking place in a Catholic church. Marina's book on the Virgin Mary has become something of a classic, but it could hardly be described as orthodox Catholicism. On this occasion I gather that, while not promising to live a Catholic life immediately, she could say with a clear conscience that she would like to believe, with her devout and charming husband; I have no doubt that her wish will be gratified.

For me during the proceedings there was a strange diversion. I was sitting at the back when a stout, working-class woman approached me breathlessly and insisted on seeing the parish priest. He was not in fact present, the service being conducted by a Dominican prior from Cambridge. The lady described herself as a battered wife and assured me and the young man sitting next to me that her husband might arrive at any time with a knife. We retired to the back of the church so as not to disturb the ceremony. The young man bravely stood guard at the door while I discussed with the battered wife what on earth could be done. I told her I knew Erin Pizzey well who runs the best-known home for battered wives in Chiswick. She said, however, that she had been there but her husband had broken in and attacked her, getting three months for his pains. She kept repeating that she wanted to go to Middlesbrough where her mother lived. If only she could get on to the Great North Road she could hitchhike her way. I ought to have mentioned that she was heavily pregnant. I salved my conscience for the moment by giving her £5. I didn't doubt the essential truth of her story.

At 5.30 p.m. I attended the Order of Christian Unity ceremony at the Press Club in which the Duchess of Kent handed the 'Valiant for Truth' award to Jon Snow. The Duchess spoke appropriately, as did Geoffrey Jackson who showed unbelievable courage himself during his long kidnapping. But inevitably they were eclipsed by the passion and eloquence exhibited both by Tony Lothian, founder and chairman of the Order of Christian Unity, and Jon. Tony, with a black patch concealing the loss of an eye, is an incarnation of courage, and so is Jon as he has proved in every continent in recent times. He modestly said that he was a coward who hated the sight of blood and paid tribute to his colleagues who ought to have been receiving the honour. A very edifying affair altogether.

Friday, 18 December 1981

Spoke without premeditation, not very coherently, in a short debate on Northern Ireland yesterday, initiated by Lord Moyola. John Brookeborough also spoke and from his point of view spoke well. I feel rather guilty when I meet him because of the nasty things that Anne and I said about his father in our book. Political things; no one who met him, as I used to at the Garter ceremonies, could dispute his friendly charm. We were just becoming involved in an argument about the humanity or otherwise – in my view otherwise – of interrogation methods in the North when Moyola and Brookeborough had to leave for the plane to Belfast.

Just in time for drinks and carols at Rupert Nevill's. A huge, pleasant South African asked me in tones of awe whether I was related by any chance to *the* Thomas Pakenham, the author of the famous book on the Boer War. This was good to hear. Lord De la Warr told the company of the wonderful exchanges between Quintin and myself recently; there seems to be a legend in the House of Lords that we have been carrying on like this since Eton days. Michael Shea, the Queen's press secretary, had been very helpful to Elizabeth about her book on the Queen the day before. I asked him who came to the press conference at which the Queen asked for more respect for their privacy, especially that of the Princess of Wales. He said all the editors of the nationals except the editor of the *Sun*, who said that he had a more important engagement. He was seeing Rupert Murdoch, his proprietor. The editor of the *News of the World*, I was aware from the Press, got really slapped down by the Queen when he suggested that a servant could go to the village shop to buy wine gums for Diana. The Queen said that she had never heard of anything so pompous. I didn't know that she spoke out so plainly.

At 8 p.m. attended for the first time for a long while the ward meeting of our Chelsea Labour Party. In homely fashion we brought up our drinks from the pub below. On the last occasion I felt very ill at ease and indeed had a suspicion that all sorts of odd things were going on beneath the surface. But this time I was made to feel at home straight away by our ward secretary and the secretary of the constituency party – both women and both very friendly.

We spent a lot of time on the usual ward business that I remember so well from the old days in Cowley. One of the best discussions arose out of the suggestion that men should be allowed to attend 'Women's Sections'. We could all join in heartily denouncing the law lords, even Scarman, our hero, for their rejection of the GLC cheaper fares. I exercised a slightly moderating influence when we made plans for protest action, but my sympathies were entirely with my indignant colleagues. I think that they were all, or mostly, supporters of Tony Benn, not through any fanatical admiration for his personality but because they considered that he was the only leader who would ever bring about any fundamental change. And unless one does desire fundamental change it is not likely that one will spend many hours at Labour Party ward meetings.

I came away, nevertheless, feeling a firm kinship with this group who expressed a strong hope that I would come regularly. We agreed, jokingly, that I would in future be able to speak with authority in the House of Lords about my life in the grass roots. What is the basis of this mutual sympathy? We recognized each other as genuine friends of the underdog and the outcast. Not only in an individual but in a political sense. For the moment this was enough. In short, a happy evening, to my surprise.

Friday, 18 December 1981

Exhilarating Christmas lunch with Antonia, Harold and all the children except Benjie, who has started work I gather as a journalist in Scotland. Then at 3.30 p.m. disaster struck. I was walking rapidly down the sharp slope from Campden Hill into Holland Park Road when I stepped on some undetected ice and in a moment was flat on my back wondering how badly I had been injured. One or two passers-by hurried away but very soon a small young woman, possibly a nurse, came to my aid. She helped me back to Antonia's, where my ankle and lower leg were seen to be painfully swollen. Antonia, effective as always, obtained a radio taxi and with the taximan's help I was soon sitting on a bench in the casualty ward at St Thomas's. I chatted for a while to a well-known pianist who was waiting while her friend and colleague, an equally well-known singer, was being examined for appendicitis. The question of whether she would or would not be able to sing on Sunday was more vital than any issue affecting me as the tickets for the concert had all been sold. I never heard the outcome as I was swept away for my own examination while my charming new friend was still reading P.G. Wodehouse.

My own X-rays looked rather terrifying with two clear fractures of a bone at the bottom of the leg. At first there was talk of my having to have an operation and staying in the hospital for several days. In the end it was decided that it would be sufficient to put me in plaster. A few hours earlier I would have regarded this fate with despondency, but every misery is relative and the threat of the operation had been a lot worse. The hospital staff were kindness itself. A male and a female nurse escorted me to Charing Cross and helped me on to the train. By this time I was on crutches but needed every bit of their assistance to clamber on board. The man next to me in the train had himself broken a leg recently and been in plaster for a long time. At Etchingham he skilfully helped me on to the platform. There I was taken over by Paddy, who himself broke a leg very seriously about two years ago and has only just recovered. So I seem to be more normal that I had supposed. Incidentally, the doctor at the hospital told me that the icy conditions had brought them an exceptional crop of accidents but most people had fallen forward and broken their forearms.

Elizabeth is looking after me with every kind of solicitude. She insists that I should practise on my crutches, which of course is correct. But I still find it easier to crawl over short distances. I have been given pain killers to be used every six hours if necessary, but so far I have been able to hold them in reserve. I had an excellent night.

Monday, 21 December 1981

Elizabeth set off for London immediately after lunch yesterday in her mini; Paddy in his larger car to transport me. Unfortunately his electrics failed. I wouldn't know what they are, but they included the windscreen wiper and the heating. In the mounting blizzard and with the roads ever more slippery, we decided after twelve miles to return to base. This morning, under conditions not appreciably improved, we reached Chesil Court in three hours ten minutes – twice par for the course. Elizabeth battled through heroically yesterday in two and a half hours. My own entry up the stairs into Chesil Court had to be effected on my bottom, although Paddy keeps insisting that one must miss no opportunity to practise on crutches. He is a gifted barrister but would have made a great schoolmaster. He and Mary are wonderful parents.

The most tragic and, at the same time, most heroic news today is of the loss of eight men and women in a coaster and of eight lifeboatmen who went to their rescue, off the Cornish coast. I rang ITN to put off Jon Snow from lunch tomorrow because of my fracture. I need hardly say that he was already at Mousehole, the scene of the disaster. Later he rang me from Plymouth and hopes to call in at the flat.

On the public plane, Poland fills all my thoughts. The Pope's envoy is in Warsaw. It is being suggested that His Holiness should act as mediator. I am almost ashamed to mention the implications this has for my book, whose page proofs have got to be finally returned by tomorrow week. Vast events are happening, or are liable to happen. The Polish Ambassador in the USA defected last night with a poignant denunciation of the atrocities under martial law. Is the right course for the West any clearer? More help? Less help?

Wednesday, 23 December 1981

One-thirty p.m.: reported at St Thomas's Hospital. Greeted by a huge, bearded porter as I hopped in on my crutches, 'Hullo, Michael Foot!' Working people seem to me more compassionate towards the disabled, but laugh at them without inhibition. A lady who works in our block of flats couldn't contain herself this morning when she saw me making my crab-like way. But there was nothing unkind in the laughter. I was wheeled into the fracture department, where Mr Smith, 'a top consultant' as the nurses refer to him reverently, took off the existing plaster and imposed a new firmer and heavier one. The old one seemed heavy enough. He detected some displacement which had to be corrected by manipulation. 'Sing out if you feel like it', he warned me. But in fact I had no great difficulty in keeping a dignified silence. He told me to place no weight at all on the bad leg for forty-eight hours. Afterwards I could walk about in moderation 'when I had to'. I must 'keep the leg up' as much as possible.

My admiration for St Thomas's is unbounded. But I must have failed to keep my leg 'up'. The foot is very swollen and might be less so if I had sat on the back seat during the three-hour trip from Hurst Green with Paddy on Monday. I report to the hospital again on Wednesday week. I came away relieved that I seem to be making normal progress.

At 7 p.m. Jon Snow visited me at the flat. He was just back from tragic Mousehole. He was sharply critical of the commercial system that led to the haggling between the tug and the doomed coaster. But he could not be sure that the coaster could have been saved in any case.

Yet once more I pressed him not to neglect his own political future. Jon is honourably ambitious. There is no reason why, apart from the laws of chance, he should not one day become prime minister. Jon has built such a national reputation on ITV that it cannot be an easy decision *when* to go all out for Parliament. He is firmly Labour; not only the label but the ideal still mean a lot to him. Commentators are just plain ignorant if they are not aware that an outstanding young man of thirty-four can still feel a powerful loyalty to Labour. Kevin, just the same age, who was actively Labour a few years ago, is today seeking an SDP nomination for Parliament. But then Kevin has spent the last few years as a merchant banker, Jon as a social investigator. Both have visited the third world many times. The angle is, not surprisingly, different.

Jon was pleased to learn that I had felt so much at home in the Chelsea ward meeting. I suppose that he would be called a 'Bennite', not in the sense of personal allegiance, but because he would feel that Bennery offers the only real hope of a true socialist change in society. The guerrillas of El Salvador are close to his heart. I remember when we were dining with him some while ago how thrilled he was when word came through that he was needed there once again.

Monday, 28 December 1981

Brought back yesterday to London by Kevin. Elizabeth's account of anything to do with the family is so much superior to mine that I choose to reproduce her version of our Christmas.

14 Dec. Ruth and Kate came by taxi to pick me up and take me with them to Waterloo Station for Sherborne, while Kevin drove Frank and Tom to Poyntington. Kevin B. met us in his huge claret Bentley, which I call his Mammoth, and to our amazement we

found the romantic Court House standing in *green* fields. Such a wonderful change. Everyone over thirty admits they hate the snow and even the children are sick of it.

We are a party of twelve – six parents and six children – a lovely party in the loveliest place for Christmas. Rachel, Kevin B., Nat, Rosie, Chloe and Caspar, Kevin P. and Ruth, Kate and Tom. Frank had to keep his foot up throughout the whole weekend, but after the first forty-eight hours he could begin to walk without a crutch. All the waiting-on he appeared to need were cups of coffee and glasses of sherry at the right intervals.

The Court House was the manor of Poyntington during the fourteenth century when the lord of the manor was Sir William Cheyney or Chenny or Chegney. In the church on the other side of the garden wall is a Cheyne tomb, a slim white marble knight in chain mail. The curious thing is that during a large part of Rachel's youth she lived in Cheyne Gardens, named after Charles Cheyne of Chelsea, who bought in 1657 what had once been Henry VIII's Chelsea Manor House.

All the Billingtons, Kate, Kevin and I went to Xmas Mass at 10.30 a.m. and the parish priest of Sherborne brought Frank Communion on Xmas Day and the Sunday after, on his motor cycle. After a wonderful Christmas lunch cooked by Rachel and Ruth we all climbed up to the top of the ridge opposite, slithering in the icy lane and avoiding snow-drifts in the fields. At the top a literally heavenly sight blazed out upon us – the setting sun disappearing slowly in a deep golden haze. We could see the silhouette of Old Sherborne Castle far away to our left. The silence was intense, a sort of active peace.

Father Christmas (Kevin P.) came before tea and crashed down according to custom under his many sacks. Tom came up and whispered to me, 'He's my Dada.' But the ringing of the outside bell and knocking on the great oak door had put them in a good apprehensive state of mind. Nat had attached a flasher to the Xmas tree lights so that they winked all the evening.

Kevin drove Frank, Tom and me back to London in his amazing German car. Frank made up a charming story about a dove who sent a hawk to sleep until Tom fell asleep and slept all the way to Richmond. They came into Chesil Court for tea and then went on to 103 Lansdowne Road.

And so ended a most happy, heart-warming Christmas. *Nothing* went wrong (despite burst pipes at the Court House the week before) and Rachel and Kevin B. bore any anxieties they may have felt with unshakable serenity (Rachel) and soaring high spirits (Kevin).

Ten days have passed since my injury. I am still hobbling about very slowly. But hobbling is a lot better than hopping. The sense of guilt which usually afflicts me because I am not doing something more energetic than I am doing at the moment is temporarily diminished, though a certain slackness creeps in, a tendency to assume that other people have nothing better to do than fetch my crutches. And I hope I now have a deeper understanding of the plight of my disabled friends. I admire their good temper more than I can say, whether they be disabled for many years or only in their latter days to a limited extent, like Quintin and Duncan Sandys. As I walk about now, slightly bent, the good leg always going in front of the bad, very slowly indeed, I identify particularly with Duncan Sandys, whose feet were crushed in the war and who has held many of the highest offices in the State since that time. For the first time I recognize the courage of him and so many others.

Tuesday, 29 December 1981

Dinner with Antonia and Harold. They were pleased to learn that I had revived my interest in bridge while laid up with my fracture. I was shocked, however, to discover that the guidance as regards bidding which is supplied in my book does not conform with the rules that Harold says all their friends play. They call 'two clubs' when they have twenty-two points in a hand: *my* book says 'two no trumps'.

There was talk of a four after dinner. But Harold suddenly revealed that he had written a short (45-minute) play – which we insisted on hearing him read. When Elizabeth heard that Harold had written a play during the Christmas holiday, she exclaimed enthusiastically, 'Harold, however did you find time?' To which Antonia, laughing merrily, said, 'It's supposed to be his profession, you know.'

The play deals with a woman who goes to sleep at the age of sixteen and wakes up twenty-nine years later. When she comes round she at once wants to know who won the war. (Curiously enough, Elizabeth dreamt recently that she herself fell asleep for twenty years. Her first question on awakening was: Who won the war? She was given the casual answer: 'Oh! didn't you know? – They did.')

Harold began by apologizing for 'not being a very good actor'. He began life as a professional actor and is obviously a better actor than nine out of ten playwrights, ten out of ten perhaps. Certainly better than Bernard Shaw, whom I once heard read *The Applecart* at Cliveden, nearly falling off his chair with amusement over his own jokes. As I expected, Harold read the play magnificently, lightening his voice for the two women's parts, deepening it for the man's. The forty-five minutes passed like a flash – a gripping experience.

It is strange what sparks off genius. The idea was suggested to Harold by a book he read about ten years ago. It has been hovering about at the back of his mind ever since. He has little doubt that his play, combined perhaps with another of his short ones, will be performed in due course at the National Theatre. He is guarded about its prospects in the West End commercial theatre. I hope he is wrong.

Thursday, 31 December 1981

I read in the *Sunday Times* that this has been a year when fear came to the world. It could as easily be described as the year of challenge, the year in which the Soviet military position, it may well be predominance, has been at last challenged by the United States, with some support from her Western allies. This Western rearmament in a desperate endeavour to recover at least parity has been in turn challenged by the strongly motivated anti-nuclear movement in Britain and other parts of Western Europe, still a minority. All of us in the West, hawkish or dove-like, accept the need for multilateral disarmament. Nineteen eighty-two may or may not produce a success of that kind.

At the moment of writing, the Polish issue takes precedence of all others. On Tuesday I handed in the page proofs of my book on the Pope. It was no easy problem to know what to say, or what will ring true when the book appears in March. One can be confident that the Pope will pursue three objectives: the heartening of the Polish people and identification with them at all times, restraint from any violence, and unwearying support for a coming-together of the Church, the State and the trade union movement. But that does not determine the correct diplomatic and strategic policy to be pursued by the Western allies. President Reagan is now imposing economic sanctions, albeit mild ones, on the Soviet Union. His European allies, including Great Britain, seem unlikely to follow suit; the dilemma of how to bring pressure to bear on the Polish and Russian Governments without damaging the Polish people is as acute as ever. If I say that I have much confidence in Peter Carrington, it is not because I think that he will produce a magical answer but because, with all the knowledge open to him, I believe that he will handle the situation better than would anyone known to me, including myself.

Even on the most limited assumptions about the significance of Britain today in the world scene, the triumphant emergence of the SDP must be for any British observer the sensation of the year. No one who has read this diary will be unaware that a year ago I had no conception of how successful they would have proved by this time.

Of course the conditions have been perfect for them. By any possible standard 1981 has been a rotten year for Britain economically speaking. In spite of Mrs Thatcher's gallant trumpetings, there is no sign of much improvement. If anything, the Labour Party has had a worse year than the Conservatives, worse even than I would have forecast a year ago, which is saying plenty. The conflict between Right and Left, personal and ideological, is sharper than ever. A new split has developed lately between 'soft Left' and 'hard Left', with Michael Foot associated with the 'soft Left', or so it seems.

An eminent man once told Tennyson that he hoped to leave the world a better place than he found it. 'And I', said Tennyson, 'seek a new vision of God.' Faint, but pursuing, I continue to aspire to both ideals.

My dear creative friend Charles [C. P.] Snow once said to me under cover of a debate in the House of Lords, 'It has suddenly struck me that it would not have made any difference to the world if I had never lived.' (He was usually far more cheerful.) The same thought must have occurred to most of us at one time or another, not necessarily in old age. Of very few can it be said that their lives have made *much* difference to the world or even their own country. Yet there is no need for discouragement here.

Writing these final words with my leg encased in plaster I am aware that while my disability lasts my power to do good in any visible sense is reduced considerably. But I am equally aware that neither age nor sickness nor frailty lessens the duty to render the utmost service in our power.

We shall undoubtedly be judged by the measure not of what we did but of what we tried to do. And no one can be much of a judge in his own case. Some of my past years stand out in my memory in terms not of glory but apparent usefulness. My book on the Anglo-Irish Treaty

(1935); my proclamation of a Christian message in Germany (1947–8); my establishment with others of the New Bridge for ex-Prisoners (1955), and the New Horizon Youth Centre for homeless young people (1969); my initiation and chairmanship of our Pornography Inquiry (1971–2). By this standard 1981 must count as an average rather than as an exceptional year. I cherish the hope that our inquiry into mental after-care will bring long-term benefits, and it has been an enormous satisfaction to write a life of the Pope at the urgent request of the Catholic Church in this country. My prevailing feeling is one of gratitude that in my seventy-sixth year I have been given strength to undertake such a wide range of activities.

And the search for God? The most impressive spiritual book which I have read in recent years is that of Cardinal Hume which deals with that precise subject. But it consists of addresses originally given to Ampleforth monks who would spend long hours every day in prayer. The adaptation cannot be easy for those of us who live in the world. John Buchan's hero Sir Edward Leithen after a most successful life was told that he had not long to live. He decided, with the evident approval of the author, to 'make his soul'. But again I am not quite in that position as yet. If I had been told at the beginning of 1981 what Leithen was told, would I have led a different life from the one described in these diaries? Not, I think, outwardly, but I suppose that I would have given much more time to prayer at home and in community. I am left pondering the moral.

Meanwhile 1982 is upon us, bringing new projects and challenges. I must hope for increased benevolence and energy not much, if at all, diminished. I can rely as always on unfailing love and guidance where they matter most.

Index

A figure 2 in brackets after a page reference means that the subject is mentioned in the entries for two separate days on the page indicated.